Eye

on the

Future

Eye on the Future

Popular Culture Scholarship into the Twenty-First Century

in Honor of
Ray B. Browne

Edited by

Marilyn F. Motz
John G. Nachbar
Michael T. Marsden
Ronald J. Ambrosetti

Bowling Green State University Popular Press
Bowling Green, OH 43403

Contents

Preface

Michael T. Marsden

A Festschrift is traditionally dedicated to the life work of an individual upon the occasion of a special event in his or her life, often retirement. But this Festschrift is dedicated to the spirit of a man who does not believe in retirement—at least in retirement from one's life work. The spirit we celebrate belongs to Ray Browne. His life's work has been both praised and condemned, for its operating principle is inclusion. His life's work is about giving voice to new perspectives on human culture, about allowing each voice a hearing, and about relegating the peer review process to the broadest spectrum of peers.

In June of 1992 scholars and friends from across the country gathered in Bowling Green, Ohio, to attend a conference on "The Future of Popular Culture Studies in the Twenty-First Century." The declared purpose of the conference was to honor the academic career of Ray Browne upon his "retirement" and to attempt to chart the directions the field of Popular Culture Studies would take in the last decade of the twentieth century and into the twenty-first century. But that conference achieved much more. It provided a public platform for the probes of contemporary scholars into future directions of scholarship in cultural analysis. It also provided Ray Browne an opportunity to present his own best professional thoughts, and many of his colleagues a chance to speak of Ray's considerable influence upon their lives. A singular theme which emerged from the conference was that Popular Culture Studies not only are alive and well, but have a bold future on the cutting edge of cultural studies.

As a "founding father" of Popular Culture Studies, Ray Browne was one of the first to see the possibilities in the uncharted territories of academic inquiry into the complexities of human culture. Imbued with that vision, he set forth, first with a group of like-minded explorers, and later with wagon train loads of merry conventioneers over well-established trails. While Ray Browne thrived on establishing these new towns across the academic frontier, he had little interest in staying around to define boundaries and draft ordinances. Like Natty Bumpo and Huck Finn before him, he felt constricted by the definitions and theories of the established communities and has continued searching out

1

new territories. Perhaps he will always be heading out for the territories, forever exploring.

What Ray Browne has done, together with the support of many other like-minded academic pioneers, is to establish a "respectable" structure for the continued exploration of culture at the margins. From his early work in Alabama folklore to his most recent efforts in describing the "New Humanities," Ray Browne's iconoclastic professional life has inspired many others to forsake the safe center of established wisdom. He has actively encouraged all whom he has touched to explore the wilderness along the moving margins of academic frontiers. Always armed with a warm welcome and an encouraging paragraph, Ray Browne has offered many previously unheard scholarly voices the vehicle of a journal or an anthology or conference to be heard.

That Ray Browne thrives on controversy and utilizes the opposition to strengthen the importance of academic explorations at the margins is a given. But he is also somewhat of a magician. His quick hand, between the blinks of academic eyes, has produced special issues of journals, new anthologies, and regional/national/international conferences. The result of this academic magic is no mere illusion, but rather recognition of Popular Culture Studies as not only a legitimate and important field of study, but also a new and invigorating interdisciplinary thrust affecting many disciplines. That his own brand of academic magic produced not illusion, but a verifiable reality must indeed be satisfying to one whose early call to "Go West" was heeded by many but condemned by a significant number.

This Festschrift is a testament to the spirit of intellectual exploration. Ray Browne is a pioneer, not in the sense of the exploitation of the resources, but in the sense of discovery. Discovery, because it cannot follow published maps, is never linear. It twists, turns, and forges new paths. It knows no boundaries or limits. This errant wandering is what makes it important, frustrating, and a great deal of fun!

Ray Browne surely knows how to have fun. He relishes the joy of discovery in his own work and that of his students. He encourages the same spirit among his colleagues. The conference on "The Future of Popular Culture Studies in the Twenty-First Century" was a celebration of what Ray Browne has come to represent among his colleagues. At a special plenary session during the conference, Ray Browne presented a synthesis of his thinking on the present state and future prospects of Popular Culture Studies. The standing ovation he received at the end of his presentation was as much for his lifetime endeavor to enlarge the scope of the study of human culture as it was for his specific remarks upon that occasion.

Let this volume of essays stand as a textual ovation to Ray Browne and his important, frustrating, and joyful spirit of discovery. Perhaps it is in the joy, importance, and frustration of discovery that we are most alive as human beings. And that is indeed cause for celebration!

Introduction

Marilyn Ferris Motz

In "What is an Author," Michel Foucault writes that "it is obvious that even within the realm of discourse a person can be the author of much more than a book—of a theory, for instance, of a tradition or a discipline within which new books and authors can proliferate." Foucault terms these individuals "initiators of discursive practices" and claims that the "distinctive contribution of these authors is that they produced not only their own work, but the possibility and the rules of formation of other texts." "They cleared a space," he writes, "for the introduction of elements other than their own, which, nevertheless, remain within the field of discourse they initiated" (457-58). Ray Browne, through his prolific writings, his creation of the Department of Popular Culture at Bowling Green State University, his organization of the Popular Culture Association, his establishment of the *Journal of Popular Culture* and the Bowling Green State University Popular Press, and his efforts to create public as well as scholarly interest in the study of popular culture as early as the 1960s, has played a major role in initiating the academic study of popular culture in the United States.

To use a metaphor from another field of discourse, Ray Browne, like the Navajo trickster figure Coyote, has served as an "enabler" who disarranges the perceived reality so as to make visible cultural assumptions otherwise hidden from view. Coyote, in the words of folklorist J. Barre Toelken, is "an enabler whose actions, good or bad, bring certain ideas and actions into the field of possibility" (222). The audacity of Coyote in challenging both the norms of behavior of his society and the apparent truth of appearances opens up to others the potential to establish new boundaries, see new connections, outline newly visible patterns. As enabling trickster (the metaphor he probably would prefer) or as initiator of discursive practice, Ray Browne has for the past 25 years cleared a space in American academia for the study of popular culture. He has provided a forum for the dissemination of research on popular culture, enabling and indeed encouraging other scholars to elaborate on, modify, and challenge his own concepts.

On the occasion of Ray Browne's retirement as Chair of the Department of Popular Culture at Bowling Green State University,

5

although not as a leader of the Popular Culture Association or an active scholar, the department hosted a conference on "The Future of Popular Culture Studies in the Twenty-First Century." When the selection of the theme of a conference in his honor arose, Ray suggested that the best way to honor him would be to look not back to his own past achievements but forward to the future of the study of popular culture; to emphasize the potential contributions to knowledge that have only begun to be explored. The participants in the conference included scholars from a wide range of disciplines and perspectives, representing all generations, many active in the Popular Culture Association and many studying popular culture in different venues. This format provided an energizing exchange of ideas centered on the directions the study of popular culture is taking and ought to be taking (or, in many cases, ought not to be). This volume includes original articles developed from 12 of the conference presentations addressing issues facing popular culture scholars in the next decades, as well as several essays written by Ray Browne throughout his career.

Discussions at the conference focussed on several key questions of concern to popular culture scholars. Issues that surfaced in many presentations, echoing areas of interest in much recent scholarship on popular culture, are:

1) How should we define popular culture?
2) What, if any, is the distinction between popular culture and elite culture?
3) How can we examine popular culture as process, practice or performance?
4) How should we study the creation and presentation of popular culture?
5) What is the relationship between politics and popular culture?
6) How is popular culture related to our understanding of the past?
7) What is the role of popular culture in the life of the individual consumer?
8) How can we examine the aesthetics of popular culture?
9) What is the relationship between technology and popular culture?
10) What new procedures of scholarly research and documentation are suited to the study of popular culture?

Probably the most basic issue facing the scholar of popular culture today is the question of exactly what constitutes popular culture. Should the definition of popular culture be based on the formal qualities of a work itself or should it be based on the relationship of the work to the society that produces and uses it? Are there stylistic or aesthetic qualities of a work that enable one to classify it as popular culture? Does the genre in which a work is classified (i.e., detective story or situation comedy) determine its status as popular culture? Or is it determined by the intent of the creator(s) to reach a large audience or to follow formulas and use techniques commonly associated with works of popular culture? Is the definition of an item as popular culture dependent on the system of its production (i.e., mass-produced or created collectively within a corporate structure), or on the means of its distribution (mass media or mass marketing)? Is it determined by the nature of the audience for the item (either in terms of the economic or educational status of the audience or in terms of the large number of people included in the audience)? Do we judge an item to be popular culture if it is evaluated in large part on the basis of its economic success and/or large sales volume? Is an object's definition as popular culture dependent on the uses to which it is put by its audience: does it fulfill a creative or symbolic function rather than a purely practical one and is it a part of daily life rather than a realm designated as elite culture? What are the temporal parameters marking the study of popular culture? Is popular culture found only after the advent of the printing press or after the Industrial Revolution of the nineteenth century? Or, as many historians have used the term, does popular culture refer to the culture of the common people in any historical period? Is folk culture which is passed directly from one person to another, is limited to a specific element of the population, has no fixed text, and is evaluated by the artistic standards shared within that group included in the definition of popular culture?

Many early studies of popular culture either explicitly or implicitly defined popular culture as those elements of culture that were not culturally designated as elite (or high or fine) art. In recent years scholars such as Lawrence Levine have pointed out that the distinction between elite culture and popular culture is based less on the formal characteristics or aesthetic qualities of a work than on the political dimensions of the work's creation, distribution, and consumption. The distinction, in other words, is based on the power of dominant groups to set apart certain elements of culture to be designated as finer in quality and therefore higher in status. Access to these elite cultural forms has been limited by the high cost of participation, the necessity of higher education in order to appreciate the forms, the enforcement of certain types of audience behavior, and the exclusion of those outside the dominant class from policy-making positions in cultural institutions. According to this argument, institutions of higher education, cultural institutions such as art museums, symphonies and opera companies, and mass media critics of the arts created and perpetuated both the distinction between elite art and popular culture and the assumption that elite art was of higher quality. These same institutions then defined this distinction as the natural result of stylistic differences in works of art that coincided with taste differences among cultural and economic groups. The dominant class thus masked, even from itself, the extent to which the distinction between elite and popular culture was the result of the operation of power differentials within society rather than differences of quality among cultural products and differences in ability to appreciate quality among different social classes.

With the historical underpinnings of the distinction between elite culture and popular culture revealed, many scholars have begun to ask whether there is in fact any real difference between the two. Dennis Hall, in "The Triumph of Aesthetics," predicts that the conflation of popular and elite culture already underway will increase, since both popular and elite culture serve as signs operating under market conditions, sold and consumed as commodities useful for their symbolic rather than practical qualities. Postmodernism, he writes, "has robbed popular culture studies of its oppositional character" in terms of both elite and folk culture. M. Thomas Inge's article, "The Art of Collaboration in Popular Culture," examines the process of collaboration in the creation of elite as well as popular culture, suggesting that the image of the author of a work of great literature as a genius working alone to create a unique expression of his insights is a false one. He describes the important role of editors, authors' spouses, and others in the creation of books that have customarily been attributed to an author alone. The collaborative, corporate mode of production common to works of popular art, Inge suggests, has also in actuality been common to many works of fine art. It is the cultural practice of assigning sole authorship to the initiator of the work, rather than the unique qualities of genius of that individual, that is responsible for the elevation of some writers to the status of "great author."

If the distinction between elite and popular culture is viewed as a result of power differentials within society rather than differences in the artistic style and quality of texts or differences in modes of production, is the distinction between elite and popular of any use in the study of popular culture? Most of the scholars whose work is included in this volume implicitly if not explicitly assume that the concept of popular culture is useful at least as a descriptive and analytical category. The term delineates a segment of culture for examination: it provides a mechanism for discussing the characteristics and functions of elements of culture distinguished by the society that produced and consumed them from other elements of culture defined as elite art. In his essay, "Popularity: How to Make a Key Concept Count in Building a Theory of Popular Culture," Harold Hinds argues that items should be considered part of popular culture not on the basis of formal, stylistic qualities or the extent to which they conform to the dictates of particular popular genres but on the actual popularity of the works as determined by the size of their audiences. Hinds suggests ways to calculate the size of the audience for a work and to incorporate the results of these calculations into studies of popular culture. This approach enables the scholar to discuss forms of popular art without needing to establish their differences from elite art in terms of mode of production, aesthetic quality, formal characteristics of the text, or status of the audience. Hinds addresses the question of whether a distinction should be made between elite culture and popular culture, arguing that sheer volume of audience provides a salient point of difference. It should be noted, however, that the use of audience size as the determining characteristic of popular culture may eliminate from consideration works circulated within a geographically or culturally defined group but not distributed nationally or works that are widely known within elements of the population but that do not reach a large percentage of the population as a whole. Did rap music, for example, become popular culture only when it reached a large, national, racially-mixed audience?

The discussion of popular culture in the terms proposed thus far assumes that popular culture is a collection of texts or artifacts whose stylistic and artistic qualities can be critiqued, whose mode of production and distribution can be described, and whose audience response can be measured and analyzed. Many scholars, particularly those approaching the study of popular culture from the perspective of folklore or communications scholarship, view popular culture not as a set of texts or artifacts but as a series of processes, practices, or performances. Scholars from these fields have become accustomed in recent decades to viewing their subject matter not in terms of fixed texts but in terms of communication among individuals or groups. In this approach to popular culture, texts are always evolving rather than static, and the audience as well as the creator of the text is involved in the creation of the meaning of the text. This concept, which has in recent years become influential in the study of elite as well as popular culture, opens up the definition of popular culture to aspects of culture in which no fixed text ever existed—holidays, children's play, improvised oral performance—as well as to ephemeral and rapidly changing aspects of culture such as fashion or advertising.

10 Eye on the Future

The Department of Popular Culture at Bowling Green State University uses a working definition of popular culture suggested by Jack Santino: popular culture consists of the expressive elements of daily life. The term "expressive" refers to the assignment of symbolic meaning to an object or event by an individual or group acting within an ideological framework, while the term "daily life" refers to the distinction between the realm of activity culturally defined as elite art and that culturally defined by default as functional, ordinary and unexceptional. This definition assumes the socially constructed and culturally specific nature of the category of popular culture. It relies on the context in which the item appears and the use to which it is put rather than, or along with, the formal characteristics of the item. Aesthetic aspects are considered in relation to the specific standards and expectations of the group participating in the popular culture rather than in comparison to an abstract, universalized ideal of artistic excellence. This definition also implies that ephemeral and local activities such as festivals are included in the category of popular culture, expanding the concept of a text, as Clifford Geertz has suggested, to incorporate a wide range of cultural practices. The study of popular culture thus includes popular uses of the mass media but also encompasses many other aspects of culture such as food, sports, clothing and jokes.

Some scholars consider the realm of popular culture scholarship to encompass the totality of daily life: in Stephen Tatum's terms, "the varied and contradictory ways in which people make sense of the everyday." In "The Heart of the Wise Is in the House of Mourning," Tatum illustrates how ephemeral fashions and performances that comprise cultural discourse can be used by scholars to capture historically specific attitudes of particular groups and examine how those attitudes were formed and expressed. He suggests that scholars can use popular culture to document oppositional views as well as dominant ones, especially if they can reconstruct the ways readers interpreted texts. Scholars must explore, Tatum argues, "how performance itself, through its duration and use of space, can produce and challenge or negotiate cultural meanings." Jay Mechling, in "Children and Colors: Children's Folk Cultures and Popular Cultures in the 1990s and Beyond," demonstrates how adults incorporate children's folklore into popular culture products such as television shows and how children then appropriate those products and transform them in their own play activities. He discusses as one example how a group of children used the characters created by *The Simpsons* television show to develop their own dramatic scenarios reflecting their concerns and depicting events and interactions in their own families.

In her study of a narrative by Garrison Keilor, "Five Ways of Looking at Aprille (With Apologies to Wallace Stevens): Analysis of Storytelling in the Twenty-First Century," Judith Yaross Lee discusses ways to approach texts which vary from performance to performance and which are transformed as they are transmitted by different media. Lee traces a narrative performed by Garrison Keilor. The narrative took shape as it emerged from Keilor's computer in a printout which presumably was already the result of numerous revisions. Keilor used the written text as the basis of his live-audience show but made spontaneous alterations as he presented his oral performance. The text was further altered for his radio and television broadcast and again for the published version. Lee, like Mechling, uses techniques developed by folklorists in the study of oral narratives and games to analyze aspects of popular culture that are most appropriately approached as performances rather than texts. The text serves only as the basis for a series of transformations performed on it, in Lee's case by a professional entertainer and in Mechling's case by the children who are the active consumers. There is no original pure text but, as in folk narrative, a series of performances in which the text appears in multiple versions.

Even when a fixed, authoritative text appears to exist, scholars examine the complex ways the structure of an industry, the interests of sponsors and other financial backers, and the negotiation for power and status by employees affect the artistic products created by popular culture corporations. The process of production involves not only the original creation of a work of art but also the reconstruction of the text by scholars. Thomas Inge discusses the extent to which the authorship of novels, those commonly designated as elite art as well as those designated as popular, is a collaborative rather than solitary activity. He describes the role of the salaried editor in the creative process and the impact of marketing considerations in forming the shape of the final artistic product. Inge argues that in attempting to recover and publish "original" texts as written by individual authors before the editorial process took place, scholars erase the contributions of the publishing industry and thus the historical context of the works as they were created within specific social and economic climates. The significant version of a text, according to Inge, was not the one existing in the mind of the author but the one that emerged from the publishing process and reached the hands of actual readers.

In "The Future of Popular Culture Studies and the Clouded Status of 'Fair Use' of Manuscripts," Thomas Cripps describes his experiences in publishing a book examining the movie industry. The copyright laws make quotation of sources exceedingly difficult and discourage scholars from revealing the behind-the-scenes details that bring to light the process of the creation of popular culture, particularly when those revelations might reflect negatively on anyone whose heirs could block the revelations simply by withholding permission to quote from unpublished documents. Thus the legal and institutional constraints of scholarly publishing today limit our own society's knowledge of the impact of legal and institutional constraints on cultural production in the past. In Cripp's case, the inability of scholars to explore fully the role of movies and the movie industry in the development of attitudes toward race in twentieth-century America hinders citizens from understanding the historical context of contemporary issues.

Stephen Tatum claims that popular culture presents the past in ways that often distort and idealize its reality and homogenize its diversity, although contradictory messages may leak through. He describes the "exhibition" of actual cowboys in a nineteenth-century museum and one cowboy's ability to break the frame of nostalgia and objectification to describe to visitors the hardships and inequities of his occupation. Popular culture scholars must examine, Tatum notes, "how the material conditions of production and the dissemination of cultural knowledge are bound up with the power of constructing historical memory." Early scholars of popular culture tended to view popular culture as either the expression of a collective mindset, as in myth-symbol approaches such as that taken by Henry Nash Smith in *Virgin Land* (and described by John Cawelti in "Masculine Myths and Feminist Revisions: Some Thoughts on the Future of Popular Genres"), or a mechanism for the imposition of the views of the dominant portion of society in an attempt to maintain its position of power, as in the Frankfurt school of Marxist analysis. In both cases popular culture texts are seen as separate from economic and social reality. Antonio Gramsci's concept of hegemony, which posits that large numbers of people inadvertently participate in accepting and perpetuating the interests of the dominant class, opens up the role of the popular culture text as an active element in the creation and maintenance of the social structure, at the same time a result of and a factor in the economic and political life of a society. It can become, to follow the thought of Michel Foucault, an element in societal discourse. Rather than expressing the shared attitudes of a society or those of a dominant elite, popular culture can be seen as the site of contention between different ideological positions, an "arena of ideological conflict," in John Cawelti's terms.

In "From Camelot to Graceland: History and Popular Culture Studies from the Perspective of the Twenty-First Century," Richard Gid Powers discusses how the invented past of movies purporting to depict historical events becomes the version of the past known to many Americans, affecting the political choices those viewers might make in the present. Popular culture thus becomes an important rhetorical tool in political discourse. Powers argues that popular culture texts are political not only in that they play an indirect role in shaping real-life actions but also in the more immediate sense that they play a major role in the discourse surrounding politics and government at the national level. Powers discusses the impact of portrayals of national figures such as J. Edgar Hoover and John F. Kennedy and argues that popular culture has replaced debate by elected representatives as the forum within which political decisions are reached. "Celebrities," he writes, "provide the leadership we once expected from politicians." Politicians and political historians must realize that increasingly popular culture is neither the reflection of social reality nor the site of debate about it: it is itself becoming the locus of political power, the mechanism through which the state is shaped.

John Cawelti, in "Masculine Myths and Feminist Revisions: Some Thoughts on the Future of Popular Genres," also discusses how images of the past become, through popular culture, a real influence on the present, although he locates this influence in fictional narratives like the Western that represent a generic and idealized past. He discusses how the Western of the early- and mid-twentieth century supported new ideals of mobility and competitiveness and depicted "the conversion of the female to the new ethos of violence and rugged individualism." In recent years, Cawelti argues, popular genres such as Westerns have reflected a desire to recapture a sense of community and family felt lacking in late-twentieth-century America. He views popular culture less as a rhetorical device used by contesting interests to influence public opinion than as the reflection and reinforcement of popular attitudes, even if those attitudes are not shared by all segments of the population. Cawelti suggests that what he terms neo-structuralist and feminist approaches to the study of popular culture lead back, through their analysis of layers of meaning found within texts, to the possibility of uncovering common messages found in popular culture. Jay Mechling notes as well that ethnographic studies may reveal that interpretations of popular culture share more of a common core than many scholars believe. We may indeed, he argues, share many elements of a common culture despite regional, ethnic, class, gender and other differences, and popular culture may serve as the narrative form through which these values are shaped and expressed. Discussions of popular culture texts as expressions of shared or conflicting attitudes lead to the question of how popular culture texts are received, interpreted, and evaluated by their audiences. How do individuals, to turn the question around, understand, assess, and use popular culture in their daily lives?

Is the meaning of the text fixed and waiting to be uncovered by the careful reader or viewer? Or do consumers participate in the construction of the meaning of popular culture, as John Fiske has proposed? To what extent are individual readings idiosyncratic and to what extent are they determined by the positioning of the consumer in society and the shared expectations voiced by members of the consumer's community? Are there any parameters outside of which a reasonable interpretation of the text cannot reach? Does popular culture, as Pierre Bourdieu suggests, serve as an aspect of cultural capital that consumers can use to establish social status or otherwise achieve pragmatic goals? Is it, as Janice Radway proposes in her study of romance readers, used by individuals to negotiate within relationships for their personal benefit? Is it part of a discourse within a community or society in which individuals can think through and discuss their views on controversial issues as those issues are acted out in commonly shared popular culture texts such as television shows? How do individual consumers relate themselves to images prevalent in popular culture texts and how do they conduct their daily lives to conform to (or reject) the models presented? How do these models affect the formation and maintenance of a sense of self?

Stephen Tatum discusses how individuals use popular culture in attempting to create personal identities out of the resources provided by mass-produced commodities, with popular culture texts serving as the primary available model for behavior and identity. "One defines one's authentic subjectivity," he writes, "by imagining the way others will regard and consume one's constructed self-image." Tatum suggests that individuals look to popular culture to provide a simulation of a community they find lacking in their real lives, attempting to construct authentic selves and authentic communities modeled on the pseudo-authenticity of popular culture texts. Mechling proposes that individual consumers can in fact successfully appropriate elements of popular culture, using them to meet their own real needs, thus converting simulation to authenticity. Children, he suggests, as relatively unselfconscious consumers, freely and actively involve themselves in the creation of meaning through popular culture texts, using popular culture as merely the raw materials with which to create their own personal individualized texts, often arrived at through the process of negotiation in small groups of their peers. He, like Tatum, suggests that scholars must look at actual consumers within their local communities to understand the significance of popular culture.

Thomas Cripps, however, points out that the copyright laws regarding unpublished manuscripts make it difficult for the scholar to present evidence of consumers' responses to popular culture in the past, as indicated by his difficulty in gaining permission to publish the comments of an early-twentieth-century movie viewer. Dennis Hall strikes a further somber postmodernist note, suggesting that as society becomes increasingly fragmented and privatized, we will be left with only individual sensory perceptions and emotional responses, devoid of the logical framework imposed by any shared interpretive community. Technological developments, he predicts, will facilitate individual adaptations of cultural products, so that the critic will be faced with a multiplicity of discrete texts and interactions with them. Rather than viewing this process as a liberating and energizing appropriation of texts by an active audience, Hall views it as an atomizing and enervating dissolution of community.

Hall explores the development of an aesthetics of popular culture. If the artistic standards commonly applied to elite art are seen as the codification of the taste of a particular group of people working within institutions supporting elite art in a particular time and place, then they represent not artistic merit in absolute terms but a culturally specific set of expectations of aesthetic experience. Clearly, different expectations have existed for the aesthetic experiences elicited by popular culture. Hall concludes that contemporary popular culture aesthetics are based on subjective individual sensory experience rather than on collectively-established community standards of quality and that this shifting of the meaning of aesthetic evaluation is part of the postmodern movement. Even scholarship, Hall predicts, will increasingly conflate personal sensory experience with analysis, a sentiment echoed by Tatum in his assertion that scholars should abandon the pretense of neutrality and distance between themselves as the subjects and popular culture and its consumers as the objects of study. Tatum further states, however, that scholars must attempt to understand the expectations held by actual audiences of popular culture in the past, expectations that most likely differed from those held by the modern-day scholar. He suggests that scholars use an ethnographic approach to determine the attitudes held and standards of evaluation applied by the consumers of popular culture rather than privileging their own scholarly interpretations. Mechling, like Tatum and Hall, sees aesthetics as established at the local level, on the basis of personal experience. Children interpret popular culture texts within the framework of the small peer groups in which they view, discuss, evaluate and re-enact them. Their aesthetic standards and interpretations often vary from those of adult consumers. Mechling,

Hall, and Tatum look to the individual's experience as a meaningful aspect of the study of popular culture. In rejecting the privileging of the critic's interpretation and standards of quality, they suggest that scholars examine the way consumers themselves interpret and evaluate the items of popular culture that they use. Hall approaches the question from the theoretical perspective of establishing a system of aesthetics that incorporates individual subjectivity, while Tatum suggests that ethnographic methods be applied to determine how meaning and evaluation are established at the local level. Mechling provides an example of how these concepts can be put into operation through his examination of the relationship of children to popular culture.

Paradoxically, as scholars turn to microscopic examinations of local and even individual manifestations of popular culture, considering how people use popular culture to attempt to create meaning in their own lives, the macroscopic study of entire systems of communication over long periods of time is also flourishing. The tandem rise of the microscopic and the macroscopic modes of analysis is not in fact as paradoxical as it might at first appear, since both have arisen as alternatives to the examination of texts as the products of single and singular authors, the depreciation of texts as the mechanism through which elite groups maintain social control, or the celebration of texts as the representation of the universal values of a unified population. It is through systems of communication that the voices of individual consumers are heard. The local merges with the national, the private with the public. It is not surprising that approaches derived from the fields of anthropology and folklore—ethnographic examination of specific contexts of cultural participation, recognition of variations in individual and community interpretation and evaluation, and definition of texts as fluid rather than fixed—would converge with approaches derived from the fields of communications and sociology—consideration of systems of communication, examination of the process of creation, transmission and reception of messages, and interest in the institutional production of culture. On an even broader scale, the tendency in recent years has been for the humanities to examine the societal contexts in which works of art are produced and consumed, while the social sciences increasingly consider the production and consumption of cultural products to be within their purview of investigation. Popular culture is located at the point of convergence of these various trajectories of scholarship. From celebrating a holiday to watching a movie, popular culture involves individual and local participation as well as national and international production, aesthetic expression as well as political motivation. Through the technologies of communication, both art and politics are removed from the province of Great Men: they become the realm of the ordinary citizen. Indeed, in the mass media art and politics have become nearly indistinguishable.

As we move from an era of texts and artifacts produced and consumed to one of information conveyed, the means of transmission of popular culture comes under increasing scrutiny. Joseph Slade, in "Technology and Popular Culture of the Future," discusses the contemporary conflation of the concepts of culture and technology as central to understanding popular culture. When the material handled by culture as well as by technology is information rather than tangible goods, the distinction between base and superstructure, technology as the production of goods and culture as the production of meaning, becomes blurred. Popular culture is no longer cast out of the realm of true "culture" by scholars on the basis of its association with the technology of the mass media and mass production. Culture, Slade writes, "is itself a technology for sorting information, interpreting messages, assigning values, and establishing meaning." Slade traces the changing metaphors for technology used throughout American history to point out how our concepts of culture and technology, often seen as polar opposites, have been intertwined. In "The Rhetoric of Media and Popular Culture as the Basis of Culture Studies: A Postmodern Critique," Carl Holmberg, like Slade, examines the form of popular culture rather than its content. Holmberg argues that it is the nature of the prevalent media that determines the character of an era. Like Slade, he is interested in the relationship between modes of communication and widespread cultural attitudes. The essential key to the pervasive mindset of an era, both imply, lies in the form of the era's rhetoric and the media in which it is conveyed rather than the content of specific texts. Holmberg and Slade argue that this approach to popular culture recognizes the extent to which traditional definitions of knowledge and of cultural eras were linked to preserving the status quo and erasing the cultural modes and messages of all but upper-class white males. Holmberg asserts that using media as a basis for periodization enables the scholar to avoid class, race, and gender bound labels for historical eras that are inappropriate for describing the experiences of large portions of the population. The use of predominant media and media formats to characterize eras combines a recognition of diversity with the concept of a common culture

Popular culture scholarship of the future, both Slade and Holmberg predict, will itself be conveyed in the rhetorical mode of the new information technology suggested by Jean Baudrillard, with data and conclusions presented not as a linear verbal narrative in which carefully selected pieces of information are presented sequentially to build to a conclusion but as a visual, spatially-related matrix in which the simultaneous multiple interrelations of bits of information are displayed. Whether this new form of communication provides a space for groups excluded from previous scholarly discourse, as Slade and Holmberg suggest, or serves as a new technological and financial barrier to replace the partially dismantled ones of access to education and employment remains to be seen. Certainly, as new forms of data and analysis emerge, new mechanisms for the conduct and reporting of scholarly research will be needed. John S. Lawrence, Tim Orwig and Marty S. Knepper have proposed a set of guidelines for including in scholarly citations a wide variety of forms of popular culture. These guidelines, "Works Cited Entries: Books, Periodicals and Beyond," take into account the ephemeral and changing nature of many popular culture artifacts and events as well as the technological changes affecting how scholars locate sources.

It is in keeping with the spirit of Ray Browne's work that these articles stimulate debate, generate ideas, and raise questions more than answer them. As popular culture becomes increasingly recognized as central to the concerns of many scholarly disciplines, the issue today is not, as it was in the 1960s or even the 1980s, whether or not popular culture is worthy of study. Thanks in large part to the success of Ray Browne in providing a forum for the discussion of popular culture within American academia, the significance of popular culture as a subject matter for scholarly examination is widely acknowledged. The issue now is in what contexts this examination will occur and whether, as the articles in this volume attest, the concept of popular culture as an analytic construct proves viable in the study of culture and society as we move toward the twenty-first century.

Works Cited

Baudrillard, Jean. "The Ecstacy of Communication." *The Anti-Aesthetic: Essays on Postmodern Culture*. Port Townsend, WA: Bay P, 1983. 126-34.

Bourdieu, Pierre. "Sport and Social Class." *Rethinking Popular Culture: Contemporary Perspectives in Cultural Studies*. Eds. Chandra Mukerji and Michael Schudson. Berkeley: U of California P, 1991. 357-73.

Fiske, John. *Understanding Popular Culture*. Boston: Unwin Hyman, 1989.

Foucault, Michel. "What is an Author." *Rethinking Popular Culture: Contemporary Perspectives in Cultural Studies*. Eds. Chandra Mukerji and Michael Schudson. Berkeley: U of California P, 1991. 446-64.

Geertz, Clifford. *The Interpretation of Cultures.* New York: Basic Books, 1984.

Levine. Lawrence. *Highbrow, Lowbrow: The Emergence of Cultural Hierarchy in America.* Cambridge, MA: Harvard UP, 1988.

Radway, Janice. *Reading the Romance: Women, Patriarchy, and Popular Literature.* Chapel Hill: U of North Carolina P, 1984.

Smith, Henry Nash. *Virgin Land: The American West as Symbol and Myth.* 1950. New York: Vintage, 1957.

Toelken, J. Barre. "The 'Pretty Language' of Yellowman: Genre, Mode, and Texture in Navaho Coyote Narratives." *Genre* 2 (1969): 211-35.

DEFINING POPULAR CULTURE

✦

The Triumph of Aesthetics

Dennis Hall

In 1971, a one-hit wonder called the Five-Man Electric Band ran to the top of the charts with a song called "Sign," a current favorite of the nostalgia merchants at your local oldies station.

> Sign, sign, everywhere a sign,
> Blockin' out the scenery, breakin' my mind.
> Do this! Don't do that!
> Can't you read the sign?

The song is a modernist assault on establishment conventions. And as did many of its contemporaries, the song celebrates the violation of those requirements and prohibitions that so energized late-hippie culture: "you have to have a shirt an' tie to get a seat," "anybody caught trespassin' will be shot on sight." In the last verse, the singer responds to an "everybody welcome" sign outside a church, wherein he thanks God for "being' alive and doin' fine."

The song, however, is itself a sign, one of the thousands of markers of the cultural shift to postmodernism that took place during the 1960s and 1970s, became firmly entrenched in the 1980s, and will likely continue well into the twenty-first century. The song's title and the refrain, "sign, sign everywhere a sign," are inadvertently appropriate, as it is unlikely the Five-Man Electric Band anticipated critical theory's passion for the term in the last two decades. But the song's theme is right on the mark, as it signals the shift in attention from ethics to aesthetics, the change in focus from doing to feeling, from action to perception, from, if you will, becoming to being that characterize the current cultural climate. And in the growing fullness of postmodernism, the collapse of what were once accepted as basic distinctions—like those between production and consumption, elite culture and popular culture, signifier and signified—will change the study of popular culture, inexorably driving it into the realm of aesthetics.

As David Harvey summarizes the point in *The Condition of Postmodernity*, "the experience of time and space has changed, the confidence in the association between scientific and moral judgments has collapsed, aesthetics has triumphed over ethics as a prime focus of social and intellectual concern, images dominate narratives, ephemerality and fragmentation take precedence over eternal truths and unified politics, and explanations have shifted from the realm of material and political-economic groundings towards a consideration of autonomous cultural and political practices" (328). Unlike its analog in the eighteenth and early nineteenth centuries, this new age of sensibility is not founded on a rejection of the rationalized economic, political, social, and cultural formations of its immediate past. Indeed, the subjectivity of the current era is a product of a fulsome embrace of the material and cultural conditions of Western, industrialized, capitalist societies. Moreover, this structure of feeling sustains the condition of late capitalism as much as it is sustained by it.

At least since the 1960s, the accumulation of vast surpluses of capital and productive capacity has resulted in radical re-conceptions and re-distributions of capital (mutual funds, junk bonds, limited partnerships, real estate investment trusts, investment tax credits, marketable pollution control credits, interstate bank holding companies, index options, leveraged buy-outs), a multitude of esoteric and common technological developments, particularly in communications and transportation (robotics, lasers, optical scanning, microwave ovens and transmission systems, personal computers, the hand-held multi-function address book appointment calendar calculator, cable television, fiber optics, fax machines, the personal telephone calling card, the Concorde, United Parcel Service), and rationalized social structures (networking, horizontal business organization, down-sizing, privatization, out-of-house production, shop-floor and consumer participation in management, project and team management structures, the single-parent family, flex-time, quality control communities, cooperative learning, long-range planning by goals and objectives, outcomes measures, the university as corporate enterprise). The radical changes in culture we loosely call postmodernism are both causes and effects of these on-going re-formations of production and consumption.

This new age of sensibility reflects the realization, in both theory and practice, that in late capitalism consumption is production. The ever increasing speed and breadth of capitalism's operations result in greater and greater dependence upon fashion and service to stimulate consumption, and thereby capitalist culture embarks upon trade in signal commodities—goods and services produced and consumed for the sake of their function as signs rather than for their use or exchange value.

Fashion provides "a means to accelerate the pace of consumption not only in clothing, ornament, and decoration, but also across a wide swathe of life-styles and recreational activities (leisure and sporting habits, pop music styles, video and children's games, and the like)" (Harvey 285). Late capitalism has plunged into services—"not only personal, business, educational, and health services but also entertainments, spectacles, happenings and distractions. The 'lifetime' of such services (a visit to a museum, going to a rock concert or movie, attending lectures or health clubs), though hard to estimate, is far shorter than that of an automobile or washing machine. If there are limits," as Harvey puts it, "to the accumulation and turn over of physical goods (even counting the famous six thousand pairs of shoes of Imelda Marcos), then it makes sense for capitalists to turn to very ephemeral services in consumption" (285).

The accumulations of capital in the 1960s, 1970s, and 1980s resulted in what Harvey calls a "casino economy with all of its financial speculation and fictitious capital formation" (322), which shows every indication of carrying the culture of subjective sensibility well into the twenty-first century, the reputed retrenchments of the 1990s notwithstanding. Casino economics spawns an ever increasing plethora of goods and services needed to drive an economy progressively even more dependent upon consumption.

This realignment of economic life, in the view of many, is founded on little if any material growth in the production of goods and services and has left a decaying infrastructure and growing numbers of people with diminished earning power or out of work, undereducated or uneducated, ill-housed or homeless, facing eroding health care, and increasingly disempowered. Yet such is the power of consumption to drive private and public decision making in terms of a structure of feelings that it has left most people progressively less willing or able to perceive such concrete particulars of daily life.

This "profusion" of goods and services, as Baudrillard suggests, has transformed them into "commodified signs" that we increasingly tend to produce and consume not so much for their utility as for their power to signify. Consumption, in this view, is a metonymic discourse that pervades the economic, political, social, and cultural fabric; signs principally refer to other signs; in consuming the signal commodity, we embrace a part that signifies the whole profusion of commodified signs that the casino economy so efficiently produces. In the process of consuming, we do not so much use up an object of attention, as deplete its power to signify, exhaust its power to represent the difference that drew it to our attention as a signal commodity in the first place. Surplus, excess, profusion—call it what we will—"is not a peripheral or occasional condition, but the constitutive rule of consumer society" (Brothers 39) that stimulates a desire for difference. The pursuit of desire results in the consumption of an interminable succession of signal commodities; we embrace signs, deplete them of their reference to other signs, only to move on to other signs. "The flight from one signifier to another," Baudrillard suggests, "is no more than the surface reality of a *desire*, which is insatiable because it is founded on a lack. And this desire, which can never be satisfied, signifies itself locally in a successions of objects and needs" (45). The bombardment of signal commodities results in the cognitive overload now commonly recognized as characteristic of the postmodern condition, the effects of which may include "the blocking out of sensory stimuli, denial and cultivation of the blasé attitude, myopic specialization, reversion to images of a lost past (hence the importance of mementos, museums, and ruins), and excessive simplification (either in the presentation of self or in the interpretation of events)" (Harvey 286).

We now easily recognize and appreciate the crucial play of signal commodities in popular culture that seem to expand at a dizzying rate—in movies, magazine publishing, radio and television broadcasting, popular music, amusement parks and "historical" sites, on MTV, in the careers of people like Michael Jackson and Michael Jordon, Madonna and Ivana Trump, in the expanding worlds of cable television, on the urban strips and in the array of stuff for sale in the shopping malls and at garage sales.

The traffic in signal commodities, however, is fundamental to late capitalism, not simply a feature of its expanding popular culture. The once commonly held distinctions between popular culture and other orders of culture, to whatever degree they may be said still to survive, are crumbling. The flood of corporate consolidation in the 1980s, for but one example, has palpably diminished the conditions of employment for millions of people and constricted the production and distribution of a host of actual goods and services, yet this phenomenon—like the S&L crisis, the Wall Street scandals, the condition of the health care system, the erosion of the infrastructure, the weakness in the retirement and social security systems, the financial crises in American cities, race relations, the state of education, the 1992 presidential campaign, and a host of others—has remained remarkably free of substantial narrative criticism of its material causes and effects. The production of this phenomenon as well as its consumption in the general culture was played out in a string of signal commodities, most commonly as images of good and evil, submerged in a succession of dioramas of life in the fast lane, in the telephone booths and board rooms of New York City as well as on the news at 6:00 and 11:00, on Ted Koppel's *Nightline* or *The McNeil-Lehrer Newshour*, in the film *Wall Street*, in Tom Wolfe's *Bonfire of the Vanities*, or in James Stewart's *Den of Thieves*. The movers and shakers of corporate and political America as fully abandon themselves to the infinite variety of the signal commodity as do the people of Peoria.

In the twenty-first century, then, I'm afraid there will be no study of popular culture as we now commonly understand it. Popular culture is no longer considered simply a matter of amusement somehow different from enlightenment and operating on the periphery of social, economic, and political life; it stands at the center. Hugh of St. Victor sought to represent God as at once the center and the circumference of a circle; late capitalism places popular culture at the center and the circumference of the human condition. We no longer produce or consume a Museum of Modern Art and a Disneyland, a book and Big Mac, an automobile and a T-shirt, the services of higher education and those of the Louisville Gas and Electric Company, or psychotherapy and lawn care as essentially distinct entities. They are all signal commodities, consumed in the infinite extension of the desire for signifiers. Subjective sensibility is remarkably democratic in both its causes and effects. Postmodernism, indeed, has robbed popular culture studies of its oppositional character, its almost definitive posture vis-á-vis elite and to a lesser extent folk culture.

The free market in signs, upon which late capitalism depends, will perforce collapse a host of conventional distinctions, just as it has erased the distinctions between production and consumption, process and product, past and present, signifier and signified. Culture, now still separable into recognizably distinct manifestations, will become even more fragmented and privatized. Atomized in a mass of mediated differences, culture will become a vast accumulation of single experiences, individual perceptions—the realm of aesthetics in the root sense of the term: *aisthetikos*, of sense perception.

The distinction, for example, between the use or consumption of popular culture and attention to it as an object of study—in effect, the distinction between experience and analysis—now still pretty much intact, is eroding at a rapid pace under the weight of the signal commodity. Those who teach in the Humanities or Social Sciences are daily made aware of this cultural pressure, as they encounter students increasingly unwilling or unable to grasp the difference between, on the one hand, their personal feelings toward *Moby Dick*, Lyndon Johnson,

Madonna, apartheid or Ross Perot and, on the other hand, an understanding of what each may mean for others, an understanding communicable to others. In the twenty-first century, this discrimination will likely collapse into a single order of experience. In the 1960s a standing joke had it that if one didn't know what a poem meant, then one guessed it was a poem about poetry. It is no longer a joke. In the metonymic discourse of consumption, self-reflexivity has become the rule; all poems are about poetry, all movies are about making movies, newscasts about newscasting, music about music, advertisements about advertising, clothing about clothing.

Under similar pressure is the distinction between the study of individual texts—inscriptions, readings, or interpretations, call them what we will—and the study of the principles of their construction— inscribing, ideology, theory, or hermeneutics. The controversy over theory and methodology, an enduring staple among students of popular culture, will become a moot point. A reading no longer simply implies a theory; it constitutes one. As signs refer only to other signs, a theory becomes a reading of still another theory, and a reading is a theorizing of still another reading. The commodified sign has crushed the concept of the text as well as that of the author in the reciprocating engine of reading<->theory.

The culture of the signal commodity will also erode the distinction, still commonly drawn, between the concepts of the individual and the category or community in both the discovery and construction of meaning. In the process of exhausting signal commodities of their fragile differences and turning to new ones, every individual product or text or person tends to be transformed into a category and every category transformed into an individual. Our understanding oscillates between the two concepts to the degree that what once seemed such a basic discrimination of "points of view" collapses under the weight of increasing privatization and fragmentation.

Central to this general collapse is the erosion of the once commonly agreed upon distinction between the objective and the subjective arenas of experience and knowledge. I use the term "collapse" in perhaps a vain search for a neutral term, for I hesitate to describe the phenomenon as a "break down" or "confusion," as is often done. Most of us are habituated to the culture of the signal commodity. The material functions of polity, economy, and society seem to stumble on, and we routinely seek to mend the frequent catastrophic failures with the stuff of signal commodities. The subject<->object has assumed the alibi of nature. And we embrace it with considerable enthusiasm, for the signal commodity has been very, very good to the majority of Americans.

The trade in signal commodities has melded objectivity and subjectivity into one lump in large measure because we are increasingly able to produce independently the signal commodities we consume. On his last show, Johnny Carson noted that in his 30 years on *The Tonight Show* the world population had increased by two and a half billion people, over half of whom now watch late-night television shows. Imagine, if you will, that we are all wired to a vast cable television network, not difficult if you have watched any public-access television programs or observed "Wayne's World" on *Saturday Night Live* or in the movie. The electronic network and the signal commodity conspire to allow each of us to celebrate our differences—Ray's world, Dennis's world, Felicia's world, or Larry's world. Each oscillates between the conditions of constituting a category and an individual, an objectivity and a subjectivity. The vast array of magazines currently available, for example, cater to every conceivable narrowly defined interest. Desk top publishing and electronic distribution will soon provide everyone his or her own magazine. The celebration of difference that these devices make possible will dissipate into a vast accumulation of barely discernable individuals and worlds, as easily discarded as created.

The collapse of these once powerful sense-making distinctions has compromised conventional efforts to describe, to explain, and, for some, to evaluate American popular culture. Our efforts to deal with the causes and effects, the structure and function, and the possible meanings of popular phenomena prove increasingly difficult and less convincing.

In the cultural economy of late capitalism—where every object may be a subject, every experience a theory, every product a process, every individual a category, every signifier a signified—we are moved more by the image than the narrative, more by paradigmatic than syntagmatic constructs, more by being than becoming. Driven by an increasingly privatized desire, our production and consumption of culture have become detached from once fairly reliable interpretive strategies— cognitive maneuvers that had enjoyed the warrant of objectivity, served to identify norms, and provided a sense of security. But necessity has given way to preference. And utility has yielded to seduction, which, as Baudrillard suggests, "operates instantaneously, in a single movement, and is always its own end" (60).

The study of culture now and into the foreseeable future demands that we seek to understand, as best we can, "a subjectivity sensitive to the logic of desire motivated by the sign, a logic founded on the metonymic features of signification, a logic of the restless and arbitrary displacement of one signifier with another" (Brothers 56). And this realm is finally that of aesthetics in its root sense of perception, particularly through feelings and emotions, rather than in the more or less philosophical sense of beauty, particularly through art and taste. Traffic in signal commodities marks, indeed requires, a return to a notion of aesthetics not common since the middle of the eighteenth century— aesthetics as the pursuit of sensation, whose goal is pleasure, as distinct from the practice of logic, whose goal was once thought to be truth.

Personal response soon may become the primary, perhaps the only, avenue to understanding cultural phenomena. The signal commodity's capacity to exploit desire in the human condition propels students of popular culture, if we are to understand it at all, to direct their attention to individuals rather than collectives, to feeling rather than doing, finally, to aesthetics rather than ethics or physics.

Works Cited

Baudrillard, Jean. *Selected Writings*. Ed. Mark Poster. Stanford, CA: Stanford UP, 1988.

Brothers, Michael. "Commodification of Discourse in the Poetry of the Age of Sensibility." Masters Thesis, U of Louisville, 1992.

Harvey, David. *The Condition of Postmodernity: An Enquiry into the Origins of Cultural Change*. Cambridge, MA: Basil Blackwell, 1989.

The Art of Collaboration
in Popular Culture

M. Thomas Inge

Individualism has often been noted by cultural historians as one of the salient features of the American character. From before Frederick Jackson Turner's celebration of individualism as a product of the frontier experience in his influential address of 1893 down to the lone figures of the film screen such as John Wayne, Dirty Harry, and the Batman of 1992, Americans have praised the solitary individuals willing to strike out on their own, take the law into their own hands, rise above the common crowd, and chart a unique path for themselves. True creativity and innovation are the products of those gifted individuals who break the pattern of tradition and the commonplace to lead us into new directions of enlightenment and achievement—or so goes this line of thought. Thus collaboration, group creation, or mass production are likely to result in the ordinary, unexceptional, and unimaginative. Who wants an assembly-line product when you can have a hand-made one? Why settle for Taster's Choice when you can grind your own coffee beans at home?

In the areas of art and literature, these ideas have connected with the concept of the creator as prophet and conduit of divine inspiration and led to the veneration of the alienated and misunderstood artist who refuses to barter his talent for the vulgar taste of the ordinary populace and the demeaning demands of the capitalistic marketplace. Herman Melville has often been cited as a case in point.

The traditional view of Melville has been to see him as a writer "damned by dollars" and the economic necessity of earning a living, who because of his individual genius and talent was unable to adapt to the prevailing patterns of popular fiction in his day, and who was rejected by his readers because he refused in *Moby-Dick*, *Pierre*, and other works to compromise by writing down to his mass audience. He has been the darling of the high-brow literary establishment because he demonstrates the fate of the artist unwilling to sacrifice his integrity for popularity. I should note, however, that this view may soon change in the light of forthcoming research that demonstrates Melville was actually drawing directly on existing popular narrative forms in these works,

31

intended to address himself to a wide readership, and was himself very much a part of mainstream antebellum popular culture. Melville collaborated with his cultural and economic world, in other words, out of intention as well as necessity.

The truth is that most of the culture of this century, probably of the nineteenth century, and possibly since the Industrial Revolution has largely been the product of the art of collaboration rather than the art of the individual. From the time movable type was developed, another individual has stood between the writer and the reader—the printer. As soon as the typesetter began to regularize the fonts and impose systematic grammar and spelling on the contents of manuscripts for the sake of expediency and readability, the books produced were collaborations.

It is the lack of recognition of this simple fact that has often led us in wrong directions in the study of popular culture. With no history of scholarship or methodology to follow in the beginning, we often relied on those approaches already established in our separate disciplines. Thus popular fiction was read by historians for its reflections of social change and historic events as one would primary documents, or by literary critics for variations in character, plot, style, and theme as one would established classics. Whatever was current in historiography or literary theory was brought to bear, more often than not with a sense of disappointment. It was quickly evident that works like *Uncle Tom's Cabin* offered neither sound history about the South and slavery nor an artistic match for such novels about the same topic as William Styron's *Confessions of Nat Turner*. Like its later sister novel *Gone with the Wind*, the importance of *Uncle Tom's Cabin* resides outside history and literature.

The very first film courses I remember being offered in universities where I taught were called "Fiction into Film" or some variation thereof. A selection of novels and films based on those novels were taught, usually by a professor of English, and both were explicated in the new critical style for plot, structure, theme, and characterization as one would literary texts. Needless to say, the works of fiction by individual authors inevitably proved superior to the films produced by the collective labors of Hollywood. The students came away convinced that reading books was superior to viewing films and that all efforts to film classic works were doomed to failure. I even heard such statements offered to curriculum committees as justification for teaching such courses in English departments—they would work to benefit literature by turning students away from movies back to books (we now know they were never even in competition with each other).

Such attitudes contributed little to a proper appreciation of the artistic qualities of film.

A film, of course, cannot be analyzed or studied as one would a novel because there is no single guiding intelligence or artistic intention. Beginning with an outline and a script, soon the talents and visions of numerous people are involved, each of whom leaves a decided impression on the final product—the director, the producers, the actors, the cinematographer, the film editor, and numerous others whose names fill the credit lists at the end, not to mention the limitations of financial backing and the market potential for films of its genre. It is purely a product of collaboration and cannot easily be done any other way.

Efforts to develop the concept of the "auteur" on the part of film critics, that is the belief that the director is the primary creative force and therefore the actual author of a film, are but misguided efforts to treat motion pictures as one would products of the solitary artist. Rather than accept film on its own terms, it is forced to fit a preconceived notion that the only worthwhile art is that produced by the individual.

Another form of popular culture where collaboration has been the order of the day almost from the start has been the comics. The very first comic strips were drawn by single artists, such as Richard Felton Outcault, Frederick Burr Opper, Rudolph Dirks, and Carl Schultze, but when their characters proved to be enormously popular with the public—the Yellow Kid, Happy Hooligan, the Katzenjammer Kids, and Foxy Grandpa—the newspapers for which they worked promptly claimed ownership of their creations on the work for hire principle and considered the creator unnecessary to the promotion and survival of the property. Legal battles in two cases over ownership of the Yellow Kid and the Katzenjammer Kids resulted in a situation in which the same characters drawn by different artists were appearing in competing newspapers simultaneously.

Whether or not they retained control of their creations, it soon became evident to the successful cartoonists that the grueling schedule of producing daily comic strips could be alleviated by taking on assistants, at first to help with incidental details and eventually the entire strip itself with the creator writing, supervising, or doing some detail himself. It was not uncommon for a cartoonist to use a writer for the gags or continuity, a letterer for the dialogue and narrative, and an assistant either to do preliminary sketches or ink the finished version. One cartoonist, Ham Fisher, creator of Joe Palooka, became notorious for his use of talented assistants who were paid very little for the contributions, among whom was Al Capp before he created his own strip *Li'l Abner*. When Fisher accused Capp of having stolen characters from his strip for *Li'l Abner*, he began a lifetime battle of mutual character assassination and acrimony which took no prisoners and became legendary in the comics community. For the public, it served to reveal the fact that most cartoonists hired others to do what readers thought they were doing on their own. A further irony was that Capp ran his own sweatshop during *Li'l Abner*'s most successful years, and among his many assistants was the future master of fantasy poster painting, Frank Frazetta. Capp claimed at least to draw the faces of the characters while others handled the rest, while he chased after talk show appearances, and the lecture circuit.

It is true, however, that some cartoonists have insisted on being entirely responsible for their features. Charles Schulz, for example, has for a record of over 40 years written, drawn, inked, and lettered *Peanuts* every day without missing a single deadline. This is a remarkable achievement which gives the body of his work a special integrity that other strips lack, but it does not guarantee consistency in quality, and he has found it necessary to turn over to teams of collaborators the *Peanuts* merchandising—animated films, greeting cards, toys, dolls, napkins, comic books, and the thousands of other items that have flooded the market and made him a multi-billionaire.

Among comic book artists, Will Eisner has always demonstrated a full mastery of all elements of the medium—plotting, writing, drawing, lettering, and inking—as demonstrated in his recent book-length graphic narratives such as *A Contract with God* and *To the Heart of the Storm*. But he has just as often collaborated with other artists and writers as in the days of his weekly feature *The Spirit*, and he established one of the early shops which hired teams of creative people to produce comic book pages to order for publishers on a mass scale. Schulz and Eisner are often cited as the ideal independent comic artists, and some artists like Bill Watterson in *Calvin and Hobbes* and Art Spiegelman in *Maus* have followed in their footsteps, but they remain the exceptions rather than the rule.

All of this simply serves to underline the fact that most comic strip and comic book features were collaborations. It was writer Jerry Siegel and artist Joe Shuster who teamed up to give us Superman, the most successful and popular superhero in American culture since Davy Crockett and Daniel Boone. It was Joe Simon and Jack Kirby together who created that quintessentially American comic book warrior Captain America, as well as other popular features such as the Young Allies, the Boy Commandoes, and the Newsboy Legion which allowed young readers to have heroes their own age. It was editor Stan Lee and artist Steve Ditko who produced *Spider-Man*, the anti-hero with personality problems, especially suited for the alienated readers of the 1960s.

A glance at the credits on the title page of a contemporary comic book suggests that at a minimum, at least seven people are involved in its creation: a general editor, a project editor, a script writer, a penciller who does the rough sketches, an inker who finishes the art, a letterer who does the dialogue and narration, and a colorist who brings the project to full-color completion. It is not unusual for further names to be added—idea people, assistants, original creators, and various associates. It is clearly not possible to identify in much comic book publishing a single guiding hand or author.

In the area of animation, one need only mention the dominant figure of Walt Disney, who had a genius for drawing into his cartoon assembly line some of the brightest talents of his generation and stamping the stunning products of their imaginations with the Disney corporate name. Disney was perhaps the most successful collaborator of this century, although it was Ub Iwerks who gave us the image of Mickey Mouse and Floyd Gottfredson and Carl Barks who made Mickey and Donald Duck into fully developed and extremely popular comic strip and comic book characters. The genuine genius of Iwerks, Gottfredson, and Barks aside, where would they have been without the inexhaustible inventive talent of Disney and his insistent concern for the quality of all products bearing his name? As another form of film making, animation is necessarily a collective endeavor.

It is not only in the so-called "lowbrow" and popular arts, however, that collaboration has been commonplace. Among the "highbrow" arts, literature has witnessed any number of successful group efforts, especially in this century. In London before and after World War I, a group of writers and artists gathered to form the Bloomesbury Group to provide mutual support for their unconventional life-styles and aesthetic theories. Several collaborative projects came out of the group, and without such support, we might not have had the remarkable novels by Virginia Woolf which helped establish modern fiction. After the war the salons and cafes of Paris witnessed the gathering of many bright and promising writers who, under the tutelage of Gertrude Stein and James Joyce, would move to the forefront of American fiction, Ernest Hemingway and F. Scott Fitzgerald among them. How much Hemingway's famous style owes to Stein and how much Fitzgerald and Hemingway owe each other are still matters of scholarly debate. Even Faulkner, who stayed away from the cafes when he was in Paris, could not escape the profound influence of Joyce and the stimulating conversations of the Lost Generation about Freud, society, art, and literature, even if it reached him indirectly through Sherwood Anderson, Phil Stone, and others.

A major collaboration to come out of this same intellectual milieu was that between expatriates T.S. Eliot and Ezra Pound. The older Pound helped get "The Love Song of J. Alfred Prufrock" into print and even took a direct shaping editorial hand in the final form of Eliot's "The Waste Land," arguably the most influential and certainly the most discussed poem in modern English letters. Without Pound, "The Waste Land" would not be the poem as we know it—the brilliant product of two exceptional talents.

On this side of the Atlantic, after World War I, a group of young students and aspiring writers began to meet in 1922 in the home of a Jewish mystic in Nashville, Tennessee, and decided to publish a magazine, *The Fugitive*. Here the early efforts of John Crowe Ransom, Allen Tate, Robert Penn Warren, Hart Crane, and Laura Riding, among others, appeared, all to become distinguished voices in American poetry. In the first issue, they didn't even sign their names to the poems, and their collaborative method of discussing and critiquing each other's poems at group meetings would inspire a system of analysis which would become known as the New Criticism and shape the teaching of and writing about literature for several generations. Four members of the Fugitive group would later become central to another Southern collaborative effort, the writing of an Agrarian manifesto called *I'll Take My Stand* in 1930. Without the impetus of the Fugitive and Agrarian movements, the shape of the Southern Literary Renaissance might have been considerably different or not have taken place at all.

Thomas Wolfe, a major writer in that Renaissance, might not have seen print had not a patient editor, Maxwell Perkins, been willing to extract and organize from Wolfe's mountain of disorganized manuscripts the novels that brought him fame and fortune. Perkins had already nursed Hemingway and Fitzgerald into print with his skillful editorial collaboration, but in the case of Wolfe, Perkin's name might appropriately have appeared on the title page. This would be even more clearly the case with regard to his later editor, Edward C. Aswell, who carved two novels and a collection of stories out of an eight-foot pile of manuscript left behind after Wolfe's untimely death and for which he even created new text when necessary. The Wolfe we know is purely the product of collaboration. There are any number of other examples that can be offered of the power of group effort in American letters, from the Hartford Wits and New England Transcendentalists to the Imagist poetry movement, the Beat Generation, the Group Theatre, and the Black Mountain Poets.

In Europe, the history of art beginning in the 1870s was punctuated by one group movement and aesthetic philosophy after another, including Impressionism, Expressionism, Futurism, Cubism, Dadaism, and Surrealism. In a burst of creative collaboration, the Impressionists Claude Monet and Auguste Renoir once set up their easels together on the banks of the Seine river and began furiously to talk and paint. They began to influence each other so profoundly that some of their paintings are remarkably similar. While involved in the development of Cubism, Pablo Picasso and Georges Braque worked so closely together that they began to think like the other and even refused to sign their names to their work. Said Picasso, reminiscing later, "People didn't understand very well at the time why very often we didn't sign our canvasses.... It was because we felt the temptation, the hope of an anonymous art, not in its expression but in its point of departure" (Gilot 75). They sought an anonymous personality in pursuit of originality. Even that violent individualist, Vincent Van Gogh, once tried to live and work with that other classic loner, Paul Gauguin, but the tensions soon terminated the experiment despite the admiration they held for each other's paintings. Obviously, the community of artists has had a strong appeal for a great many painters and sculptors and has provided them with a creative energy and sympathetic inspiration difficult to attain on one's own.

Some of the recent efforts in literary textual scholarship to rescue the writer's primary intentions reflect, I think, a misconception of how literature has been produced in the late nineteenth and twentieth centuries. The writer is clearly the originator of the manuscript, but he or she does not stand in any direct relationship to the reader. Generally speaking, between the creator and the receiver there stand several influential people—the author's agent, the acquisitions editor, the primary reader who evaluates the manuscript, the copy editor who prepares it for the printer, the typesetter, the proof reader, the promotion editor, the marketing manager and sales staff, the book reviewer, the wholesaler, and finally the book store retailer. The whole structure is a complex series of negotiations and compromises dedicated to introducing the best book possible for the given market and thereby make a living if not enrich each participant in the process. Sometimes the process works to the detriment of a book and no one benefits, but most often it succeeds. Otherwise, it would have been abandoned long ago. This is not to say that this is necessarily the best possible process and that good literature inevitably results. But it is the way literature has been done in this century, and to pretend that we live in a society where the artist is totally free to address the patrons and exercise full control over the creation is not realistic. The concept of the artist as complete individualist is a romantic notion whose day has passed and perhaps never really existed anyway except in our imaginations.

Yet much of modern textual criticism and scholarship is determined to bring us back as readers to the author's original impulse as if the whole process described above has been a corruption of some noble ideal. We are asked to give primacy to a version of a novel that was never meant really to exist outside the archive. The Pennsylvania edition of Theodore Dreiser's *Sister Carrie* is a case in point. Four textual critics have meticulously restored in all its massive length the author's original version using the manuscript and the typescript of the text. In the preface, they note:

> Dreiser's wife and his friend Arthur Henry cut and revised the manuscript and typescript. The typists and the publisher's house editors made further changes. The *Sister Carrie* that was published in November 1900 was marred by this editorial interference and censorship and has been the basis of American editions and foreign translations until the present. (Dreiser ix)

As they go on to admit in the historical commentary at the end of the edition, these were considered by Dreiser as welcome intrusions or "interference." Both Dreiser and Henry were beginning writers who decided to write their first novels simultaneously so "they could share the experience" (Dreiser 505), and they swapped portions of their work, providing advice and editorial suggestions to each other as they proceeded. Always happy to have all the help he could get, especially with spelling and grammar, Dreiser enlisted the aid of his schoolteacher wife Sara, nicknamed "Jug," to offer corrections and criticism:

> Throughout the composition of the manuscript, in fact, Dreiser offered his drafts to Jug and Henry for revision and editing. This practice was by now habitual: during his apprentice years as a newspaper reporter, Dreiser had become accustomed to working with copy-editors and rewrite men, and he had never developed much sensitivity about his prose. He had always been a poor speller and an indifferent grammarian: Jug, who knew the mechanics of the language from her teaching days, could correct demonstrable errors in his drafts. Henry's function was different; he was a published author with some feeling for the style and rhythm of English prose, and Dreiser allowed him to identify and revise awkward spots in the drafts. The manuscript of *Sister Carrie* therefore exhibits, in nearly every chapter, markings by both Jug and Henry. (Dreiser 506-07)

The typists also added punctuation and corrected spelling errors but sometimes misread his difficult handwriting or skipped over sentences in the manuscript. Except for these latter changes, which Dreiser himself allowed to stand, all the other alterations were accepted or approved by the author. When the publisher required that 30,000 words be excised from the lengthy novel, unable to face the task himself, Dreiser asked Henry to do the job. The textual critics admit that "almost without exception his cuts quicken narrative pace and tone down sexual passages" (Dreiser 520). In other words, Henry made the novel more readable and suitable for the turn-of-the-century marketplace.

If ever an author benefited from editing and excising, it was Dreiser, in my opinion. Given to rambling Germanic sentences, difficult syntax, overwhelming detail, and endless digression, not to mention a poor grasp of the rules of spelling and punctuation, we wouldn't want to read him at the manuscript stage. Dreiser was gifted when it came to characterization, narrative development, realistic detail, research into social milieu, and thematic power. As had Walt Whitman earlier, Dreiser gave voice to the enormous economic, political, and ethical struggles that were the birth throes of a major new world-class nation. He is an influential and unavoidable presence on the American literary scene, but a polished prose stylist he was not. To my mind, he is the perfect example of the kind of writer who needed the guidance and refinement offered by the American publishing system. Dreiser seems to have known this too. I find it ironic that the textual editors note in their preface, "The Pennsylvania Edition of *Sister Carrie* has been, since its inception, a collaborative effort" (Dreiser ix). They would rescue Dreiser from the very process essential to their own work.

The new edition of *The Great Gatsby*, in the Cambridge Edition of the Works of F. Scott Fitzgerald, is another case in point. Fitzgerald relied heavily on Maxwell Perkins to help with technical and structural problems in the manuscript, which took him almost three years to see through to publication. He would write his editor three months after the book appeared, "Max, it amuses me when praise comes in on the 'structure' of the book—because it was you who fixed up the structure, not me" (Fitzgerald xviii). One of the most effective features of *The Great Gatsby*, then, was attributable to Perkins.

Apparently Fitzgerald used a minimum of punctuation and what he did use was inconsistent and idiosyncratic, especially commas. While removing most of the punctuation inserted by the house editors at Scribner's does not impede our understanding, in a few instances, this is not the case. Take for example the restored version of the first sentence of chapter IV.

On Sunday morning while church bells rang in the village along shore the world and its mistress returned to Gatsby's house and twinkled hilariously on his lawn. (Fitzgerald 49)

I had to read this sentence three times before I understood it clearly because of the uncertainty as to the subject of the verbs of the main clause. How much better is the version with the house-supplied punctuation in the 1925 text:

On Sunday morning while church bells rang in the village alongshore, the world and its mistress returned to Gatsby's house and twinkled hilariously on his lawn.

There is an openness and fluidity in the "lite," punctuation-free *Gatsby*, but I cannot say I prefer it to the original comma-ridden text. I'd rather risk the calories. The textual critic in this case, Matthew J. Bruccoli, who is noted for his intelligent and common-sense textual practices, did resist following Fitzgerald all the way in returning to authorial intentions. Fitzgerald had various titles in mind as the novel progressed: "Among the Ash Heaps and Millionaires," "Tramalchio in West Egg," "The High-bouncing Lover," and "Gold-hatted Gatsby" among them. Fortunately both Perkins and Bruccoli had the wisdom to resist Fitzgerald's final, desperate plea in a telegram: "CRAZY ABOUT TITLE UNDER THE RED WHITE AND BLUE STOP" (Fitzgerald 207). *The Great Gatsby*, the title Fitzgerald placed on the manuscript, was clearly the best choice, and authorial intention was contrary to the best interests of the novel. Bruccoli notes, "it is too late now to retitle a classic novel" (Fitzgerald 180). I am also wondering it it isn't too late to be re-editing a classic novel.

    The texts of Faulkner's novels have also been under similar reconstruction by another astute textual critic, Noel Polk, who has returned in each case to the typescript of the work after Faulkner did his final revisions and corrections and before the copy editors at Random House began their process of regularization and alteration. This, itself, is a compromise since everyone agrees that Faulkner's final intentions, if he had any, cannot be determined. *Sanctuary* presents a particularly thorny dilemma. When his publisher registered shock upon seeing the original text of *Sanctuary* in proof stage, Faulkner broke the galleys down, reorganized, and rewrote the novel. In the afterword to his edition of the restored text, Polk admits that "the revised *Sanctuary* is a smoother, faster-paced, and more dramatic novel than its heretofore unpublished predecessor" (Faulkner 304). Polk goes on to say that had Faulkner decided to rewrite *The Sound and the Fury*, the revised version "would almost certainly have been a different book from the early one, although not necessarily superior to it" (Faulkner 305). The business of determining what text at what stage should be the authoritative one is unresolvable, and the author's final intention may seldom be the best guiding principle, if it matters at all.

All of these versions of standard American novels—*Sister Carrie*, *The Great Gatsby*, and *Sanctuary*—are books which really have no place in American literary history. They are anomalies and belong, if anywhere, on the shelves of research libraries and the desks of specialists interested in the working habits of our major writers and the textual histories of their novels. They are treasure houses of information about the ways of creativity and genius and the sources of fiction that lay claim to greatness. But they are *not* the novels that were issued in their respective historic periods; they are *not* the books that were reviewed, read, and discussed by generations of critics and teachers; they are *not* the novels which, despite the tamperings of market-place publishing in America, have emerged as books of lasting value; and they should *not* serve to replace them among general readers or in the classroom. The original texts remain impressive monuments to the abiding power and ability of writers able effectively to deal with the compromises of a largely collaborative industrial society and emerge victorious.

There are numerous other examples of the importance of collaboration in all types of modern culture that I can mention only briefly. In comedy, one might take note of Laurel and Hardy, the Marx Brothers, Abbott and Costello, Monty Python, and Saturday Night Live; in popular music, Lerner and Lowe, Rogers and Hammerstein, the Beatles, and the Rolling Stones; in comic opera, Gilbert and Sullivan; in popular philosophy and history, Will and Ariel Durant; in sexual research, Masters and Johnson; etc. Such a list can be continued indefinitely.

My conclusion, of course, is clear by now and my statement is a simple one. We must begin to find ways to address and evaluate the influence of collaboration in cultural studies, whatever our areas of specialization and the disciplinary bases from which we work. In the study of popular culture, it is especially important to recognize that in nearly all of its forms, we are talking about things which came into being by cooperation and delicate negotiation between creators, producers, and consumers. Individualism as an ideal will remain important in the hearts and minds of those who will sustain the American democratic experiment, but it can only obscure the visions of those who insist on seeing it as the primary source of creativity and place a premium on its cultural value. We must make allowance for the dynamics and the vital power of the art of collaboration. This I see as a major direction in which the study of popular culture must inevitably move.

Works Cited

Dreiser, Theodore. *Sister Carrie*. Pennsylvania ed. Eds. John C. Berkey, Alice M. Winters, James L.W. West, III and Neda M. Westlake. Philadelphia: U of Pennsylvania P, 1981.

Faulkner, William. *Sanctuary: The Original Text*. Ed. Noel Polk. New York: Random House, 1981.

Fitzgerald, F. Scott. *The Great Gatsby*. Cambridge ed. Ed. Matthew J. Bruccoli. Cambridge: Cambridge UP, 1991.

Gilot, Françoise and Carlton Lake. *Life with Picasso*. New York: McGraw Hill, 1964.

Popularity:
How to Make a Key Concept Count
in Building a Theory of Popular Culture

Harold E. Hinds, Jr.

What approach or approaches should be adopted in the study of popular culture? The first generation of theorists believed that popular culture was especially characterized by formulas and its own aesthetics. Although both of these conceptual approaches have been subjected to a convincing critique (Rollin, "Against"; Rollin, "Son"; Feldman), they continue to enjoy currency among those, mainly critics writing for the popular media, who believe there are fundamental differences between "elite" and "popular" works of art, and by some scholars, e.g., Thomas J. Roberts' 1990 *An Aesthetics of Junk Fiction* and Arthur Asa Berger's 1992 *Popular Culture Genres.*

In my 1988 essay "Popularity: the *Sine Qua Non* of Popular Culture," I argued that popularity was the most promising concept for future theory building in popular culture studies. While the essay's main emphasis was on demonstrating that prior definitions of popular culture were too inclusive and that alternative conceptual approaches, e.g., those of aesthetics and formula, were seriously flawed, the concept of popularity itself was minimally developed. As a point of departure for theory building I suggested "that popularity at a minimum demands adoption/consumption in more than one regional culture and by more than one narrow socio-economic group" (211). This essay will further explore the complexities and differences associated with defining popularity, and then, in light of these, suggest both a minimal and an ideal standard for applying the concept to popular culture studies. One basic question concerning popularity is: what exactly is to be counted, and how?

What constitutes a "text"[1] is a critical problem for any approach involving quantification. What is it exactly that will be counted? In one sense, a text would not appear to be problematic. Tonight's television sit com, this morning's sports page, the local movie theater's current feature film, a new country LP that is number one on this week's *Billboard* charts, and Monday's chapter of the comic strip *Doonesbury*, all are easily identifiable texts. Or are they? For each might well appear, not in a single format, but in several, and if so, which one (or ones) should be considered the unit of study? For example, the film will eventually be seen not just as a feature movie in a movie theater, but on Home Box Office, and then as a video that can be purchased or, most likely, rented. And the movie originally shown at a cinema may well differ from the video release, for at a minimum most videos significantly crop the rectangular movie to make it fit the squarish television screen. Content, perhaps significant, is lost. Today's *Doonesbury* strip will appear on the comics page in some papers, but on the editorial page in others, and some papers will elect not to run it at all, if the paper's editors deem its content too objectionable, and might well substitute an older episode in its place. And at a later date it will be collected in one, perhaps many, collections of Gary Trudeau's work. In general, though, the problems here are not of too great a consequence, for the "same" text is presented "relatively unaltered" in either a different format or a different context.

Many texts, however, *are* significantly altered when presented anew. Subsequent editions can be quite different. Illustrations may be added to a print text, as when Big Little Books transformed pulps into lavishly illustrated novels; consequently the text was both enhanced and expanded. Paperback editions, on the other hand, not infrequently delete most, or even all, of the original hardback's illustrations. Bowdlerized texts, *Reader's Digest* novels, and children's editions can even more radically alter by deleting original text. Altered texts also result from translations into other languages; from the modernization of archaic language, e.g., the Revised Standard version of the King James version of the *Bible* or high school editions of Shakespeare plays; and from the addition of explanatory text or annotations to another period's classics. Syndicated television programs, or later rebroadcasts, use different ads, creating a new text. Many types of popular texts, when presented in alternate mediums, result in quite different texts, e.g., the novelization of movies, postcards of famous vistas, Classics Illustrated comic books based on established literary works, and radio ads using only the audio part of television ads.

In addition, the very act of consumption alters the text. A text does not inject meanings into its consumer, rather there is a complex set of interactions, a give and take, between a reader/viewer/consumer and the popular text. The consumer's values, opinions, beliefs, and the like interact/collide with those of the text to create a new text, one potentially quite different from that intended by the text's author(s). And these new texts may resemble those of other consumers with similar cultural and socio-economic backgrounds, or they may be highly individualistic (Fiske 62-83).

Incidentally, the problem of what constitutes a text applies not only to individual works, but to groups of texts, such as a popular author's complete corpus or a genre. But to the problems of how to count different editions or translations or appearances in new formats or mediums is added that of the degree of inclusiveness: just how similar to the prototype of a modern, adult Western, the *Virginian*, must a work be to be counted? Is Louis L'Amour's origin novel for the Sackett clan, *Sackett's Land*, which is set in Elizabethan England, a Western? Or are the adventures of a flying cowboy, Sky King?

What then is to be counted, if a title's, or a category's, popularity is to be summed up? All appearances by an individual title, despite its being abridged, condensed, modernized, illustrated, or censored, should be added together. Also counted, but separately, should be all appearances in alternate mediums, such as movie novelizations. It seems reasonable to be at least this inclusive, even if noting the difference between the above two categories. In addition, it would be useful to also at least note appearances which in some sense model or mold themselves upon the original text, e.g., parodies such as Mel Brooks' movie *Young Frankenstein*. One might also conceptualize these three groups as a text's field of popularity, with the original and near-original texts occupying the center, with appearances in other mediums occupying an inner ring just beyond the center, and with an outer ring being composed of works bearing a strong family resemblance to the original.

If it can be decided what to count, how should the text's popularity be reported? Basically when stating that a given text is most popular or ranks X or Y on a given list, one of two variables is used: how many were bought, viewed, etc., or how many dollars, pounds, etc. were spent on sales and/or rentals. Both of these measures, when given as crude figures, can be highly misleading. If a bestseller sells one million copies, or the Superbowl draws an audience of 100 million plus, *and* both are labeled popular culture, as is often the case, *both* are *not* equivalent in popularity. One reaches less than half of one percent, the other about half, of the United States' population. Likewise, if a movie grossed 50 million dollars in 1928, and another movie in 1990 grossed 100 million, and one simply listed movies in rank order of total receipts, with ticket sales not given in constant units of currency, i.e., if inflation is not taken into account, then one would incorrectly list the 1990 movie as more popular than the 1928 flick. Popularity, whether stated in terms of total audience or gross income, should always be stated both as raw figures *and* either as a percentage of total population or in terms of constant units of currency.

Furthermore, available data on sales or consumption may not always agree or be reliable. Competing surveys using different definitions and measurement techniques, or surveying different populations, or even questioning the same population but at different times and/or under alternate circumstances, can produce data which range from confirming each other to differing significantly. For example, there does not exist an agreed-upon set of criteria for how many copies a hardback or paperback book must sell to be placed on a "best-seller" list, or even which book sellers or publishers should be consulted in determining sales (Atlas). Frequent discrepancies between such lists should, then, come as no surprise. To cite another example, the Nielsen ratings for television programs can produce estimates of popularity different from those of the Gallup polling organization. Gallup, unlike Nielsen, does not produce an estimate of who is watching which programs, but asks a statistically valid sample of viewers which programs they enjoy. Both rank their findings, but in 1992 Nielsen rated the new television comedy *Home Improvement* sixth, while the show did not even make Gallup's list of top comedy programs, and the new comedy *Davis Rules* ranked 56th according to Nielsen but topped Gallup's list in the new-television-comedy category (Dorsey). The fact that statistics are neither as complete as desired, nor always consistent, nor gathered for the purpose(s) scholars wish to use them for, should not deter cautious, judicious use of what is available. Failure to do so will only perpetuate the confusion of marginally popular texts with those texts that do reach far greater audiences.

If total audience or sales for a text, or group of texts, can be ascertained, some attention, if possible, should also be given to who bought, who consumed the text. Assuming for now that the basic geographical unit of consumption is the modern nation state (see discussion on geography and popularity below), the "who" is generally stated, if addressed at all, in terms of a typical or average consumer, or as a demographic profile of all consumers, or as a statistically valid sample of consumers. Since consumers of a product or category of goods are a highly varied lot, a profile of an average or typical consumer may seriously distort the demographic basis of popularity. When data permit, a portrait of consumers should be given in terms of the variables of race, ethnicity, gender, and class/income, and a description of a typical consumer should be balanced by attention to the range of consumers. For instance, my sample of the purchasers of the Mexican superhero comic book, *Kalimán*, revealed the average buyer to be a subteen lower-middle-class urban boy, but the age ranged from 12 to 60, and the socio-economic status (SES) from an illiterate shoeshine boy to lawyers practicing before a state supreme court (Hinds and Tatum 32-34). Unfortunately, data sufficiently abundant and reliable to enable popularity to be stated in terms of a demographic profile often either are proprietary, and thus not accessible, or simply have never been collected.

A number of caveats, however, are in order about demographic profiles of consumers. First, in at least some cases purchase, possession, or presence does not mean the text is in fact consumed. Too many books litter my own study, bought with the best of intentions, but only partially read, or awaiting some never-to-be parallel life with a surfeit of reading time, for me to ever confuse purchase with consumption. Some consumers just enjoy shopping, but cannot limit themselves to window shopping: such purchases often end up in attics or yard sales. Some purchases function more as status symbols, used only for display, than as vehicles for either knowledge or entertainment, e.g., coffee-table books. The Italian semiotician, Umberto Eco, believed his first novel, *The Name of the Rose*, would appeal to about a thousand readers, yet it sold nine million copies, most of which probably remained unfinished. Indeed Eco has become the master of "a trend in modern publishing: the unread best seller." He followed his first novel with *Foucault's Pendulum*, a volume so dense and intellectually complex that he hoped 500 of the millions purchased would ever really be read (Stille 125, 128)! And is everyone really listening to all those turned-on radios and televisions? Evidently, at least many Americans and Britons use these media as background noise or pay only nominal attention until something is broadcast of "real" interest (Morley). Are all those books purchased for prospective readers by your local public librarian ever read by more than a few, or always read when checked out? The British scholar, Peter Mann, argues that most literary, i.e., "serious," novels are not purchased by individuals, but by libraries, and probably have multiple readers, but he also notes that very little is actually known about "what use is made of...[a purchased book] when it gets into the public libraries" (12). Finally, some purchases force the consumer to accept an entire package or collection when he or she is in fact only interested in one or two stories, songs, etc. For example, the Book-of-the-Month Club's offering of a special package deal which the consumer cannot resist, but which leaves that extra "bargain" unopened, points to selectively realized consumption.

Second, consumption is not always by choice. Sales of Shakespeare's more popular plays, *Hamlet* and *Macbeth*, are probably in the main to high schools and to college bookstores. Assigned texts should not be confused with those purchased and consumed by choice. Items purchased as Christmas or birthday gifts are not always received by choice, or even necessarily freely consumed. And, of course, every family has its collection of gifts relegated to a back closet, never consumed, but which no one will risk not having at hand should they be needed for display to the giver.

Third, pass-along consumption often goes unrecorded, or its being recorded depends a great deal on the delivery medium. Purchased books often are passed along to family and relatives, fellow workers, or neighbors. For example, a Mexican comic book, it is estimated, may on average be reread by ten additional readers other than the original purchaser. They either acquire it on the used market, rent a reading, hear it read aloud, or borrow it. These consumers largely remain uncounted. Samples of home TV audiences, on the other hand, do attempt to factor in entire households, and to account for just who does watch.

The above examples strongly suggest that in at least some cases a demographic profile of consumers based on "official" data may well provide only a partial picture of actual consumption. Sophisticated counts, and discussions of available data, should take into account such inadequacies and anomalies, even if the issue(s) cannot be satisfactorily resolved.

Demographic profiles of consumers, however, need to be placed within a geographical and historical perspective. A strictly regional culture would not qualify as popular, any more than one restricted to a narrow socio-economic group, e.g., recent Ph.D.s. The concept of a "region," however, has not been easy to define even for geographers. Peter Haggett in *Geography: A Modern Synthesis*, the most widely adopted college-level introductory geography textbook in the English-speaking world, simply states that "a region is any tract of the earth's surface with characteristics, either natural or of human origin, which make it different from the areas that surround it" (262). Cultural regions have both physical and cultural characteristics, and are the products of diffusion of generally multiple characteristics from a cultural hearth outward. For example, Donald Meining in a classic essay envisioned a region composed of three concentric areas: core, domain, and sphere; the core being the cultural hearth and having the highest concentration of the region's signature characteristics, the sphere being farthest removed from the regional center of diffusion and including the places where the defining characteristics have not yet been generally adopted. Regions may be rather small, as are those pockets of America targeted by nine-digit ZIP code mailings. Michael Weiss has identified some 40 neighborhood types based on the target mailing system developed by the Claritas Corporation, e.g., working-class row house districts or small towns based on light industry and farming.

Regions of interest to popular culture scholars will undoubtedly be considerably larger than Weiss' neighborhood types which incorporate about one to five percent of the population. Wilbur Zelinsky's cultural areas, broadly inclusive cultural regions, number only five for the entire continental United States: New England, the Midland, the South, the Middle West, and the West, although he is not certain just where to place Texas, much of Peninsular Florida, and Oklahoma. When data is available for the United States on a state-by-state basis, aggregates of data can provide a good approximation of Zelinsky's cultural areas and even reveal cultural hearths. Most sources of data available on popular culture use the predominant geographical statistical unit of the modern world, the nation state. Of course, some cultural regions embrace supra-national areas of the world, e.g., the Islamic world, but data at this level is generally less available. Whenever statistical data for the popularity of some text is available and is broken down into sub-national regions, the fact that consumption is not restricted to a narrow cultural region should be demonstrated. When data is only available at the national level and only a small percent of the population is reached on a first-hand basis, e.g., the case for a "bestseller" novel with sales of one million, the fact that this might represent consumption for only a quite limited cultural area and/or socio-economic status group should be acknowledged. That is, the study may really belong to regional, not popular, culture. In any case, the geographical scope of adoption/consumption should always be given, if known.

My 1988 minimal conception of popularity ignored the temporal or historical dimension, a serious deficiency in the original essay. Clearly different popular texts have very different life spans. Much of popular culture is ephemeral, throwaway culture. Pet Rocks, individual Harlequin romance titles, Hula Hoops, and the like are only momentary blips on the cultural scene.

Some previously ephemeral popular culture, due to new technologies or a multiplication of delivery channels, has gained a second life: rebroadcast of vintage television programs on superstation channels or on cable has given new life to programs such as *Dragnet* or *Andy Griffith*. New video technologies have vastly expanded the temporal range of our choices for an evening's cinema entertainment: older movies which many of us might never have had the opportunity to see are now readily available, whether an Academy Award Winner, a critic's favorite, or a trashy "B" film. Indeed, "new" editions can significantly prolong the popular life of a text. Reissuing a hardback in a paperback edition, adoption as a *Reader's Digest* Condensed Book, selection by the Book-of-the-Month or Quality Paperback clubs, for example, can significantly boost sales and extend the longevity of a text.

Some texts may never, if the time unit used is a month or even a year, appear on "bestseller" or such lists. Yet they are slow, steady sellers whose lifetime sales may well top even the most attention-getting short-term success stories: *The Bible* is easily *the* all time best seller in the United States. Many category books (Westerns, Romances, Mysteries) are slow, steady sellers. And in some of these cases, it will make more sense to count the life-time sales of the entire category, e.g., Harlequins, or the entire corpus of an author, e.g., Louis L'Amour, than sales of individual titles. Classics frequently sell especially well when first introduced, then sell at modest levels indefinitely, e.g., James Frazer's *The Golden Bough* (Beard 216-23, 227).[2] Since the periodicity of popularity is so variable, popularity should always be expressed in terms of a specific period, whatever is appropriate and provides the fullest and most accurate portrait, whether the temporal unit is a month, season, decade, year, century, or even millennium. And, if possible, it should also be expressed in terms of periodic totals or periodic averages.

If attention to popularity may be necessary for building theories and methodologies unique to popular culture studies, then popular culture scholarship should incorporate estimates of popularity. As a *minimum* those estimates should include the total number of consumers as a percentage of total population, attempt to determine who the consumers are and their geographical distribution, and be sensitive to just when an item is popular. If figures are given not for consumers, but for total sales, then sums should always be corrected for inflation (e.g., given in constant dollars). *Ideally*, consumer profiles will include information on typical consumers, as well as the diversity of consumers in terms of gender, race, class, and income; geographical data will attend to sub- and supra-national distributions of consumers; all appearances, regardless of format or medium, of a text or a group/category of texts will be taken into consideration; and the conditions under which consumption takes place, or fails to take place despite purchase, will be considered.

A perusal of the articles appearing in the flagship journal of popular culture studies, the *Journal of Popular Culture*, reveals that often not even the minimum is attended to, and the ideal almost never. This undoubtedly reflects the lack of confidence that popular culture scholars, overwhelmingly either literature or history professors, have in working with statistics. Yet the rewards for such attention could be considerable. Imagine a data base which gives at least minimal attention to popularity. Popular culture could then be presented not as a crude, homogeneous whole or as divided only along the lines of genres or categories of goods, but as stratified, with strata composed of texts of similar degrees of popularity, and within a stratum clusters of texts with distinct demographic, geographical, and temporal characteristics. Such information on, and organization of, popular culture might well allow sufficiently meaningful comparisons and conclusions to be drawn to build theories, models, and methodologies unique to popular culture. Perhaps with such a comparative base popular culture studies might yet suggest plausible answers to such questions as when, under what conditions, in which versions, and by whom do texts become accepted and consumed by some, a majority, or nearly all of a culture?

Finally, the model outlined in this article both incorporates recent theoretical concerns in humanities scholarship *and* transcends them. Any careful treatment of a text and its adoption/consumption, I argue, must reflect the concerns of post-modernist critics and social science scholarship: texts are not stable, often appear in multiple forms and mediums, and are appropriated by diverse audiences rather than by average consumers. The process of appropriation, which this essay has not focused on, in turn fashions new texts.

Then my argument parts company with these theorists, as this newer scholarship also posits that in the post-modern world traditional cultural hierarchies, such as elite vs. popular art, have dissolved. It also states that whether culture as a whole, or particular aspects of it, is the subject of study, the analytic method(s) used should be applied symmetrically (Collins, Sarchett, Mukerji and Schudson). Thus, while older approaches based on formula and aesthetics failed to establish the distinctiveness of popular culture, and while at least some post-modernist analytical models, e.g., semiology, can be profitably applied to a wide range of texts, including those commonly labeled popular or elite, my approach promises to salvage popular culture as a distinctive category. A great deal of empirical research, with careful attention to degrees of popularity, will first be necessary, but rather than resulting in the dissolution of popular culture into culture in general, it might yet provide an analytical foundation for this important category.

Notes

[1]In this essay, "text" refers to concrete physical objects, e.g., books, television programs, movies, print ads, and children's toys; to mental thoughts or images, e.g., beliefs, values, myths, lore, customs, and common knowledge; to events, e.g., the assassination of a political leader and rituals; and to experiences, e.g., watching the Superbowl and eating a Big Mac.

²In particular see Beard (216-23, 227) where she makes a case for *The Golden Bough*'s "extraordinary and immediate popularity" upon publication, and its contemporary popularity which "rests on the undeniable fact that it is so rarely read," as indeed are many classics.

Works Cited

Atlas, James. "Making the List." *The Atlantic* 252.6 (Dec. 1983): 108-12.

Beard, Mary. "Frazer, Leach, and Vigil: The Popularity (and Unpopularity) of *The Golden Bough*." *Comparative Studies in Society and History* 34.2 (1992): 203-24.

Berger, Arthur Asa. *Popular Culture Genres: Theories and Texts.* Newbury Park: Sage, 1992.

Collins, Jim. *Uncommon Cultures: Popular Culture and Post-Modernism.* New York: Routledge, 1989.

Dorsey, Tom. "People Choose Favorites Tonight." *The Courier-Journal* (Louisville) 17 Mar. 1992: C1-2.

Feldman, David N. "Formalism and Popular Culture." *Journal of Popular Culture* 9.2 (1975): 384-402.

Fiske, John. *Television Culture.* London: Methuen, 1987.

Haggett, Peter. *Geography: A Modern Synthesis.* Rev. 3rd ed. New York: Harper & Row, 1983.

Hinds, Harold E., Jr. "Popularity: The *Sine Qua Non* of Popular Culture." *Symbiosis: Popular Culture and Other Fields.* Eds. Ray B. Browne and Marshall W. Fishwick. Bowling Green, OH: Bowling Green State U Popular P, 1988: 207-16.

Hinds, Harold E., Jr. and Charles M. Tatum. *Not Just for Children: The Mexican Comic Book in the Late 1960s and 1970s.* Westport: Greenwood, 1992.

Mann, Peter H. "The Romantic Novel and Its Readers." *Journal of Popular Culture* 15.1 (1981): 9-18.

Meining, Donald W. "The Mormon Culture Region: Strategies and Patterns in the Geography of the American West, 1847-1964." *Annals of the Association of American Geographers* 55.2 (1965): 213-17.

Morley, David. *Family Television: Cultural Power and Domestic Leisure.* London: Comedia, 1986.

Mukerji, Chandra and Michael Schudson. "Popular Culture." *Annual Review of Sociology* 12 (1986): 47-66.

Roberts, Thomas J. *An Aesthetics of Junk Fiction.* Athens: The U of Georgia P, 1990.

Rollin, Roger B. "Against Evaluation: The Role of the Critic of Popular Culture." *Journal of Popular Culture* 9.2 (1975): 355-65.

___. "Son of 'Against Evaluation': A Reply to John Sheldon Lawrence." *Journal of Popular Culture* 12.1 (1978): 113-17.

Sarchett, Barry W. "The Joke Is On Us: The End of 'Popular' Culture Studies, And It's A Good Thing Too." Paper presented at "The Future of Popular Culture Studies in the Twenty-First Century." Bowling Green State University, Bowling Green, OH, 4-6 June 1992.

Stille, Alexander. "The Novel as Status Symbol." *The Atlantic* 264.5 (Nov. 1989): 125-29.

Weiss, Michael J. *The Clustering of America.* New York: Harper & Row, 1988.

Zelinsky, Wilbur. *The Cultural Geography of the United States.* Rev. ed. Englewood Cliffs: Prentice-Hall, 1992.

POPULAR
CULTURE
AS
PROCESS

✦

"The Heart of the Wise
Is in the House of Mourning"

Stephen Tatum

As I walked out in the streets of Laredo
As I walked out in Laredo one day
I spied a cowboy wrapped up in a story
Immersed in a novel by Mr. Zane Gray [sic].

'Oh, beat the drum slowly and play the fife lowly
And play the Dead March as you give a look,
Take me to the green valley and pile the sod o'er
For I'm a young cowboy, was reading a book.'
                    "The Streets of Laredo (The Book-Worm's Lament)"
                                              (qtd. in Thorp 177)

When the call for papers honoring Ray B. Browne's distinguished career and his retirement from Bowling Green State University was announced, I was at the time particularly immersed in reading both a fairly ancient and a fairly recent critic of what might be called popular pleasures. On the one hand, I was working through the teacher's wisdom in Ecclesiastes, a reading selection chosen as a consequence of a trip to Texas to bury my grandfather. On the other hand, I was studying Walter Benjamin's "Theses on the Philosophy of History" and his essay "The Storyteller," writings which had been assigned as supplemental readings for a course I was teaching in Native American autobiography and fiction. Though my grandmother, being a good Christian woman, found more comfort in reading the verses from I Corinthians which announce Paul's belief in the diversity of gifts issuing from the same spirit, I rather found *counsel*, to borrow Walter Benjamin's word for the wisdom imparted by storytellers, in the proverbs from Ecclesiastes—particularly the one arguing that, because the way of all humans is death, "It is better to go to the house of mourning, than to go to the house of feasting" or, to quote the full verse from which I draw my title for this essay, "The heart of the wise *is* in the house of mourning; but the heart of fools *is* in the house of mirth" (7:2, 4).

57

Such sentiments, beyond the immediate context of enduring a death in the family, seemed particularly appropriate, upon my further reflection, both for honoring the career of a distinguished scholar and teacher of popular culture and for interrogating the future of popular culture studies. This appropriateness is so not simply because the generic name for the speaker in this Old Testament book is often translated as "teacher." Although it might at first glance seem strange or maudlin to celebrate Ray Browne's retirement with textual utterances focusing on death and mourning, we should first consider how this Old Testament critic of popular pleasures raises issues central to contemporary popular culture studies in academia. I am thinking here of issues such as the *worth* of popular pleasure, the fate of wisdom or the virtues of possessing knowledge, the ends of labor on this earth, and, of particular concern for this essay's purposes, the nature of the relationship between past, present, and future. Consider that for the teacher who speaks in Ecclesiastes, "The thing that hath been, it is that which shall be; and that which is done is that which shall be done." And since in the teacher's estimation "there is no new thing under the sun" (1:9), the future of popular culture studies—what it is which shall be and which shall be done—seemingly can be, indeed should be, found by interrogating the *past*, not prophesying the future. The problem, though, is this: because human thought is vexed by desires of the flesh and for material gain, and because words insufficiently represent reality, the pursuit and acquisition of wisdom brings on greater worry. As a result, the teacher further argues that "there is no remembrance of former things; neither shall there be any remembrance of things to come with those that shall come after" (1:11). Rather than ever knowing the past, and hence according to his logic knowing something also of the shape of the future, the teacher argues that what we actually experience is a *present* moment expanded merely in space and time, continuously rewriting the past in its own image, whorelike, to use the image from Ecclesiastes 7:26-29, in the way its rendering of the face of the past is seductive and yet ultimately barren. Or perhaps I should simply say this is what "Nick at Nite" is all about.

I am tempted to remark further on how the teacher's remarks seemingly belie his conclusion about our inability to remember the past or to forecast the future, since such past remarks diagnose precisely the contemporary anxiety with, and manipulation of, time that characterizes such recent movies as *Back to the Future* and *Peggy Sue Got Married*, as well as the public's selection of the "young" Elvis stamp. However, what we should recognize is that the teacher's notable melancholy, this caused—as Benjamin would argue—by his despair at ever grasping and knowing a *genuine* historical image, proceeds from a root desire to *empathize* with the past. My point here is that though we should seriously consider the pathos present in Ecclesiastes' sense that history is a parodic repetition of the same, which is of course another way of describing the elite critic's view of the "popular," such consideration does not *necessarily* mean we must settle solely for the satisfaction of food, drink, and doing one's work well. Perhaps sensing, as does Benjamin centuries later, that the dominant social order can and will always employ soothsayers to interpret the future so as to justify the present *status quo* (cf. Eagleton 146), the teacher appropriately stresses how the future lies in the past. But as Benjamin would add, the past needs to be interpreted against the grain, not connected in any *positive* dialectic between past and present as we see in, say, the recent *Back to the Future* movies. The task of the teacher or critic or scholar is thus not to retreat to the satisfactions provided by full stomachs and artisanal values. Nor is it to provide a commodified memory for a consumer culture full of faulty memories and disposed always to value the "now." The intellectual task is rather to forge a *radical* remembrance, one which regards past moments of popular texts and/or practices as sites for seeing the contestation of values, not simply the dissemination of hegemonic power or the transparent expression of a democratic public's will.

In reading Ecclesiastes through Benjamin, then, I want to stress that the future of cultural studies—"popular" or otherwise—in the academy will depend upon both individual and institutional efforts to recover the popular culture of the past, particularly its recovery of those sociocultural moments in which cultural definitions of "high" and "popular" culture are in flux, their territorial boundaries indeterminate and in the process of being stabilized by the social order for different reasons at different times. This is to say by way of critique that academic popular culture studies to my mind has too often been overly involved in what has been an uncritical promotion of the present or the near-past, a promotion that proceeds as if the mere citation of a popular cultural artifact guarantees or validates the triumph of democracy. "Uncritical" promotion means a critical trajectory which usually traces two arcs: on the one hand, the critical trajectory of such "presentism" takes a ride on what Raymond Williams has called "the nostalgic escalator,"[1] or, on the other, generally views popular culture as basically a ritual management of social differences that always produces, if only in fantasy, an ultimate consensual harmony. The result is a view of popular culture as working along the lines of a Coca-Cola-world-singing-together-in-perfect-harmony ad. Or even if a critique *is* offered during a reading of the popular in the present, the recurrent problem is that, whether from the left or right sides of the political spectrum, such interpretations often simply update, with different degrees of astuteness, of course, the Frankfurt School argument that the culture industry invariably and essentially manipulates the desires of willingly-duped audiences. This view we might call the "something's going on here but you don't know what it is, do you Mr. Jones?" approach to everyday life.

Consider for a moment two items from contemporary everyday life culled from daily newspapers, my selections predicated on the fact that both report on citations from cowboy culture by the world of entertainment and fashion. In the "Trends" section of the 29 May 1992 *Salt Lake Tribune*, it was reported, under the headline "Brave fashion wilds in a hat with hair," that designer Rene of Paris has created a "hat with hair" for urban cowgirls, this feat accomplished by his sewing a long, curly Kanekalon fiber braid of hair to the bottom of a hand-blocked cowgirl hat. "The look and feel of the hair belies the fact that the fiber is synthetic," the article states and for a mere $185 *you* can fulfill not one but "two cowgirl fantasies at once—having luxuriously cascading long hair and having the bravado to wear a cowboy hat." Indeed, as the fashion report notes, "Pop on the hat and—yeeee-haw—you could star in a Guess jeans ad."

The second item comes from a 15 May 1992 cabaret review in the *New York Times* headlined "Happy Trails in New York." It seems that the Rainbow and Stars cabaret atop 30 Rockefeller Plaza in New York City has booked a revue of western songs and cowboy poetry, this called "Cowboy Logic" (after the title of a recent Michael Martin Murphy record), for a four-week stint. The booking coincides with the establishment of Warner Western, a new record label devoted to reviving authentic Western music and folklore. In the rambling trailside musical three cowpersons—country-pop singer Michael Martin Murphy, cowboy poet Waddie Mitchell, and Texas troubadour Don Edwards—sit around an ersatz campfire taking turns singing songs and telling stories in a manner that consciously attempts, the reviewer notes, to link their own lives to late-nineteenth-century cowboy history and mythology. Thus, running through the material—and what apparently defines "cowboy logic" for these cowpersons—is "a deep strain of fatalism, because, as Mr. Edwards explained, 'the cowboys lived with death all the time.'"

Now, the notorious problem facing the critic of popular culture is precisely how to make sense—assuming one wants to make sense—of such anecdotal evidence from an everyday life that one is currently living in and through. This constitutes a problem simply because the popular culture critic generally does not enjoy, as is the case in other academic fields of inquiry, either the temporal or spatial distance with which to offer new, epitomizing knowledge about some preferred object of study, and because popular pleasures are associated with the body, not the intellect. But of course, in a manner similar to the teacher's rhetorical position in Ecclesiastes, the "something is going on here but you don't know what it is, do you Mr. Jones" approach generally does declare itself immune from the allures of such recent commodification of the cowboy figure, and from this separate, uncontaminated high moral ground better able to view and tell Mr. Jones what *is* going on here. Thus, in the case of "Cowboy Logic," what *seems* to be going on is a refurbishing of the West as a commodified image of therapeutic escape, a renovation grounded in a nostalgia for both the residual values of the historical frontier, particularly its ideology of pragmatic masculinity, and for the retro-50s dude ranch/television West of the baby-boomer generation's childhood. From this perspective, "Cowboy Logic" emerges as a kind of refried "Sky King" meets "Riders in the Sky" or as a *City Slickers* in reverse, since in this instance West comes East in a time-honored pattern pioneered by Buffalo Bill Cody or, perhaps of more relevance given Ray Browne's training in folklore, by John Lomax, who in 1911 traveled from Austin, Texas, to Ithaca, New York, to address the Modern Language Association about the songs of the cowboys (*Adventures* 82-85). Since one of the things the West is always about is the production of gender ideology, it would seem also the case that what's going on here is an affirmation of what has been called in other contexts a "new age" masculinity, one that combines a sort of working class male bravado with the softer masculinity provided by the contours of culture and sentiment. And the explicit identification here with previous male cowpersons as important figures authorizing the entertainers' present work and identity suggests that "Cowboy Logic"— like such recent movies as *Field of Dreams, Dances with Wolves, The Untouchables* and *City Slickers*—is preoccupied with repairing Oedipal rifts generated during the 1960s through the projection of ideal substitute fathers.

Furthermore, if cowpersons were somewhat fatalistic because they lived with death all the time, the cowgirl "hat-with-hair" invention, for those who particularly believe popular culture texts enact a ritual management of desire in the interests of harmony and disclose a conspiracy on the part of producers—this synthetic creation by Rene of Paris stinks of death. Harmonizing connotations of leisure and work, elegance and ruggedness, the artificial and the natural, this product, like the fashion system in general, of course promotes an illusion of personal renewal, this via a narrative of future adventure in the sexual selection jungle, which disguises the infinite sameness involved in the act of commodity consumption. The promised erotic sport with synthetic matter (Kanekalon fiber) prostitutes the body to the inorganic world, and in the process reveals a fetishistic psychic economy which flees from death by according an external object the power to fill the felt gap between an individual's present lack and future fulfillment. What's going on then, Ms. Jones, is the intended erasure of death by the fetishized object—but the imputing of redemptive power to the consumable object ultimately illuminates the inner blankness of the human subject.

Now what I mean by "the inner blankness of the human subject" can best be explained here by considering both how the "Cowboy Logic" outfit cites previous western popular songs and mythologies and how the ad copywriter fantasizes that one "could star in a Guess jeans ad if one possessed the cowgirl 'hat with hair.'" Such gestures reveal how a presumably desirable authentic experience is always subordinated to emblems or to cultural representations of experience. The cultural function of surveying cowboy and cowgirl performers would seem to be to offer up to our gaze the sight of the "authentic" or the "natural," since cow culture—as the name implies—is identified as close to the instinctual, not intellectual, world of animals and nature. Ironically, this surveillance is both a cause and consequence of what John Berger in *Another Way of Telling* names as our lost social subjectivity.[2] That is, we who have the leisure to gaze at displays of primitives wearing exotic dress and speaking an exotic, picturesque language—cowboys, peasants, indigenous peoples—desire to "see" what we have "lost" as a result of living in a devitalized, banal urban present, and in doing so displace our anxieties into the very act of looking, one which gives pleasure to the extent that the hungry eye is gratified by the visual possession of commodities.

Even more ironic, of course, is the sense that, as the musical revue's very existence indicates, the primitive, the authentic, or the natural has been lost from view, gradually and yet inexorably eradicated by the commodification of the cowboy in wild game haunts such as Manhattan cabarets. From this perspective, buying the "hat with hair" or consuming the cabaret experience cannot but disappoint since what we buy or go to discover as a result of having lost it—the "real" me; authentic life; an organic society—is not to be had or located, has been removed by the very process of modernization of which leisure time, places, and record labels are both practices and effects. Since the cowperson past in "Cowboy Logic" is rewritten to expel the traces of heterogeneity or of difference in cow culture, and since the desirable end of one's taking the place of the actual Guess jean model displaces any coincidence of being and meaning—prevents any self-identity—the identification and authority of *origins* is troubled. In terms of the "hat with hair," we should consider how its marketing strategy illustrates not only *intertextuality* in the sense that the desire to express the "real" me (or allow it to emerge) binds one to a series of textual representations beginning with the Debra Winger character in the movie *Urban Cowboy*. It also illustrates how the "natural" gets displaced by *representation*, in the sense that one defines one's authentic subjectivity by imagining the way others will regard and consume one's constructed self-image. In a word, both items illustrate what we've been in the habit of calling the postmodern condition, a condition in which the inability to experience origins due to a pervasive immersion in *simulacra* has caused a loss of faith in any larger, grand, totalizing narrative explaining everyday life. In this view, the temporary solace provided by the musical review and the "hat with hair" points up the various and fragmented ways cowpersons and other people make sense of everyday life under the sign of the commodity.[3]

As others have written in recent years—remember, as the teacher in Ecclesiastes says, there is nothing new under the sun—Western society's loss of faith in the power of totalizing or grand metanarratives has shifted our attention to the ways of worldmaking in local practices, particularly how these can trouble the top-down model of power relations. Thus, the second point to make here, in addition to my earlier one defining the future of popular culture studies as lying in a radical remembrance of the past, centers on the need for popular culture studies to commit itself to studying *how* groups use cultural resources to make sense of experience, to articulating how in practice such uses can be said to resist as well as accept the full domination by the commodity form. While both the teacher in *Ecclesiastes* and Benjamin offer different counsel on how humans should live in a world in which, like our own, expressions are ephemeral and in which human effort cannot guarantee desired results, the emergent issue both these critics of the popular implicitly raise in their writings concerns not just that of the fate of wisdom and the worth of labor, but also that of the degree of *tolerance* each is willing to grant the pleasure of others. Or, to put what's at stake here in the form of a question: when addressing the popular pleasures of either the past or the present, must we invariably repeat the kind of hygienic policing of popular desire that we see emblematized in Ecclesiastes and enacted in my above interpretation of "Cowboy Logic" and Cowgirl "hats with hair"? Must we always position ourselves, like the teacher in Ecclesiastes, as once a willing participant but now a privileged knower of truths beyond the ken of the mystified masses immersed in popular culture and everyday life? Can the worth of studying the popular thus be demonstrated without recourse in an earlier popular culture studies moment to campy trendiness or more recently to scapegoating the masses who supposedly fall prey to the manufactured illusions and profit motives of producers?

Though I'm afraid my own forays into interpretations of the popular have not for the most part argued this case, the answer to these questions can of course be "yes." In effect, this shift in emphasis to how consumers create popular culture can and should lead our critical work in two directions: one, if we still wish to examine cultural texts from the producers' perspective as a managing of popular desires so as to legitimate the dominant ideology, then more critical attention must be paid to how a surplus of utopian meanings, even in the most "degraded" cultural forms, as Ernst Bloch's work reminds us, can and does leak through the text; and two, if we wish to examine how consumers act as agents in making "popular culture," then it seems clear that the traditional humanities' orientation of popular culture studies needs to be more closely aligned with developments in cultural anthropology and, perhaps, even sociology. On the one hand, we truly need to think *dialectically* about the work of popular culture texts, which is to say that popular culture studies, to have a future, must resist the "just do it" mentality and disclose how popular texts and practices possess complexities which belie their status merely as formulaic reproductions of the dominant ideology. And on the other we need to utilize, among other skills, *ethnography* in order to make sense of the varied and often contradictory ways in which people make sense of the everyday.[4]

At this point I'm afraid that my recourse to the imperative mood makes me sound like a "preacher," to use the other prominent word identifying the speaker in Ecclesiastes. But consider how such a cultural text as "Cowboy Logic," like cowboy iconography in general, does not solely exhibit a theatricality associated with the alluring power of spectacle, but also, as part of its appeal and force, articulates a deep-seated desire in the contemporary social order to re-experience the merger of kinship *and* occupational affiliations. Consider how *this* particular commodification of the cowperson way cannot be said solely to privatize experience, precisely because the songs or poetries or tales also locate both performers and audiences in a community that the performing act provisionally brings into existence so as to repair the everyday's corrosive social fragmentation. What is too little interrogated is how *performance* itself, through its duration and use of space, can produce and challenge or negotiate cultural meanings. And with relevance to my title consider how the utopian impulse of comradeship coursing through cowboy songs and poetry ultimately moves in diametrical opposition to the desire for mirth, passes within and through feasting and laughter until it settles, like the trajectory of Ecclesiastes and of Benjamin's thought, on happiness gained through both intimate knowledge and remembrance of suffering and misfortune and death.

The point I'm moving toward with this observation is not simply (of course!) the familiar one concerning how life is savored to the fullest as it comes into close proximity to death. It is rather that the aesthetic of melancholy emergent in cowboy songs and poetry complicates popular cultural memories of the cowboy's energetic physicality, narcissistic individualism, and resistance to social control and social commitment. Here I'm returning by degrees to Benjamin's basic distinction between *memory*, the dominant culture's organized system of ideas and commemorative practices evoked to nourish the present, and *remembrance*, which—as Terry Eagleton has described it—depends on the critic's prognosticating the present and then deciphering the past's images before they sink into oblivion, a tactic which—as I've described it earlier in this talk—searches out the fragments of the past that keep alive its heterogeneity and refuses to substitute future liberation for memories of past oppression and inequalities. What I would like to do in closing is illustrate my major points: 1) the future of popular culture studies lies in remembering the past; 2) the need for critics to retrieve utopian impulses seeping out of texts and practices; 3) the need to jettison the pose of a neutral, unbiased, viewing critic whose transcendent gaze works to distance seeing subject from seen object in sensual, intellectual, and spiritual ways; 4) the further need to build into our methodological pursuits a commitment to seeing popular culture from what Clifford Geertz would call the "native's" point of view. These four points I would like to *begin* to set in motion by remembering the cowboy's emergence as a cultural figure of significance a little over a century ago.

I turn to 1886, the year when Theodore Roosevelt was adventuring in Dakota Territory; when Karl Marx's daughter Eleanor was in this country with her husband Edward Aveling lecturing on behalf of the Socialist Labor Party of North America; and when Jack Thorp, the eventual collector and publisher of the first volume of cowboy songs, was out West buying stock horses for polo players back East—and heard for the first time "The Cowboy's Lament." Roosevelt devotes extensive attention to the cowboy in his *Ranch Life and the Hunting Trail* (1888), illustrated by Frederic Remington, then a newcomer to the New York art scene. In his autobiography and semi-documentary history of range life, Roosevelt overdetermined the cowboy's workingman status with codes emphasizing his warrior and aristocratic heritage and tastes. The result was a classic incorporation: the cowboy's residual individualist traits were yet depicted as serving the interests and needs of an expanding, corporate industrial society. In 1886, for instance, Roosevelt found the cowboys patriotically eager to form a troop cavalry when rumors of war circulated through Dakota Territory, and he adds in a footnote that in the following year, "on the day the Anarchists were hung in Chicago, my men joined with the rest of the neighborhood in burning them in effigy" (109). Thus, as a result of Roosevelt's portrait of the cowboy as a guileless figure who shared his overseer's views and who was better, morally speaking, than the desperadoes and buffalo-hunters he encountered in Dakota, Roosevelt identified, as did Wister and Remington in the next few years, the view of the cowboy as the unacknowledged, but pure, racial type. The "Bad Man" in his books is not the westerner who resists social commitment but Wall Street bankers, Populist farmers, and labor radicals. One measure of the transformation in the cowboy's stature that Roosevelt—with Remington's help—inaugurated can be seen in the fact that only a few years previously President Chester Arthur, in commenting in 1882 on range wars in the West, used "cowboy" as a synonym for outlaw or desperado.

Now Roosevelt's discourse was responding in part to the dime novel tradition, and his celebration of an exotic working primitive functioned ambivalently. Though the cowboy's work and so-called code legitimated the dominant culture's economic, political, and moral interests, his "untrammeled individualism"—or at least that was what Roosevelt selected for value at the time—critiqued the increasingly corporate consequences of the modernizing process that was foreclosing on the cowboy's peculiar independent manliness. By contrast, the Avelings discovered, in a Cincinnati "dime museum," that the cowboy's anti-modernist potential did not always get managed. The chief attraction at this "dime museum" was a group of cowboys *on exhibit,* "sitting in two and threes on various little raised platforms, clad in their picturesque garb, and looking terribly bored." "To our great astonishment," they report in *The Working-Class Movement in America* (1888), one cowboy, John Sullivan—*alias* Broncho John—a man with a "singularly handsome face and figure, with the frankest of blue eyes," rose up and "plunged at once into a denunciation of capitalists in general and ranch-owners in particular" (157). According to Broncho John, cowboys were increasingly fed up with dangerous work, isolation, and economic oppression by cattlemen, and many desired to form a cowboy union along the lines of the Knights of Labor. For their part, the Avelings conclude that the cowboy who works out-of-doors is as oppressed as the factory worker who works indoors in either Old or New England.

What interests me here is how the exotic primitive on display in a "museum" devoted to exhibits of "curiosities" breaks the distance between seer and seen, disrupts not only the conventions or the "rules" of the exhibit, but also the emergent cultural representation of the cowboy as the last true, free individual. Broncho John's and the Avelings' ultimate failure in contesting the cowboy's cultural representation in both the Roosevelt-Wister-Remington line and the dime novel entertainments provides a case study in how the material conditions of production and the dissemination of cultural knowledge are bound up with the power of constructing historical memory. What I want to retrieve here is a sense of the cowboy's collective identity or social subjectivity as something more significant for the culture's participants, more democratic, in fact, than that *part* of the cowboy code stressing an individual's honorable consistency in treating others which has been promoted as the *whole* of the cowboy's essence. With this in mind, I want to turn to the classic cowboy song Thorp heard first in 1886, "The Cowboy's Lament," sometimes entitled "The Streets of Laredo." Its lineage traced to the venerable "Unfortunate Rake" tradition, the song appears in Thorp's 1908 edition, as well as—though bowdlerized—in Lomax's 1910 edition, which is dedicated to Theodore Roosevelt. The song would seem to be of special interest for popular culture students, since its narrative of sin, death, and remorse indicts popular pleasures—in this case drinking and gambling—in a manner that reminds us of how an underlying sense of Christian righteousness persistently locates the cowboy's life in service to an official bourgeois morality. Indeed, on the surface its project seems to be that of enforcing a melodic Ecclesiastes type of complaint about the vanities of this world. But what needs further to be said has two aspects: 1) how the song identifies—as do many cowboy songs—the merger of kinship and occupational values in the face of death, this desired merger accomplished through an oral performance; and 2) how the utopian impulse to comradeship coursing through the songs takes substantial shape precisely because of and in opposition to the absent but felt presence of an official morality.

Consider the song's opening stanza, in which the dying cowboy lying on the streets of Laredo notes a passing stranger's "get-up," or outfit, identifying him as a fellow cowboy and hence endowing him, and not others in this public space, with the status of an auditor worthy to hear the dying cowboy's lament. In its various versions the song proceeds as the narrator looks back to his origins, confesses his sins of gambling and drinking, and expresses remorse over having left family and, in at least one version, a "good" woman and a potentially stable marriage for the adventurous cowboy life. Most of the song's verses, however, detail the dying cowboy's various requests of his cowboy auditor(s): for example, for a surgeon to mend his wounds; for a minister to pray for him; for a letter to be sent to his parents and former loved one; for his auditor to shield him so his "shame" will not be noticed by passing strangers. Certainly on one level the song is structured by a dialectical tension between the body in pain in the present and the body projected as a corpse in the future needing to be covered with flowers so as to counter the smell of its decomposition. The lament takes on power not only because the sense of instruction here is charged by its proximity to life's end, but also because of the cowboy's remorse, expressed early in the song, over both his previous forsaking of his actual family and his future forsaking of the reconstituted authentic family of cowpunchers with whom he took pride in his work. Interestingly, the narrator's projection of his body diffused into fragments ultimately allows him to sequester his imagined and real losses and transform them into a cultural representation disclosing redemptive meaning. In the face of the mystery of death, in the face of the ultimate indeterminacy of meaning, and with the recognition that individuals cannot control, however hard they try, the interpretation of their existence, the narrator can be overheard desiring to bequeath to his fellows a *fully* comprehensible and comprehensive sign: flowers on his coffin will indubitably proclaim that here is a cowboy "cut down in his pride."

However, the beauty of the song lies elsewhere than in its seemingly sentimental effort to discipline the worker's body who dallies in popular pleasures. We should notice, first, how the dying cowboy's narrative is shot through with a tender solicitude for his cowboy listener(s), this emotion marked by his request that the cowboys not grieve for him and by his anticipation that their burden of carrying his corpse will be eased, as I mentioned above, if flowers are strewn to stifle the smell of death and if the clods of earth to cover his coffin are dropped gently so as not to overpower onlookers with an aural reminder of death's hollow blankness. This is to say that as much as the song situates the teller before fate and destiny, it is equally—if not more so—concerned with placing the listener before the task of resuming a life in the world. The latter concern is particularly highlighted by the verse in which, having finished his "sad story," the dying narrator asks for a glass of water from his fellow cowboy auditor. The song's power intensifies at this point, for the failure of one mission—the wounded cowboy dies before his compatriot can return with the water—leads directly into the accomplishment of another. The auditor now becomes narrator and finishes the story, which centers on the forging of an occupational family of men and women (six cowboys and six maidens) united by their fulfillment of the dead cowboy's request for a particular funeral:

> We beat the drum slowly and played the fife lowly
>   And we bitterly wept as we bore him along.
> For we all loved our comrade, so brave, young, and handsome,
> We all loved our comrade although he'd done wrong. (Thorp 159-60)

Benjamin describes an aesthetic of melancholy characterized by a single protagonist, alone, amid ruins, whose identification with a desolate scene precludes feeling, whose gaze is unresponsive, cryptic, withdrawn, enigmatic. Although he obviously could not have had *Lonesome Dove* in mind, this aesthetic of melancholy certainly is embodied by the figure of Call and his particular way of honoring Gus' dying wish. What "The Cowboy's Lament" illustrates—and what has been overlooked in discussions of the song—is the wisdom that comes from being in the house of mourning, one predicated on resisting the privatization of everyday life, one predicated on experiencing an intensity of heart (the grace of love and comradeship) through a sense of misfortune. The song should not be regarded as an exercise in sympathy or empathy—nor is it at bottom a story of a chance meeting. My phrase "resisting the privatization of everyday life" is prompted not only by the shift in the final stanza from the individual "I" to the collective "we" who express their love and respect *in the face of* the cowboy's having done wrong. The recovery of social subjectivity the song traces in my account of it is inaugurated by its taking place in a *public* space. The oral performance enacted in and by the song does not focus on the cowboy's muteness, his invisible internal life or thought. Feelings are expressed visibly and audibly, and the lyric, insistent repetition of words and sounds intensifies the sense that all that is spiritual and internal is being made manifest in terms of the body and words and tears and physical movements.

As Bakhtin has said of the early Greek romances (134-35), the individual in this cowboy song is entirely visible and audible, his exteriority ultimately grounded in an organic human collective: He is there for the others whose companionship he laments losing; the others are there for him, and in the act of mourning they form an expanded mirror image of the initial dyadic relationship of the opening stanza. In the course of the song the teller becomes less active, finally becoming silent, while the listener becomes more active, ultimately becoming a narrator. And we who at the song's outset are situated as auditors overhearing the "sad story" passed along become the specific audience addressed by the final stanza's listener-turned-narrator. In the public space of Laredo, in the temporal space of the song, then, a field of co-existence is created, one whose stress on interdependency and intersubjectivity belies the lonely isolation of death. In this regard, finally, the song reminds us of how a "parting" is at the same time a "meeting," in that within its temporal and spatial boundaries, an act of recognition occurs in which each participant hopes to cache an image of the other so that nothing—particularly the moralists' voice—can efface it (cf. Berger 109).

Nevertheless, before I forget too quickly one of my points about the future of popular cultural studies being connected with its practitioners' interrogation and account of the "native's" point of view, let me introduce here cowboy Teddy Blue's remark in his autobiography that he always had to stop and laugh when he heard "The Laredo song" sung, in spite of its sadness. As he remarks, "'I first took to drinking and then to card playing'—and they'd all be drunk when they was singing it, most likely" (Abbott 222-23).[5] Knowing that Broncho John refused to be an immobile curiosity for visual consumption by those who can afford to pay for a spectacle, knowing these cowboys' appropriation of the song, recognizing how the song redeems, via the proximity of death, social subjectivity rather than narcissistic individualism, and knowing that parting with Ray Browne on the occasion of his retirement can be, as "The Cowboy's Lament" instructs us, another form of meeting—knowing these things reminded me above all that the future of popular culture studies needs, on the part of its devotees, to include a dose of humility in thinking about how we frame our assertions about how the popular is produced and consumed. Whether or not this essay lives up to its own exhortations, its beginnings were definitely influenced by my learning from my grandmother that during the 1920s and 1930s she and her husband, my maternal grandfather, both of whom would be called working-class readers, would read Zane Grey *aloud* to each other at night before dropping off to sleep, a practice which certainly troubles my own received wisdom about gender and class issues in the distribution and consumption of the popular.

Notes

[1]Williams means by the term "nostalgic escalator" the tendency for critics to push some sense of a viable "organic" community further and further back in time "as a stick to beat the present" (367). 'Old England' and its timeless pastoral rhythms, for instance, is located in the early nineteenth-century by twentieth-century critics, the eighteenth century by Victorian critics, etc. Beyond the need for us to notice the universal and persistent strain of the nostalgic, Williams argues that we should interrogate how the desire to locate an organic society means "different things at different times, and quite different values are being brought to question" (367-68).

[2]I want to thank Reggie Twigg for this source and for insights about this relevant book for anyone interested in the matrix of subjectivity, commodities, consumption, and cultural spaces for resistance.

[3]The further point here would be to note how in a culture supposedly devoted to the present or the "now" the structure of commodity consumption and the economy of desire in actuality evacuates the experiential present, voids it as the press of desire anticipates a future (or a past, if nostalgia is the key mode) more satisfying than the present.

[4]Here I'm thinking of the instructive insights offered by the work of Geertz and especially Clifford on the virtues of and the obstacles to avoid when trying to see from the native's point of view, particularly discussions that center on the need to develop an ethnographic method which moves away from the mode of "salvage," or redemptive, ethnography, which assumes "that the other society is weak and 'needs' to be represented by an outsider (and that what matters is its past, not present or future)" (Clifford 113). In institutional terms, I'm obviously recommending here a rethinking of the curricular organization of training for students in popular culture studies.

[5]In recovering the popular culture of the past, one obvious danger is that the scholar's effort at radical remembrance can in the end produce instead a form of critical nostalgia for the past, seen as the location of wholeness and authenticity in contrast to the scholar's inauthentic, fragmented present. In this context, I should stress that the implicit point in *my* reading of this song and my citation of Teddy Blue's response concerns our discovering, to cite Burke, "the grammar of motives" in the responses to the song at different times by differently-constituted audiences. Teddy Blue's participant "ethnography" clearly is situated with and against another, more sentimental reading disseminated in the culture, and points us to consider further the interaction of working-class and bourgeois audiences whose modes of response, whether nostalgic or ironic, occur at a particular moment in the modernization of the nation. Similarly, as far as I can tell, my own textual selection and effort to recover the utopian impulse of comradeship in the song and to define a

particular aesthetic of melancholy emerges of course as cowboy poetry, cowboy music, and cowboy fashions have been recently revived by fashion and entertainment arms of the economy. A fuller, differently framed essay on these texts, then, should trace various appropriations of the song at different cultural moments to probe the cultural function of nostalgia.

Works Cited

Abbott, E.C. ("Teddy Blue") and Helena Huntington Smith. *We Pointed Them North: Recollections of a Cowpuncher.* 1939. Norman: U of Oklahoma P, 1971.

Aveling, Edward and Eleanor Marx. *The Working-Class Movement in America.* 1888. New York: Arno, 1969.

Bakhtin, M.M. *The Dialogic Imagination: Four Essays.* Ed. Michael Holquist. Trans. Caryl Emerson and Michael Holquist. Austin: U of Texas P, 1981.

Benjamin, Walter. *Illuminations.* Ed. Hannah Arendt. Trans. Harry Zohn. New York: Schocken, 1969.

Berger, John. *Another Way of Telling.* New York: Pantheon, 1982.

"Brave Fashion Wilds in a Hat with Hair." *Salt Lake Tribune* 29 May 1922: C1.

Burke, Kenneth. *A Grammar of Motives.* Berkeley: U of California P, 1969.

Clifford, James. "On Ethnographic Allegory." *Writing Culture: The Poetics and Politics of Ethnography.* Ed. James Clifford. Berkeley: U of California P, 1986: 98-121.

Eagleton, Terry. *Walter Benjamin, or, Towards a Revolutionary Criticism.* London: Verso, 1981.

Geertz, Clifford. *Local Knowledge: Further Essays in Interpretive Anthropology.* New York: Basic Books, 1983.

Holden, Stephen. "Happy Trails in New York." *New York Times* 15 May 1992, National ed.: B3.

Lomax, John A. *Adventures of a Ballad Hunter.* New York: Macmillan, 1947.

___. *Cowboy Songs, and Other Frontier Ballads.* New York: Sturgis and Walton, 1910.

Roosevelt, Theodore. *Ranch Life and the Hunting Trail.* 1888. New York: Winchester P, 1969.

Thorp, N. Howard ("Jack"). *Songs of the Cowboys.* Eds. Austin E. and Alta S. Fife. New York: Clarkson & Potter, 1966.

Williams, Raymond. "The Nostalgic Escalator." *Contemporary Critical Theory.* Ed. Dan Latimer. New York: Harcourt Brace Jovanovich, 1989: 364-68.

Children and Colors:
Children's Folk Cultures and Popular Cultures in the 1990s and Beyond

Jay Mechling

Americans take their blurred genres in stride (Geertz 19-35). Like Alvin Toffler's 12-year-old daughter, who returned home from a trip to the store to inform her father rather too nonchalantly that the store that had been there a week earlier was gone, simply gone (56), most Americans of the 1990s live comfortably in a postmodern world of pastiche, ironic juxtapositions, and self-reflexive parody. On Monday, May 18, 1992, the popular CBS television sitcom character Murphy Brown, played by Candice Bergen, gave birth to her son, an event watched by nearly forty million Americans and, for those old enough, a television text that, itself, recalled the off-camera television birth of Lucy's baby on *I Love Lucy*. Thirty-five years earlier 44 million American watched the episode in which Lucy gave birth to Little Ricky, far many more Americans than watched Eisenhower's inauguration the following day (Diggins 188). And that text (the birth of Little Ricky, not Ike's inaugural) itself resonated with the media coverage of the real birth of Lucille Ball's baby, though in the "real" case the baby was a daughter, an accident of birth that needed fixing by the writers.

On Tuesday night, May 19, 1992, Vice President Dan Quayle, in a speech before the Commonwealth Club in San Francisco, used the birth of a child to an unwed Murphy Brown as evidence of the moral decay responsible for, among other things, the Los Angeles rioting (only a few weeks earlier) in the wake of the verdict in the Rodney King case of police brutality. That verdict, a culture text fixed forever in our memories, took its salience in large part from the fact that the event in dispute was videotaped. And, as our American proverb holds, "seeing is believing" (Dundes, "Seeing" 86-92). Just as months earlier seeing was believing in the videotape of the altercation in a Los Angeles convenience store leading to the fatal shooting of a black teenage girl by the clerk, a middle-aged Korean woman.

And then, just one week after Quayle's attack on Murphy Brown, President Bush himself cited a new study juxtaposing two facts: first, that children watch on the average of three hours of television each day, and, second, that children are reading less and that children's reading comprehension (as measured by standardized tests) continues to decline. President Bush joined a long line of public figures in concluding that television is to blame for what's wrong with American kids.

Let me shift my gaze, now, from the intertextual forest of the public debate over the salience of television in the morality of Americans to the equally public debate within the university over multiculturalism and "political correctness." A month after the Los Angeles riots Leo Marx, the distinguished American Studies scholar most famous for his book, *The Machine in the Garden* (1964), spoke before the university teachers gathered at a national conference on "American Studies and the Undergraduate Liberal Arts Curriculum," held at Vassar College and sponsored by the National Endowment for the Humanities. Marx voiced ambivalent concern over the present culture wars in the United States. After rehearsing in detail the history of American Studies's and America's move from 1950s consensus to 1960s conflict, Marx characterized the present state of our wars over multiculturalism. Although Marx finds salutary the effects of multiculturalism within the academy, he also finds something of value in the calls by figures such as historian Thomas Bender for a new synthesis in American history (120-36). When our retreat into particularism starts to look like the dangerous Balkanization we see, literally, in the war in the former Yugoslavia, said Marx, then isn't it time we ask whether intellectuals can contribute somehow to a revitalized sense of nationhood in the United States? Marx noted that he was not calling for the revitalization of the old grand narratives privileging White Anglo-Saxon Protestant male experience, but for the recapture of some sort of grand narratives that stress what we share rather than what makes us different. Echoing Bender's theme that we have lost perspective and balance in our talk of parts and wholes in American culture, Marx asked if we who call ourselves American culture critics cannot return to the initial American Studies project of understanding better the whole.

The audience for Marx's address responded pretty much as one might guess, finding an uncomfortable nostalgia in Marx's project. But what was most remarkable about Marx's talk and about the discussion thereafter was that *popular culture was mentioned not even once!* Nevermind that television provides continuous narratives about what it means to be an American in a multicultural society, from the gang on Sesame Street to the new society encoded as a new generation of Star Trek characters. Nevermind that the films of George Lucas and Steven Spielberg provide self-consciously mythological narratives of American experience, or that the films of Spike Lee speak directly to our discourses on race and gender. Nevermind, in short, that popular, mass-mediated culture contains exactly the sorts of narratives—exactly the sorts of hypotheses about the relations of parts to wholes—that Marx wants to see coming from American Studies scholars.

So here are the strands I wish to begin weaving together in this essay—Leo Marx's question whether there isn't some way to talk about wholes as well as parts in American culture and others' questions whether children would be better off watching less (or no) television. Actually, I wish to recast these questions in the scholar's more familiar terms of culture criticism. Grand tradition in culture studies leads us to see the totalizing force of the mass media, to see television and film and a dozen other genres as complicit in creating the cultural hegemony (Antonio Gramsci's term) underlying rather trivial expressions of difference. A newer tradition focuses instead upon the consumption of popular culture texts as sites of resistance. Reader and audience response theories and approaches cast aside the portrait of the reader or viewer depicted as a passive, uncritical consumer of texts and paint instead the picture of people engaged in the active social construction of meaning, sometimes with and sometimes against a popular culture experience (Davis and Puckett 3-33). My interest in children's lives leads me to focus these questions upon the experiences of children. Are children's experiences with popular culture only totalizing, or do children have at their disposal cultural resources for resisting popular culture? Do gender, race, class, or any other particularities of children matter in the ways they "take" popular culture texts? How might the ethnographic study of children's lives in natural settings help answer these questions?

I shall begin with the general landscape of our scholarly thinking about the consumption and resistance of popular culture, and then move quickly to what happens to that thinking when we cast our gaze upon the lives of American children. Finally, I shall want to draw some broader theoretical, methodological, and even political conclusions from my examination of children's encounters with mass-mediated cultures. My title, "Children and Colors," evokes for me these multiple meanings—of children watching color television, of children of different colors watching television, of children of different colors thinking about human differences, and even about some children who must choose their "colors," which for them means choosing a gang.

Hegemony and Resistance

Popular culture critics are now familiar with Gramsci's notion of hegemony, a concept developed by the Italian Marxist as a way of revising Marxist theory to account for the puzzling ways domination seems to operate in Western societies in the twentieth century. Gramsci characterized hegemony as "the 'spontaneous' consent given by the great masses of the population to the general direction imposed on social life by the dominant fundamental group; this consent is 'historically' caused by the prestige (and consequent confidence) which the dominant group enjoys because of its position and function in the world of production" (12). This sounds simple enough, but historian Jackson Lears cautions us that Gramsci had in mind a very subtle system in which consent and force (or the threat of force) always coexist, but in different proportions. "Ruling groups," explains Lears, "do not maintain their hegemony merely by giving their domination an aura of moral authority through the creation and perpetuation of legitimating symbols; they must also seek to win the consent of subordinate groups to the existing social order" (569). The primary devices for engineering this consent, of course, lie in the "discursive practices" (Foucault's term) of dominant groups, of groups that have the means to make their own narratives more pervasive and more compelling than the narratives of less powerful groups.

Lears notes that for Gramsci consent "involves a complex mental state, a 'contradictory consciousness' mixing approbation and apathy, resistance and resignation. The mix varies from individual to individual; some are more socialized than others. In any case, ruling groups never engineer consent with complete success; the outlook of subordinate groups is always divided and ambiguous" (570). This opens the public space to the possibility of "counterhegemonies," discourses that are oppositional to the dominant discursive practices. English Marxist historian and culture critic Raymond Williams points to two sources of alternative and oppositional sources. He uses the term "residual cultures" to describe the result when "some experiences, meanings, and values which cannot be verified or cannot be expressed in the terms of the dominant culture, are nonetheless lived and practised on the basis of the residue—cultural as well as social—of some previous social formation" (10). Folk cultures often live in these interstices, serving to maintain (we might say) the diversity of the gene pool for the future possibility that the residual culture will emerge as a better cultural practice than the present, dominant one. "Emergent cultures" are Williams's second source of potential opposition and counterhegemonic discursive practices. By emergent Williams means "that the new meanings and values, new practices, new significances and experiences, are continually being created" (11). The dominant culture usually attempts to incorporate—to co-opt—emergent practices and cultures, as we see so often in popular culture. The dominant culture seems less interested in incorporating residual practices and cultures, but folklorists see this process when dominant discursive practices latch onto and commodify folklore or, in the case of "the invention of tradition," use thin understandings of folk cultures to justify new practices (Hobsbawm and Ranger). The folk usually abandon their folklore once its oppositional power is diminished by its appropriation and incorporation. That was the fate of break dancing and, one suspects, could be the fate of rap music. By way of summary, Lears notes that

To resort to the concept of cultural hegemony is to take the banal question—"who has power?"—and deepen it at both ends. The "who" includes parents, preachers, teachers, journalists, literati, "experts" of all sorts, as well as advertising executives, entertainment promoters, popular musicians, sports figures, and "celebrities"—all of whom are involved (albeit often unwittingly) in shaping the values and attitudes of a society. The "power" includes cultural as well as economic and political power—the power to help define the boundaries of common-sense "reality" either by ignoring views outside those boundaries or by labeling deviant positions "tasteless" or "irresponsible." (572)

The next stage in the development of critical thinking about these cultural processes was the emergence of audience response theory and criticism. Radway's *Reading the Romance* stands as the exemplar of reader-response approaches, as she offers both a formalist reading of the romance novel texts and a fieldwork-based (though not quite ethnographic) analysis of the social construction of the meanings of the novels by women who read them. At the same time, media critics were developing an audience response reception theory which, for example, led Ien Ang and others (e.g., Lull; Seiter et al.) to chart the differential meanings constructed by people watching television narratives, such as *Dallas*. John Fiske's work and ongoing work in British cultural studies in many ways dominate scholarly discourse on reception theory, as Fiske has operationalized through his criticism such key notions as "resistance." For Fiske and others, popular culture events are sites of struggles over meaning, as the text works to narrow and close the range of its meanings and the audience actively works to resist one interpretation and to open the text by constructing alternative and oppositional understandings of the text's messages (Fiske 62-83).

As attractive as reception theory may be, it faces some serious problems. For example, it would be generous to call the method "ethnographic," for in most cases the researcher is not engaged in anything like an ethnographic method. Interviews and mailed questionnaires do not amount to ethnographic surveillance of the social construction of meaning in natural settings, and a great deal of the scholarship that passes for audience reception research actually relies more upon the researcher's inferring the audience's resistances rather than actually discovering them in discursive practices.

But even if we improve our ethnographic practices in reception research, we still face challenging conceptual problems. Some critics see characteristic American optimism in overblown claims about the range of freedom audiences have in constructing the meanings of popular texts. Todd Gitlin has voiced this criticism most dramatically, perhaps, when he complains that

"resistance"—meaning all sorts of grumbling, multiple interpretation, semiological inversion, pleasure, rage, friction, numbness, what have you—is accorded dignity, even glory, by stamping these not-so-great refusals with a vocabulary derived from life-threatening political work against fascism—as if the same concept should serve for the Chinese student uprising and cable TV grazing. (191)

A most interesting criticism of reception theory comes in Celeste M. Condit's discussion of "The Rhetorical Limits of Polysemy." Reception theory argues that popular culture texts are "polysemic," that is, that texts actually permit and may even invite multiple interpretations, thereby making them more open texts that create space for oppositional cultures. Condit complains that this view overstates the actual ways in which an audience can "read" a text. Texts themselves may have more power than we think to constrain readings, but Condit's real contribution is to draw our attention to a number of other factors constraining the ability of an audience to make multiple readings of texts. Using as a case study the responses of two college students, one pro-life and the other pro-choice, to an episode of *Cagney and Lacey* dealing with the debate over abortion, Condit shows how two viewers may agree on the "meaning" of a text but suffer from a number of constraints on their ability to resist the text. Condit's constraining factors are the "audience members' access to oppositional codes, the ratio between the work required and the pleasure produced in decoding a text, the repertoire of available texts, and the historical occasion, especially with regard to the text's positioning of the pleasures of dominant and marginal audiences" (103-04). Condit concludes that

To assess the social consequences of a mass communication event requires...that we dispense with the totalized concept of "resistance." It is not enough to describe a program or an interpretation of a program as oppositional. It is essential to describe what particular things are resisted and how that resistance occurs. (117)

So, to summarize our current state of criticism of mass-mediated culture, while we willingly replace old-fashioned consensus theory with a conflictual understanding of the dynamic process of hegemony and resistance, we no longer take for granted the victory of either dominant or oppositional cultures. Our ethnographic practices in these studies are so thin and crude that they hardly deserve the name. So the goal of further research must be to gather "thick descriptions" (Geertz's term) of the reception of mass-mediated narratives by audiences in their natural settings. Until we begin that work, we cannot begin to answer some of the questions I raised at the outset, that is, questions about the degree to which Americans may "share" a common culture. Do gender, race, ethnicity, social class, sexual orientation, and other human particularities create or permit radically different readings of mass-mediated texts? Or are there factors—some internal to the texts themselves, some external— that constrain our readings of the texts, so that gender and all the rest matter relatively little?

Children's Culture(s) as Repertoires for Resistance

Having stated (too briefly, I fear) our present practices in thinking and writing about mass-mediated texts and audiences, I am prepared now to turn to the material that interests me most. Audience reception theory addresses only adult audiences or, at best, children as part of larger family audiences. As usual, we ignore children because we are so certain *a priori* how they "read" mass-mediated texts. So presumably there is no need actually to do the ethnographic work of looking at the ways in which children may engage in their own social construction of the meanings of mass-mediated texts. This is a version of a common fallacy among scholars, most of whom construct in their imaginations and writing the "child" they want to see rather than the child who may contradict their expectations. What is needed in these circumstances is a fresh look at children and their encounters with popular culture. We may find that our view of the passive child mesmerized by television, for example, is thoroughly wrong, but we won't know that until we study children's lives in natural settings. It turns out that folklorists are the adults who are doing this kind of study, so let me offer an assortment of tantalizing studies that may raise more questions than they answer; but, at least, the questions they raise are far more interesting than the stale assumptions that govern our writings and silences about children's lives. What links these examples is the child-centered view that asks how children actually read mass-mediated texts. These examples may encourage us to undertake the research we should be doing in the twenty-first century—that is, research into the relative importance of particularities (gender, ethnicity, social class, and so on) in constraining or opening up children's social constructions of the meanings of mass media texts.

Some researchers have shown the proper respect for children's perspectives on mass media texts. Notable, for example, is Robert Coles's lengthy discussion of the film *To Kill a Mockingbird* (1962) with the white and black New Orleans children he was interviewing during the stressful days of integrating that city's schools (66-76). Black and white children, it turned out, read the film very differently, the white children focussing on the main plot of race relations, while the black children focussed (much to Coles's surprise) on the subplot involving Boo Radley, the ultimate protector of the children.

It is folklorists who have the best perspective on children's lives in natural settings, so my main examples come from those sources. Folklorists know that children construct peer cultures that are very powerful socializing institutions. Peer cultures are folk cultures, and as such they are primarily oral cultures, so children learn the dynamics of communication in a setting where the structures, poetics, and aesthetics of the communication are oral. Children learn in their oral folk cultures that communication is dialogical, that most oral performances (of a story, of a riddle, of a joke) blur the boundaries between performer and audience, such that the telling of a story is interactive—really, a collaboration between the narrator and the audience. We would be quite surprised, therefore, if we found children attracted to a communication event (say, watching television) without bringing to that event a sensibility that one can enter a conversation with that performer, even if the performer seems to lack the feedback loops we normally expect in a conversation (see Caughey).

Folklorists also know that children's folklore is (in Brian Sutton-Smith's word) highly "antithetical." Children are relatively powerless beings, but they are also highly resourceful, taking power in those areas under their control—namely, their talk and their bodies. Children's folklore mocks adults and adult institutions, often engaging in the parody we find in modernist critiques of culture (Mechling 91-120). Moreover, children's folklore evidences what Gary Alan Fine has called "Newell's paradox," that is, the paradox that children's folklore is simultaneously conservative (in its fixed formulas, for example) and dynamic ("Newell's Paradox" 170-83). In Raymond Williams's terms, the folk cultures of children are both residual and emergent.

Now, what might the folklorist say to the worry of Neil Postman and others that television is the enemy of children's folk cultures? The folklorist greets this worry with skepticism, seeing it more as a projection of adult anxieties than a real threat to children (e.g., see Best). Children are extraordinarily resourceful and resilient human beings who are quite adept at understanding power relations in their dealing with adults. In the dialectic between mass-mediated culture created by adults for children and children's folk cultures, children take more power than adults realize.

There are really two "moments" in this dialectic. In the first moment, adults take children's folklore and turn it into a commodity that, in turn, is sold back to the child. Both folklore and popular culture rely heavily upon traditional formulas for their structures and themes, so the appropriation of children's folklore works rather well. For example, the frightening figures of fairy tales and, later, of adolescent urban belief legends like "The Hooked Hand" serve important psychological and social functions (Dundes, "Psychology"). Children conjure and react to "monsters" as part of a natural process of taming fears. Children hear and retell these stories, playact the stories, and use toys to enact the stories as part of this process of exciting and then taming fears. It is, in the folklorist's view, a small step toward creating commercial toys (like "Transformers") and commercial narratives (like the *Friday the Thirteenth*, *Nightmare on Elm Street*, and similar films) that are extensions of the children's own folk narratives. Media critics like Neil Postman insist that this is a large step, that the media have a logic, aesthetic, and power qualitatively different from face-to-face communication, but the folklorist would remind Postman that children usually play with Transformers in play groups and that teenagers usually watch *Friday the Thirteenth* in groups. True to Newell's paradox, those films and the television narratives (cartoon shows) accompanying toys like the Transformers turn out to endorse quite conventional morality.

Put differently, we might say that a commercial toy or narrative becomes most popular not because children have been seduced into some adult agenda but because the toy or narrative is *familiar* to the child. The Teenage Mutant Ninja Turtle phenomenon has been so great because the narratives are those of the preadolescent boys who are their primary audience (Fine, "Ninja Turtles" A19). Similarly, the Garbage Pail Kids stickers were enormously popular in the 1980s because they served children's fascination with "gross" things. Some adults made a great deal of money by recognizing children's desire to invert and ridicule the Cabbage Patch doll and to explore forbidden topics of dirt, disorder, and bodily mutilation.

We might say, then, that the first moment—the moment of commodification—in the dialectic between children's folk cultures and mass-mediated culture shows us that children in the late twentieth century find their folk cultures mirrored in the commercial popular culture. Popular culture is comfortable and comforting because it is so familiar. Television is an aesthetically and poetically "friendly" medium for children, resembling the aesthetics and poetics of children's oral cultures much more closely than the unfriendly medium of the printed page (see Ong; Gronbeck, Farrell, and Soukup, eds.).

The familiar and friendly nature of mass-mediated narratives makes easy the second moment of the dialectic, the moment wherein the children turn the tables and appropriate commercial culture into their own folk cultures. This appropriation is an important element of the dynamism we see in Newell's Paradox. Brian Sutton-Smith's extensive project at the University of Pennsylvania on "The Folkstories of Children" yielded some interesting examples of the ways in which both the content and the poetics of television narratives entered children's own folk narratives. Boys apparently were more affected by television narratives than were girls, and the research team made a particular case study of the ways in which exposure to the trickster formula of Bugs Bunny cartoons enhanced the ability of children to render their own competent versions of trickster narratives (Abrams and Sutton-Smith). In an ethnographic study of playfighting in preschool children, Sutton-Smith and his students found that television seemed to provide the children richly textured fantasy frames (such as names, costumes, and props) for what the researchers recognized as the traditional play of "good guys versus bad guys." Two of the researchers

carefully noted the way in which non-aggressive children used the fantasy of the symbolic content to tone down and contain the physicality of the more aggressive children. Here was a stage in which they sought to capture violence, if not the conscience of the Kings. Interestingly, when play therapists rationalize the use of war toys to evoke violence in their child patients, they apparently are making use of a similar expectation that the "wild beasts within" can be tamed through well-ordered fantasy, which is to say, in our case, "folk games." (Sutton-Smith, Gerstmyer, and Meckley 172)

Folklorist Margaret Brady discovered that television narratives affected the traditional Navajo skinwalker narratives told by Navajo children exposed to the Anglo media, and other folklorists working with children can cite many similar examples from their own fieldwork, examples that show how creative and subtle children can be in mixing mass-media elements with traditional play.

Patricia Banez offers a different sort of example that also stands for many others. She studied closely the daily play of a group of five children (ages 7 through 13 from two families) who created an ongoing fantasy play scenario based upon the popular television show, *The Simpsons*. Calling themselves "The Simpletons," these children assumed roles from the show and constructed elaborate plots based in part upon real plots from the show and in part from their own imaginations. The children wove together in these dramatic texts three separate sorts of narratives: the media narrative of a television family, the everyday narratives of the children's two families, and the everyday narratives of the social relations in their play group. Like the preschool children who used fantasy frames to control an unruly child, these older children used play roles and fantasy narrative frames borrowed from television in order to work through the troubles they had in their relations within their families and within the peer group. Sometimes the improvised television scripts permitted children to play roles and assume powers otherwise denied them; at other times, the children used the fantasy frame to make quite astute and poignant commentary about their home families.

Banez's study should warn us how dangerous are generalizations based upon textual criticism alone. Many parents and teachers watching the Simpsons see only negative "role models" and feel especially threatened by Bart Simpson's sassy, antithetical ways. Many parents forbid their children to watch *The Simpsons* and several school districts, stunned by Bart's critique of the schools, actually have banned the wearing of Bart Simpson tee-shirts. Banez's ethnographic eavesdropping on children's actual interpretations and uses of the television show help us see the audience's social construction of meanings from the texts, meanings that textual analysis cannot yield.

As everybody knows, video games are the latest example of what adults see as, in Gary Alan Fine's wonderful phrase, *fun noir*. The latest entrants in adult complaints are two books purporting to understand the conspiracy of media represented by video games. The first, Eugene Provenzo's *Video Kids: Making Sense of Nintendo*, is easiest to dismiss quickly, for Provenzo's attack is so full of the adult's thin reading of the violence and aggression in video games, so full of the romantic nostalgia for "free play," and so empty of the children's perspectives on the game that the book is more useful as a psychological projective test of adult anxieties than of the meaning of Nintendo. Marsha Kinder's *Playing with Power in Movies, Television, and Video Games* is a more sophisticated book, but once again it is a book about *adult* readings of the intertextuality between the texts of television and of video games. Kinder muddies things by seeming to have asked kids about the games and television and movies incorporating video games (e.g., *The Wizard*, *Teenage Mutant Ninja Turtles*), but a close reading of her book reveals that most of her generalizations come from talking with her preadolescent son, Victor, and then not letting us hear much of Victor's voice. In short, Kinder offers us the semiotician's formalist and Lacanian reading of the video game, television, and movie texts, uninformed either by reception theory's issues of resistance or by folklorists' issues of the creative appropriation of adult texts by kids. There is no ethnography here. Consider, in contrast, the following example closer to the folklorist's approach.

Syndy Slowikowski observed her kindergarten-age son and three of his friends build a "fake Nintendo" game in the absence of the real thing. The children drew a television screen with a number of Nintendo game sequences and characters on a large piece of cardboard and connected that piece to two smaller cardboard "control panels" with shoelaces. "To the outsider," writes Slowikowski, "the screen was an indecipherable code of stick figures, scribbles and what appeared to be clouds and plants. But the children remembered each figure, and uninitiated children immediately recognized the figures and story-line" (8). The children continued to play with the "fake Nintendo" even when the family finally bought a real version. To Slowikowski's inquiry why they continued to play with the "fake" game, the children answered that they actually preferred their own creation, and their responses confirm the power and control they felt in playing with their folk version:

> "This is better than real Nintendo because it is fake."
> "Yeah, you don't have to die."
> "You don't have to miss any duck birds."
> "I can change into anything."
> "You get to go wherever you want."
> "Things don't have to eat or kill you."
> "Or you can kill what you want. Not like the other Nintendo."
> "And, you can go slow." (11)

Indeed, Slowikowski observed that the "fake Nintendo" made it possible for several children to participate at the same time, for the play group to adjust the pace of the play to suit an individual player or group mood, and to change the game from a "zero-sum game" to one where "no one loses, or runs out of time." The children sometimes would stop the play in order to draw new figures, so the "fake Nintendo" is truly interactive with the children. Folklorists often see children manipulate the rules of their folk games in order to accommodate the younger or less-capable players, and the "fake Nintendo" game simply lays the Nintendo fantasy frame on top of very traditional games and negotiations (e.g., Hughes). Fantasy role-playing games appeal to teenagers for the same reasons (Fine, *Shared Fantasy*).

Conclusion

So how do these examples return us to the questions I posed at the outset of this essay and to the larger question of an agenda for the study of the dialectic between children's folk cultures and mass-mediated, popular culture? President Bush's worry is the easiest to address. Adults would make better use of their time working to ameliorate the material conditions of millions of American children—of homeless children, for example—than fretting over the effects of television and video games. Children are quite resilient and resourceful in the symbolic realm; they are more at our mercy when we let them go hungry or put them in genuinely awful institutions "for their own good."

Leo Marx's worry is a different matter. Have our attentions to the particularities of experience in local cultures led us to contribute to a dangerous political situation where Americans are no longer united (if they ever were) by a sense of peoplehood and citizenship? Is there a way to recapture some sense of what we share, without discovering that what we share is some hegemonic mythology scripted by those whose interests are served by our believing in the grand narratives they spin?

My answer to these pressing questions is perfectly postmodern in its mood. That is, my answer is emergent, incomplete, and dialogical.

There may be serious reason to believe that children—and, therefore, probably adults—share more than we think they do. Marjorie Harness Goodwin returns to this theme at the conclusion of her wonderful book, *He-Said-She-Said: Talk as Social Organization Among Black Children*. Goodwin's ethnography of the play groups of children (aged 9-14) in a black, working-class neighborhood in Southwest Philadelphia is attuned to the very subtle ways those children used talk to construct their peer culture. Since race and social class are constants in Goodwin's groups, she focuses her attention primarily upon gender differences in the discursive practices of the children, but she also draws upon other scholarship (most of it based upon white, middle-class children) to help her understand how ethnicity and class may be at work in the peer cultures she is studying.

Goodwin discovered some differences in the discursive strategies of girls and boys, but overall Goodwin came away impressed more by the ways in which girls "may build differentiated speech actions that are appropriate to the situation of the moment, and speak in a range of 'different voices'" (64). Thus, *contra* Gilligan, girls are quite capable of showing the moral concerns of "justice and rights" as well as those of "care and responsibility." Goodwin believes that we have put too much emphasis upon *differences* in our study of children's cultures, and her own ethnographic experience suggests that there is a great deal of sharing that crosses our traditional thinking about gender and race (social class may be a different matter).

I share Goodwin's suspicion that children are more alike than we imagine. My own ethnographic work with a troop of white, middle-class Boy Scouts reveals a peer culture not far removed from the cultures unpacked by recent ethnographic work among black and Latino gangs (Fine and Mechling). The dynamics and ethics of Boy Scout troops and gangs may not differ much. The problem is that our scholarly and lay adult mindset is to look for differences and to overlook similarities. The problem also is that we usually don't bother to look at children's peer cultures with a sensitive, ethnographic eye as clear as possible of the adult bias to see children as we expect to see them. We simply don't know enough about the peer cultures of children to know what they share. We have scant ethnographic knowledge of the ways children interact with and may resist mass media. So a possible agenda carrying our research into the twenty-first century is for folklorists and other ethnographers of children's lives to explore the dialectic between children's folk cultures and mass-mediated, popular cultures.

Or we could leave the kids alone. That is a tempting option, but, unfortunately, there are too many well-meaning adults determined to "protect" and "save" children according to their own adult agendas of what childhood should be. Ethnographic research into the lives of children in natural settings can serve the crucial purposes of child-advocacy, especially if the advocacy is to leave the kids alone. Hunger, homelessness, juvenile AIDS, and a dozen other conditions of the lives of American children show us how silly are the concerns of adults who want to "protect" kids from popular culture.

A final warning: we must also beware of romanticizing the power of resistance that any audience has, including children. It is possible that the diabolical cleverness of hegemonic processes lies in their ability to carve out space for harmless oppositions and resistance. As Raymond Williams shows us, the dominant culture of late capitalism has an uncanny ability to absorb and domesticate residual and emergent countercultures. Ann Kaplan, at the conclusion of her semiotic analysis of MTV, argues that, unlike Europe, the United States never has had a truly oppositional youth culture, that the "opposition" really has been crafted and contained by media managers (152).

We adults may feel so powerless in the face of hegemonic forces that we want to find genuine oppositional cultures and vicariously identify with their resistances. Our own work—creating fantasies of resistant, oppositional cultures (if that's what we're doing)—may be abetting the work of hegemony. This possibility should not paralyze us, but it should make us humble and energize us to link our scholarship with social action meant to make a more humane world for children, children such a Murphy Brown's new son.

Works Cited

Abrams, David M. and Brian Sutton-Smith. "The Development of the Trickster in Children's Narrative." *Journal of American Folklore* 90 (1977): 29-47.

Ang, Ien. *Watching Dallas: Soap Opera and the Melodramatic Imagination.* London: Methuen, 1985.

Banez, Patricia D. "The Simpletons: An Ethnographic Study of Children's Use of Media Narratives." Unpublished senior thesis in American Studies, U of California, Davis, Apr. 1991.

Bender, Thomas. "Wholes and Parts: The Need for Synthesis in American History." *Journal of American History* 73 (1986): 120-36.

Best, Joel. *Threatened Children: Rhetoric and Concern about Child-Victims.* Chicago: U of Chicago P, 1990.

Brady, Margaret K. *"Some Kind of Power": Navajo Children's Skinwalker Narratives.* Salt Lake City: U of Utah P, 1984.

Caughey, John. *Imaginary Social Worlds.* Lincoln: U of Nebraska P, 1984.

Coles, Robert. *The Moral Life of Children.* Boston: Houghton Mifflin, 1986.

Condit, Celeste Michelle. "The Rhetorical Limits of Polysemy." *Critical Studies in Mass Communication* 6 (1989): 103-22.

Davis, Dennis K. and Thomas F.N. Puckett. "Mass Entertainment and Community: Toward a Culture-Centered Paradigm for Mass Communication Research." *Communication Yearbook/15.* Ed. Stanley Deetz. Newbury Park, CA: Sage, 1992: 3-33.

Diggins, John Patrick. *The Proud Decades: America in War and Peace, 1941-1960.* New York: Norton, 1988.

Dundes, Alan. "On the Psychology of Legend." *American Folk Legend: A Symposium.* Ed. Wayland D. Hand. Berkeley: U of California P, 1971: 21-36.

___. "Seeing is Believing." *Interpreting Folklore.* Bloomington: Indiana UP, 1980: 86-92.

Fine, Gary Alan. "Children and Their Culture: Exploring Newell's Paradox." *Western Folklore* 39 (1980): 170-83.

___. *Shared Fantasy: Role-Playing Games as Social Worlds*. Chicago: U of Chicago P, 1983.

___. "Those Preadolescent Ninja Turtles." *New York Times* 1 June 1990: A19.

Fine, Gary Alan, and Jay Mechling. "Child Saving and Children's Cultures at Century's End." *Identity and Inner City Youth: Beyond Ethnicity and Gender*. Eds. Shirley Brice Heath and Milbrey W. McLaughlin. New York: Teachers College P, 1993: 120-46.

Fiske, John. *Television Culture*. New York: Routledge, 1987.

Geertz, Clifford. "Blurred Genres: The Refiguration of Social Thought." *Local Knowledge: Further Essays in Interpretive Anthropology*. New York: Basic Books, 1983: 19-35.

Gilligan, Carol. *In a Different Voice: Psychological Theory and Women's Development*. Cambridge: Harvard UP, 1982.

Gitlin, Todd. "Commentary: Who Communicates What to Whom, In What Voice and Why, About the Study of Mass Communication?" *Critical Studies in Mass Communication* 7 (1990): 185-96.

Goodwin, Marjorie Harness. *He-Said-She-Said: Talk as Social Organization among Black Children*. Bloomington: Indiana UP, 1990.

Gramsci, Antonio. *Selection from the Prison Notebooks*. Ed. and trans. Quintin Hoare and Geoffrey Nowell Smith. London: Lawrence & Wishart, 1971.

Gronbeck, Bruce E., Thomas J. Farrell and Paul A. Soukup, eds. *Media, Consciousness, and Culture: Explorations of Walter Ong's Thought*. Newbury Park, CA: Sage, 1991.

Hobsbawm, Eric and Terence Ranger, eds. *The Invention of Tradition*. New York: Cambridge UP, 1983.

Hughes, Linda A. "Beyond the Rules of the Game: Why Are Rooie Rules Nice?" *The World of Play*. Ed. Frank E. Manning. West Point, NY: Leisure P, 1983: 188-99.

Kaplan, E. Ann. *Rocking Around the Clock: Music Television, Postmodernism, and Consumer Culture*. New York: Routledge, 1987.

Kinder, Marsha. *Playing with Power in Movies, Television, and Video Games: From Muppet Babies to Teenage Mutant Ninja Turtles*. Berkeley: U of California P, 1991.

Lears, T.J. Jackson. "The Concept of Cultural Hegemony: Problems and Possibilities." *American Historical Review* 90 (1985): 567-93.

Lull, James. *Inside Family Viewing: Ethnographic Research on Television's Audiences*. New York: Routledge, 1990.

Marx, Leo. *The Machine in the Garden: Technology and the Pastoral Ideal in America*. New York: Oxford UP, 1964.

Mechling, Jay. "Children's Folklore." *Folk Groups and Folklore Genres*. Ed. Elliott Oring. Logan: Utah State UP, 1986: 91-120.

Ong, Walter J. *Orality and Literacy: The Technologizing of the Word*. London: Routledge, 1982.

Postman, Neil. *The Disappearance of Childhood*. New York: Dell, 1982.

Provenzo, Eugene. *Video Kids: Making Sense of Nintendo*. Cambridge: Harvard UP, 1991.

Radway, Janice A. *Reading the Romance: Women, Patriarchy, and Popular Culture*. Chapel Hill: U of North Carolina P, 1984.

Seiter, Ellen, et al., eds. *Remote Control: Television, Audiences, and Cultural Power*. New York: Routledge, 1989.

Slowikowski, Syndy. "The Culture of Nintendo: Another Look." *Journal of Play Theory and Research* 1 (1993): 8-11.

Sutton-Smith, Brian, John Gertsmyer and Alice Meckley. "Playfighting as Folkplay amongst Preschool Children." *Western Folklore* 47 (1988): 161-76.

Toffler, Alvin. *Future Shock*. New York: Bantam, 1970.

Williams, Raymond. "Base and Superstructure in Marxist Cultural Theory." *New Left Review* 82 (1973): 3-16.

Five Ways of Looking at Aprille
(with Apologies to Wallace Stevens):
Analysis of Storytelling in the Twenty-First Century

Judith Yaross Lee

A slippery problem facing scholars of popular culture involves how to analyze examples that exist as multiple texts or performances rather than as a single stable artifact. Stable artifacts include the texts of popular fiction, tapes of radio or television broadcasts, and theatrical films or videotapes. The comic strip or book is somewhat less stable, since a scholar may have to grapple with the historical authority of the newspaper feature page versus the narrative authority of the anthology or comic book, but one can make a case for studying either version or both. A similar problem exists for some television series, which broadcast videotapes of live performances before a studio audience. *All in the Family* (1971-79), for instance, exists in two video forms: the master tapes of the live performances and the edited tapes of the broadcast series. Although the edited tapes captured most of the live performance's spontaneity—various pratfalls and glitches in performance became evidence of the taped show's authenticity—the cuts not only kept the show within necessary time limits, but also altered its substance: the off-color remark or gesture, long laughter from the audience. Still, a scholar can distinguish between the master and broadcast tapes in much the same way as between an author's manuscript and the published text. Despite the limitations of the broadcast tapes, which (among other things) obscure whether the audience laughed for 15, 30 or 55 seconds—they nonetheless are the authoritative texts for studying the work of producer Norman Lear and his cast. They represent commercial television, whereas the master tapes record only a studio performance.

By contrast with stable artifacts such as these, consider standup comedy and public storytelling. Both involve multiple performances that vary the material in many ways. Some variations are minor; others, substantive. Some represent a refinement; others, simply a variation with only subtle shifts in sense. Folklorists have made progress on but not really resolved the interpretive problems that result from multiple texts.

91

Richard Bauman and Sandra K.D. Stahl have focused on the relation of each telling to its narrative context, for example, accounting for differences in the tellings in terms of the different narrative events.[1] Contextual criticism thus downplays variations in phrasing and concentrates instead on theme, structure, and cultural significance. Seeing narrative details mainly as elements of a cultural message, however, gives the criticism a didactic thrust more appropriate to fairy tales than to the monologues of Johnny Carson or Spaulding Gray. Under the circumstances, it is not surprising that even folklorists have found the thematic and structural approaches limiting. As Dell Hymes observed in his examination of a pair of transcriptions, "Each telling makes use of common ingredients, but it is precisely in the difference in the way they are deployed and shaped that the meaning of each is disclosed" (392).

Variations matter even more in popular performances, which have become commodified as commercial art. Whereas the traditional folk narrator served as a medium of transmission, today's standup comedian or storyteller is the author of the material as well as its performer. The oral narratives of the standup comedian or public storyteller may sound like folklore, particularly the genre known as the personal experience narrative, and the anecdotes may in fact have originated in experience, yet the comedian and professional storyteller have no obligations to truthfulness. Audiences grant these performers the novelist's license to invent, and willingly suspend their disbelief. Variations from performance to performance are therefore more substantive than variations among performances of a folktale, even though traditional tellers commonly had their own, distinctive ways of telling a tale.

They are also more significant than variations in the performances of a scripted play. Whether introduced accidentally or deliberately by actors, director, crew, or performance space, variations on a script give different audiences different experiences of the play, but theoretically, at least, the performance remains somehow distinct from the play itself. Just as the musical performance is recognized as the approximate rendering of the ideas in the score (Dehnert), the dramatic performance is recognized as an approximate rendering of a definitive text. Such a text does not even exist for standup comedy and public storytelling, although we tend to behave as if it does. For a recent example of this phenomenon, consider the efforts by Lenny Bruce's producer, Don Friedman, to recreate the comedian's 1961 Carnegie Hall performance in commemoration of what would have been Bruce's 67th birthday. The fifteen actors who auditioned in July 1992 based their impersonations not on Bruce's own monologues, which were of course ephemeral, nor even on Bruce's own recordings, which are more stable, but on the stable 1974 text of Dustin Hoffman's re-enactment of unstable routines in the film *Lenny* (Weber).[2]

As oral genres grounded in colloquial talk and tending toward improvisation, standup comedy and storytelling reverse the stage play's implied priority of written text over live performance. And not only is the performance more definitive than the written text: the various oral performances of a single story or routine vary in authority in relation to one another. Unlike the multiple video-texts of the television broadcast, one public performance will not have more authority than others, unless some are designated rehearsals or trials. Unlike the successive drafts of a manuscript, the most recent performance does not always stand as the artist's last word.

A particularly illuminating case in point is Garrison Keillor's 1986 story "Aprille," which nearly defies classification. The story takes its inspiration from *The Canterbury Tales*, builds its theme on a passage from the New Testament, and blends his wife Ulla Skaerved's recollection of a childhood game on the bus with half a dozen fictional Lake Wobegon anecdotes—all the while purporting to tell his own experiences. So, "Aprille" is not folklore, not even "literary" folklore like the personal experience narrative (Stahl 12-28), though it imitates folklore: the monologue is a professional performance presenting fictional personal experiences of narrator Garrison Keillor of Lake Wobegon, Minnesota (a fictional town)—all of these created by writer Garrison Keillor of Anoka. Nor is "Aprille" a short story, since it was composed primarily for oral performance, not for print. Nor is it television, since the Disney cameras that recorded the show (originally transmitted live via cable and later shown over public television) shot it from the vantage point of the studio audience—as a radio program being witnessed by an audience, not as a show that was meant to be telecast. But the monologue is not conventional radio, either, since the speaker engages in intimate conversation and lies instead of the public and factual material that make up normal radio talk. All these modes of storytelling contribute to the tale's humor by inviting and then frustrating our generic expectations.

More important, the tale itself invites us to examine relations between oral and written storytelling, since Keillor structured "Aprille" around the ten-line opening of Chaucer's "Prologue," giving the oral story a thoroughly literary grounding. The recitation not only reminds us that *The Canterbury Tales* itself presented purportedly oral stories as written texts, but also calls attention to the difference between the text-bound activity of memorization and the performance-based activity of improvisation in Keillor's own narration. In addition, as Chaucer's words set the springtime Minnesota scene for the main story—how Lois Tollerud, a young woman troubled by the existence of evil in the world, does not find her faith on Confirmation Day, yet nothing happens as a result—Keillor also establishes a series of thematic parallels among the three pilgrims of the tale. Lois, Keillor, and Chaucer all undertake spiritual journeys that turn into occasions for storytelling, and in "Aprille" as in *The Canterbury Tales*, the pilgrims' stories become more important than the religious goals inspiring them.

Despite the seriousness of its themes and structure, "Aprille" remains typical of Keillor's work: it is also a very amusing story. Narrator Keillor's own pilgrimage fails when he arrives in Lake Wobegon and finds that his whole family apparently ran out the back door, at which point his journey to see them devolves into a quest for a toilet. His goddaughter Lois is also on a quest (she's looking to regain her faith in God), but at first they find only each other. As one anti-climactic anecdote leads to another, the humor builds in a conversational, apparently unstructured way that belies Keillor's intense labor on it.

The monologue was the centerpiece of a performance celebrating the grand re-opening of St. Paul's World Theater on Friday, April 25, 1986, and it was broadcast live the following night during his regular Saturday evening radio show, *A Prairie Home Companion* (1974-87). Keillor's popularity in 1986, soon after he agreed to allow the Disney Channel to cablecast the weekly show, made the April 26 broadcast extremely important to him, and even after the opening "concert" (i.e., non-broadcast) performance on Friday evening he continued tinkering with the details and themes of the story all the way up to broadcast time on Saturday night. Before each oral performance, he worked at his word-processor, printed out a draft, and edited it by hand. The result of this process is five variants of the tale: the Friday computer printout with handwritten emendations (version 1, 4/25/86), the Friday evening broadcast (version 2, 4/25/86), the Saturday computer printout with handwritten emendations (version 3, 4/26/86), the Saturday evening broadcast (version 4, 4/26/86), and the published *Leaving Home* story (version 5, 230-37).[3]

The first text (version 1) contains all three of the main stories— Lois's lost faith, Einer Tingvold's lost binoculars, and young Gary's fear of being isolated from family and friends—along with a fourth anecdote about the Tolleruds' agnostic Uncle Gunnar, which remained in all three written versions but was never included in an oral rendition. But several crucial details in Lois's story changed after the first performance, and the ending of the narrative continued to evolve through the second performance (version 4). Several of the most significant changes in his second performance did not, however, find their way into the published version of "Aprille," which appeared in *Leaving Home* (1987), a collection of Lake Wobegon tales published shortly after *A Prairie Home Companion* went off the air. Although Keillor's introductory "Letter from Copenhagen" described *Leaving Home*'s stories as "written for performance on the radio" (xvi), this fifth, published version of "Aprille" is neither a transcription nor a reworking of either oral performance, but rather a minor revision of the second printout (version 3).

Together the five variants of "Aprille" illustrate the problems inherent in analyzing the unstable texts of oral popular culture and point the way toward more systematic and sensitive analysis of storytelling in the twenty-first century. We need to find techniques appropriate to these texts and to understand the increasingly important roles of print, broadcasting, computers, and audio tape in defining them.

"Aprille" illustrates the fundamental difficulty of identifying exactly what is the story, since unlike the successive drafts of a manuscript the five variants of the tale do not exist in simple chronological relation to one another. Additions to the written text carry over thematically, if not always literally, into the next oral telling, yet improvisations in the oral tale are seldom incorporated into the next draft. The process thus underlines the greater importance of the oral versions, and their greater autonomy, and suggests that the final written version of the story (version 5) remains less significant than the second oral performance (version 4).

The first printout, for example, shows Keillor working to expand the description of springtime in Lake Wobegon at the beginning of "Aprille." Next to the typed remarks about trees and birds, he added a handwritten note in the margin: "The NBFs are washing their sheets, a sure sign" (version 1). In the first oral performance that same evening, he provided an even fuller description, saying, "this last week the Norwegian bachelor farmers washed their sheets, which is a sure sign that the cold weather, cold weather is over, and they're starting now to think about the danger of, the danger of infection" (version 2). The repetition of the phrases "cold weather" and "the danger of" work like "um" or "uh," as voiced pauses suggesting that Keillor invented the phrasing on the spot, and this implication of spontaneity asserts the authenticity of the storytelling event: the speaker hasn't prepared his remarks in advance. In this case the phrasing almost certainly was spontaneous, however, since none of the other variants repeats it exactly.

The next day, the second printout (version 3) shows Keillor integrating into his electronic text the marginal note from the first printout, but *not* the remark about "the danger of infection" from the previous night's oral performance. Instead, the text notes merely, "and now the Norwegian bachelor farmers are washing their sheets—" (version 3). The remark remains in that form in version 5, the version published in *Leaving Home* 15 months later. In the second oral performance (version 4), however, Keillor altered not only the phrasing of the item but also its placement and details. He postponed mentioning the Norwegian bachelor farmers until after he had described Lake Wobegon's springtime scenery in detail, finally noting, "the Norwegian bachelor farmers hung out their sheets, this last week, finally washing their sheets after those long winter months. Now it's finally safe to do em" (version 4).

These variations in such a simple matter demonstrate that Keillor's weekly monologue had more in common with a jazz performance than with an impromptu speech. That is, the monologue was a planned performance featuring spontaneous talk. The demands of live radio made this risky enterprise all the more precarious, since a live broadcast cannot be edited if the program runs too long. In all his years on this tightrope, Keillor fell only once, in Juneau, Alaska on July 12, 1986, when he just could not bring his monologue to a close, even though he had written a nine-page text for himself (Miller). Keillor worked out the components of "Aprille" carefully but nonetheless embellished and altered it in performance. His written drafts therefore represent prompts for the performance, suggesting the directions of his thoughts and his thematic intentions, but remaining subordinate as texts to the public performances.

For example, consider the different reasons that the bachelor farmers finally do their laundry. In the first telling they wash the sheets because it's warm enough for the bacteria in them to breed; in the second telling they wash them because it's finally warm enough to risk coming in contact with water. Keillor does not seem simply to have changed his mind here; the two jokes are equivalent. The point is the eccentric variation on the traditional obsession with spring cleaning. The exact rite is less important than the fact that a rite exists because the rite is more ritualistic than practical. In the case of the Norwegian bachelor farmers, spring cleaning accomplishes very little. Washing their sheets—for whatever reason—will not appreciably raise their level of hygiene. Perhaps more important for a theory of oral narrative, equivalent variation is possible because oral tellings do not supplant one another in the same way that successive drafts do. Whereas interpretation of writing rests on the principle of final intention, in which the authoritative text is the last of successive written drafts, interpretation of oral storytelling requires a principle of simultaneous authority, in which each telling has equal validity.

If the substance of these differences matters very little, the fact that the differences exist matters very much, indeed. The anecdote is full in the oral performances and sketchy in the printouts, in a progression typical of oral retellings. Richard Baumann notes that stories tend to grow when retold (81), especially when the teller commands the attention of the audience without having to seize it from other parties present—the difference, for example, between yarn spinning around a campfire or in conversation and the full performance of a storytelling festival, in which the featured storyteller is expected to demonstrate virtuosity (101-06). But the relationship between Keillor's written texts and the next telling reflects the complexity of the hybrid genre within which he works. Although details become more elaborate in the retellings, episodes may be rearranged, truncated, or eliminated. For example, both oral performances of "Aprille" mention the day of a rainstorm, and in the second performance Keillor elaborates the detail by making a show of searching his memory for the exact day—"[I'm] thinking about an afternoon, like—well, Tuesday, or Wednesday aft— Wednesday afternoon, after that tremendous rain that we had in the morning" (version 4)—but none of the written versions, including the version published in *Leaving Home*, refers to a specific day of the week. By contrast, Keillor apparently considered Daryl's Uncle Gunnar important enough to devote about 250 words to his eccentricities in each of the written texts, including the *Leaving Home* version, but Uncle Gunnar does not make even a brief appearance in either oral performance. We cannot know whether Keillor dropped the anecdote to keep the monologue within the allotted time (one aspect of his virtuosity was surely his ability to work within the finely calibrated time intervals of live radio), or whether he lost interest in the material but failed to delete it from the computer file that ultimately became the text in *Leaving Home*. Any analysis of the story must take this inconsistency into account, but it points to the theoretical difficulty of assuming that versions in two media stand in strict chronological succession to one another.

Other differences, however, clearly show the artist changing his material and sharpening his vision of it. Apparently dissatisfied with the tale he told on Friday night, Keillor sat down on Saturday and made two major changes in the computer text that became version 3. He deleted three suspected miracles that inspired Lois to keep an open mind about her lost faith, and moved the anecdote about Einer Tingvold to follow rather than precede the tale of playing strangers on the bus. Integrating these changes led to others, resulting in very different themes and meanings between the Friday and Saturday versions, oral and written.

In Friday's versions 1 and 2, the possibility of miracles tempers Lois's crisis of faith. The hot water does not run out as usual on Saturday night, her mother manages to get a stain out of Lois's confirmation dress, and her father's arm does not burn when his new sweater catches fire from the candles on her cake. These events strike her as possible evidence that God does exist, and they allow "Aprille" to end with some optimism for Lois and for all the faithful. Removing them, on the other hand, diverts the tale from questions of God's existence to questions of human faith. It also allows Keillor to emphasize the parallels between Lois and himself: she becomes terrified when her prayers echo without response, just as he had been frightened as a child when another Lois, his aunt, pretended during their game of "Strangers" that she did not know him.

As deleting the miracles diminished the tale's optimism, so moving the Einer Tingvold anecdote altered the story's original theme. An example of faith sure-to-be-found in versions 1 and 2 became a warning about faith abandoned in versions 3 through 5. With the story of how Tingvold threw away the next day's breakfast eggs and his own beloved binoculars just because he was frustrated that an unruly group of Boy Scouts wouldn't learn semaphore signals, Keillor provides a highly comic parable on the dangers facing Lois in her doubts about God on the eve of her confirmation. The anecdote's new position after the story of playing "Strangers," a game in which a young Keillor and his aunt Lois pretend not to know one another until the boy feels frightened and lost, emphasizes the consequences of throwing away one's religious values in the heat of a moment's disappointment. At the same time, the binoculars need not symbolize faith or even integrity to provide a reason for telling Einer's tale, since its details offer the considerable pleasures of comic retribution.[4] As a result, "Aprille" not only implies the orthodox conclusions that Lois's faith in God matters less than God's faith in her, and that neither God nor faith will abandon her if she does not throw them away or try to become someone she is not, but also insinuates the downright blasphemous notion that faith is irrelevant to a good story. In this context, the parallel between Lois's story and Einer's also intensifies relations among the three storytellers in "Aprille": Keillor, Lois, and Chaucer.

Eliminating divine intervention (or the perception of it) also required changes to the ending of the monologue. In the first oral

performance, he started with the simple conclusion of his written text—
"For the fourteen year olds of this world, I'm glad to get old so they can
grow up and we'll see what they do with themselves" (version 1)—and
extended it into a comment on how the world as a whole benefits from
the courage of the young, "who having lost their faith could stand on the
edge of darkness and wait for it to return" (version 2). By the next day,
however, his written text proposed that loss of faith has less to do with
God than with ourselves. People get caught up in games like "Strangers"
and, after a time of playing at being someone else, forget who they really
are. Nonetheless, God's grace remains as reliable as the signs of
springtime: "the sweet breath, the tendre croppes, and the smale fowle
maken melodye—God watches each one and knows when it falls, and so
much more does He watch us all" (version 3). The power of Chaucer's
poetry and Keillor's rhythmic line, a resolution to the question of evil,
and the storyteller's virtuoso control over an apparently formless tale
bring the third version of "Aprille" to a powerful close.

But although Keillor carried over this ending from version 3 to
version 5, the text published in *Leaving Home*, he did not repeat it in
version 4, his final oral performance. Apparently on inspiration in that
Saturday night broadcast, he loosened the connection between spring
and reborn faith. Instead, he proposed a more generalized power in "this
world, and each other, and the people in it": "Well, I'm transformed by
this world, the one that I look at. It's so beautiful. I believe that it has the
power to make us brave, and to make us good. This world, and each
other, and the people in it. It has the power to give us faith, the sweet
breath of the wind and the tender crops, and the small fowles maken
melodye that slepen all the nycht with open eye" (version 4). Whereas
the written texts of versions 3 and 5 offer the traditional Christian
insistence on faith in spite of doubt, the oral text of version 4 offers
consolation through poetry, not doctrine.

My point is not simply that Keillor declined to revise the second
written version to incorporate changes made in the second telling, or
even (as I suspect), that at some level of consciousness he chose an
orthodox conclusion for his stable written texts and a more ambiguous
ending for his unstable oral texts. Rather, the issue is, what finally is "the
story"? The lesson of "Aprille" is that scholars of storytelling need to
answer that question on an individual basis for every tale and teller. For
now we must conclude that the story is not, to borrow terms proposed by
Barbara Herrnstein Smith, some "basic story" consisting of elements
common to the five variants, nor a Platonic ideal of the tale constructed
from bits and pieces of the variants (209-32). Moreover, a reliable
analysis cannot look solely at the published text of an oral tale, no matter

how much one would like to replace multiple unstable texts with a single stable one. Any reconstruction of "the story" must take into account sequential, substantive changes that amount to revisions, as well as accidental variations, like the bachelor farmers' laundry day, that represent what Erving Goffman calls "fresh talk" (188).

"Aprille" is, therefore, a different story in each of the two media that its author worked in and in the different versions in each medium. The tale of faith lost and found clearly belongs to the stable world of print texts, as represented in *Leaving Home*. The more ambiguous quest for faith in the oral versions of "Aprille" remains, appropriately enough, unresolved in the unstable texts of the performances. We cannot really understand "Aprille" if we do not know whether the ending envisions a world made wonderful by God or by the people in it, whether the answer to the problem of evil in the world lies in religious faith or in awe over nature. Yet the nature of oral storytelling means that instead of choosing one ending, we must somehow—like Keillor himself—embrace both.

The discontinuity between the fourth and fifth versions—that is, between the second performance and the published version in *Leaving Home*—reminds us that every oral telling begins afresh, whereas successive printouts from a word processor reflect only changes wrought upon the electronic text. The five variants together illustrate the creative process of a single mind, but as texts the oral and written versions of "Aprille" stand somewhat independent of one another. Instead of looking at the five versions as a single series, then, we need to see a more complex relationship among the variants. The three written variants (versions 1, 3, 5) have an evolutionary relationship to one another, yet the second printout has a special significance. It incorporates ideas stimulated by the first oral telling and plots out the most important changes incorporated into the second telling. For similar reasons, the second telling has somewhat more authority than the first, since Keillor incorporates into the Saturday night version ideas first used in the Friday performance and the Saturday draft. On the other hand, Keillor's practice of improvising his narratives like jazz performances rather than memorizing his texts like scripts means that every oral telling is an authoritative text somewhat autonomous from the most recent written text. An oral telling has an evolutionary relationship to previous performances yet stands independent of them.

The different endings of different versions thus offer yet another contrast between the unstable texts of oral stories, and such stable texts as Chaucer's poetry and the Bible. Oral stories are unidirectional, unlike written texts, which allow a reader to flip back and forth among the pages. And whereas the intent listener concentrates on the last joke only at risk of missing the next gem, a reader has the leisure to explore implications between the lines. In the context of three subverted pilgrimages, the dominant theme of the written tale, whether God loves Lois seems not so much paradoxical (the implication of the oral story) as irrelevant. In the end, the "Aprille" of the written texts characterizes religion as the narrative means to a narrative end—a subject for tales and an excuse for storytelling. Perhaps the goal of the oral yarn was to encourage religious faith, perhaps not: the end at once promotes and suspects piety. But in the written tale, which acquires a different emphasis, religion itself has a goal, and that goal undoubtedly is storytelling itself.

For this reason, transcription will never provide a satisfactory solution to the problems of studying oral performance. The process of transforming an oral text into a written one also gives the unstable oral text the appearance of a stable printed text. On that basis, audio tape is probably not the answer, either, though it represents a tremendous improvement over the inadequate transcript. Audio-visual CD-ROM technology, on the other hand, offers a superior means of storing, retrieving, and perhaps even quoting excerpts from oral narratives, since it can evade some problems of transcription by using the speakers already installed in personal computers (a sound board will improve the fidelity), and CD-ROM technology already in use makes it possible to search for specific phrases and hear them recited while the text also appears on the screen. With appropriate software, scholars could input their own material for such random access and analysis, which would offset the unidirectionality of live and conventionally recorded storytelling. Ideally, we could search not only for keywords but also for inflections, pauses, and mannerisms—all of them represented as digitized patterns—without the trouble of optical scanning or other forms of data entry. In this utopian scheme, the oral source will continue to be examined as an oral source, not as a visual representation of an oral source. Newer technologies may offer better alternatives.

While transcription therefore threatens any oral performance, it is particularly damaging to "Aprille," whose oral performances rely on devices for which no print-based equivalents exist. How can the printed page express the unselfconscious tone of voice, the appearance of artlessness and spontaneity, or the perfectly timed pause? Keillor's practice of plotting out his monologues but not scripting or memorizing them gave the tales elements of literary composition while fostering genuine improvisation in performance. When he structured "Aprille" around a ten-line passage from *The Canterbury Tales* and lengthy verse from the New Testament, he intensified this already risky game of memory and improvisation. A printed quotation cannot convey the least degree of artlessness or spontaneity. Nor can it demonstrate Keillor's remarkable memory, which produces these effects in the first place. By contrast, in the oral performance of "Aprille," Keillor's memory not only sustains him through a long recitation in passable Middle English, but also enables him to embellish the prepared story on the spot. Without this display of memory, the story loses other crucial elements: our awe of the storyteller, apparently spinning this yarn just for us as we sit enchanted by his gift; and our delight in language, perhaps the most powerful oral gratification. Seven pages of reading cannot match the rhetorical impact of Keillor's 30-minute performance—he called it a séance—for the very medium of print inhibits, though of course it does not entirely obscure, the tale's celebration of words—Chaucer's, Keillor's, and the Bible's.

In the oral performance of "Aprille," even *scrip*ture is oral. Several times the storyteller recites parts of Lois's confirmation verse, relishing its sounds, but he quotes the full text only once, when describing how Marilyn Tollerud inscribed all 31 words—"Be not conformed to this world: but be ye transformed by the renewing of your mind, that ye may prove what is that good, and acceptable, and perfect, will of God"—in blue frosting atop Lois's cake. One could hardly ask for a more oral use of a text than to turn it into food, and then to turn the food into a joke for oral performance. This gentle ridicule of the Tolleruds' celebration quite literally, and not so gently, reduces the Bible to a mouthful of words, of which Keillor's share on his square of cake reads "Con but for"—a hint at the humorist's con-game. The long recitation of the verse on the cake exploits the advantages of oral performance by demonstrating the teller's prodigious memory, all the more impressive at the end of the narrative when he reasserts his control over all his apparent digressions by reciting Chaucer's poetry.

But no moment of "Aprille" better illustrates the essence of oral yarn spinning, and Keillor's brilliance at it, than his modulations and pauses at a key point in mid-story. (The phrasing varies from version to version, but the episode exists in all five variants.) Slipping from his role of observing narrator, he adopts Lois's point of view to relate her thoughts on good and evil during a solitary walk in the woods after lunch, while her family eats the cake. He continues to tell the story from Lois's perspective as he describes her frantic efforts to run away from a man standing by the road, whom "she knew...was put there by an evil force...and that this was Evil roaming the world, and looking for whomever it may devour" (version 4, 4/26/86). Tension increases as she falls, begging him for mercy. "'Please, please,' she said, 'don't do it.'"

Keillor's voice drops to a whisper in the tension. Then he pauses, raises the pitch, and in a slightly bewildered tone, adds unexpectedly, "Which surprised me...."[5] In the pause following this wrenching shift of perspective, we realize that our storyteller was the man standing there, that Lois made a mistake; the revelation rescues Lois and the tale comically as it evades the question of evil. Nonetheless, this exquisite moment from the oral performances, a rhetorical tour de force, does not appear in *Leaving Home.* In the printed version of "Aprille," a new paragraph just under Lois's words begins simply and directly, "I hadn't seen her for five years" (235). Whether or not he had added the remark about his surprise, Keillor might still have revised the written text to startle his readers as he had shocked his listeners—that is, to translate the oral-aural experience into a literary one. But he didn't. In place of the stunning oral performance, the printed text offers the aesthetic compensations of print, careful construction and themes worth reflection.

The power of the monologues also derives from a number of non-narrative elements in their performance. Keillor's voice—intense, sincere, companionable—was a major factor in his stories' appeal, much enhanced by the intimacy of radio as a medium and his understanding of how to exploit it. The monologues portray one colloquial, confessional voice speaking directly to the individual radio listener—one companion chatting to another.[6] The obviously live, unscripted performance added to the illusion of spontaneous conversation. So did the choice of "panned mono" technique for the stereo broadcasts, since this sound mix emulates live, directional, non-broadcast speech (Larson and Oravec 234). But Keillor's genius lay in matching his message to the medium. As he worked out the Matter of Minnesota for oral storytelling, he borrowed techniques from oral narrative traditions. In these traditions, Walter Ong observes in "Writing is a Technology That Restructures Thought," oral stories link present and past, memory and orality, knower and known—all in the "simultaneous present" created by live narration (39). The fundamental orality of "Aprille," despite its literary structure and literate story material, points to the source of the Lake Wobegon monologues' appeal: they mimic our most beloved kinds of folklore.

"Aprille" and Keillor's other apparently improvised monologues, like those of many standup comics and professional storytellers, are invented stories masquerading as personal experience narratives. That is, they are literary fictions imitating folk legends and artistic performances imitating unpremeditated talk. Autobiographical experience inspired many Lake Wobegon anecdotes, yet Keillor consistently subordinated facts to his narrative purpose, fully fictionalizing them (Lee 81-83, 150-53). Similarly, interaction with his audience helped shape the narration of his oral stories even though the rules of professional storytelling performances allow a studio audience only the limited responses of laughter and applause. In conversational storytelling, by contrast, listeners may ask questions if they're interested, and seize the floor from the speaker if they're not. They may also cue the performer in any number of nonverbal ways to alter the pace of the tale. But just as his stories are not folklore, neither are they "radio talk," as Goffman terms it (197). Announcers are supposed to talk about real events of moment in the real world, not invented anti-climaxes in an imaginary town, and at least part of the monologues' humor from the very beginning stemmed from their violation of listeners' expectations. Radio storytelling separates teller and listener even further than the professional story performance. A radio audience has no active role to play during narration. Neither the performer nor anyone else notices if a listener falls asleep, walks away, or even turns off the set (commercial radio has a vested interest in identifying programs that cannot hold their listeners, but public radio, lacking sponsors, has no such audience research). Despite such odds against him, Keillor at the height of his popularity drew an estimated audience of some four million listeners to the weekly broadcast of *A Prairie Home Companion*, and they certainly were not passive. Each new story in the Lake Wobegon saga brought letters of commentary, suggestions for stories, and gifts to the storyteller.

Keillor's success as an oral storyteller came largely from his transformation of the personal narrative into a narrative genre appropriate for the electronic age. In that sense, he finally accomplished in the 1980s the return to tribal orality that Marshall McLuhan first predicted some 20 years earlier in *Understanding Media* (1964), although it is his skill as a writer that makes this achievement possible. But of course Keillor's stories belong to the *electronic* hearth, and as a result they exemplify the ephemerality of communication in an electronic age. Radio stories leave no artifactual texts. Computers allow writers to write and overwrite the same text, bringing us many authoritative texts, even though some revisions will remain invisible, existing only on a disk. In this sense, despite its origins in such canonical literature as the Bible and *The Canterbury Tales*, "Aprille" belongs to the world of post-modernism, in which instability, ambiguity, and multiplicity rule.

In its liminal position between the literate and the oral, "Aprille" challenges scholars to move beyond reductive transcriptions that put oral texts into print. Instead, we must interpret the artifacts of popular culture—print, broadcast, computer texts, audio and video tape—in the terms of whatever media they use. For broadcasts and other unstable artifacts, that means acknowledging simultaneous authority of multiple texts rather than seeking the stable meanings of a writer's last intention. The list of popular narrative media will surely grow in the twenty-first century, and our theory must be ready to meet them.

Notes

To the memory of Susan Golla (12/23/48-1/9/93):
scholar, storyteller, and friend

[1]Bauman offers the fullest example (see esp. 78-111), but interest in the subject goes back at least as far as Albert Lord. Stahl mentions the occasional variant performance and recognizes the role that different audiences may have in shaping the teller's tale (see, for example, 56), but for the most part treats individual tellings as representative for purposes of interpretation.

[2]Another stable source of Bruce's material is Albert Goldman's biography.

[3]Photo and audio copies of the four nonpublished versions were provided to me from the Prairie Home Companion Archives at Minnesota Public Radio. The tapes, which were made for my study from the audio masters at MPR, were not edited in any way, in contrast to the monologues presented in *News from Lake Wobegon* (1983), *Gospel Birds* (1985), and other audio collections, which excised bits of silence or laughter, speeded up the master tape, or featured partial monologues to manage the length of each recording for commercial release.

[4]This sort of playing with didactic and aesthetic narration explains Keillor's appeal to both rural and urban audiences. It also suggests that the yarn spinner sometimes uses religious material as he uses tuna hot-dish—as an element of local color.

[5]In the first performance, he said, "which amazed me" (version 2).

[6]Erving Goffman compares this "direct" announcing with the telephone call, an attempt to simulate a conversation between two parties, and contrasts it to the imaginary "three-way" conversation of the talk-show or interview, which casts the audience in the role of a mute participant in the conversation (234-35).

Works Cited

Bauman, Richard. *Story, Performance, and Event: Contextual Studies of Oral Narrative*. Cambridge Studies in Oral and Literate Culture. Cambridge, England: Cambridge UP, 1986.

Dehnert, Edmund. "The Consciousness of Music Wrought by Musical Notation." *Beyond the Two Cultures: Essays on Science, Technology, and*

    Literature. Eds. Joseph W. Slade and Judith Yaross Lee. Ames, IA: Iowa
    State UP, 1990: 99-116.

Goffman, Erving. *Forms of Talk.* Philadelphia: U of Pennsylvania P, 1981.

Goldman, Albert. *Ladies and Gentlemen, Lenny Bruce!!* New York: Ballentine
    Books, 1974.

Hymes, Dell. "Language, Memory, and Selective Performance: Cultee's
    'Salmon's Myth' as Twice Told to Boas." *Journal of American Folklore*
    98 (1985): 391-434.

Keillor, Garrison. *Leaving Home: A Collection of Lake Wobegon Stories.* New
    York: Viking, 1987.

Larson, Charles U., and Christine Oravec. "*A Prairie Home Companion* and the
    Fabrication of Community." *Critical Studies in Mass Communication* 4
    (1987): 221-44.

Lee, Judith Yaross. *Garrison Keillor: A Voice of America.* Jackson, MS: UP of
    Mississippi, 1991.

Lord, Albert. *The Singer of Tales.* Cambridge, MA: Harvard UP, 1960.

Miller, Rosalie. Letter to Judith Yaross Lee. 22 July 1989.

Ong, Walter, S.J. "Writing is a Technology That Restructures Thought." *The
    Written Word: Literacy in Transition.* Ed. Gerd Baumann. Oxford:
    Clarendon, 1986: 23-50.

Smith, Barbara Herrenstein. "Narrative Versions, Narrative Theories." *On
    Narrative.* Ed. W.J.T. Mitchell. Chicago: U of Chicago P, 1981: 209-32.

Stahl, Sandra Dolby. *Literary Folkloristics and the Personal Narrative.*
    Bloomington: Indiana UP, 1989.

Weber, Bruce. "The Iconoclast as Icon: Actors Vying to Be Bruce Stay Within
    the Lines." *New York Times* 24 July 1992: B12.

CONSTRUCTION
OF
HISTORICAL
MEMORY

◆

The Future of Popular Culture Studies and the Clouded Status of "Fair Use" of Manuscripts

Thomas Cripps

In a recent book, *Making Movies Black* (Oxford University Press, 1993), I led off a paragraph with the following sentences: "Once research has been completed, much of the credibility, reliability, authenticity, voice, and flavor of a book are derived from quoting directly from archival sources. This is particularly so in writing the social history of twentieth century popular culture." Such a simple thought: that the sense of the past should be brought home to the reader by drawing verbatim from the eyewitnesses to history. And yet, in recent years the entire notion of an academy free to make "fair use" of manuscripts has been so called into question as to threaten the historian and the literary critic with a daunting censorship at the hands of authors, their survivors, and, in our litigious society, their lawyers and the executors of their wills.

In view of this suddenly chilling shift in the rules of scholarship, my editors counseled me so urgently as to constitute a command: seek permission for *every* quotation gleaned from a manuscript source or delete the quotation in favor of a characterless paraphrasing. A scholar's right to quote brief passages, either for purposes of the advancement of knowledge or to include in a review, had always seemed protected by the ancient doctrine of "fair use" as long as the use did not poach on the original author's market or misrepresent his work, and the quotation contributed to a work of scholarship or serious journalism. Manuscripts in public archives were construed as being even more accessible.

Under this system, creators were protected from copyright infringement by decades of jurisprudence that permitted "fair use" only under conditions that recognized the creator's right to market his work and the obligation of the user to adhere to scholarly canons of seriousness of purpose. Then, in 1976 the equilibrium of the world of authorship was shattered by a new federal law meant to clarify copyright principles. At the same time the law seemed to refine and protect the scholar's right to quote from manuscripts for use in commentary, criticism, and historical writing. Thus, on its face, the law seemed not only benign but even

109

progressive in the eyes of the scholars, authors, and publishers who had testified on its behalf in congressional hearings. Briefly, the revised law extended the doctrine of "fair use" to unpublished manuscripts on deposit in all archives to which a public had untrammeled access.

As we shall see, the new law as interpreted by a judge sitting on the Second United States Circuit Court of Appeals, the federal bench in Manhattan where, willy-nilly, most cases involving publishers would be heard, soon grew into a thicket that constrained the scholar's ability to do the business of freely copying archival materials for later reading in the privacy of his own study and freely quoting snippets from unpublished manuscripts. Taken together, two such opinions placed a subsequent burden upon the scholar to collect written evidence of his diligent search for the heirs and assigns of any author of any fugitive letter that might shed light on, capture the flavor of, or speak in the ideology of a bygone era. Indeed, the thrust of the cases was so compelling that in the event that an heir proved elusive, his lawyer proved unforthcoming, or the archive in which a document was held adopted a policy of disallowing all requests for permissions to quote (or asserted its powerlessness to act), the scholar would be better served by abandoning the quest or by quoting from a letter published before the weight of the new law had quashed scholarly inquiry.

Why should these changed rules of the game affect students of popular culture in particular? After all, researchers into all literatures have customarily taken up matters such as authors' intentions, audiences' and critics' responses, and other contextual references to the written word. And of course, often the most savory of such commentaries were written as private records in manuscript letters, diaries, and journals. In addition, however, we live amidst a rage for studying culture from the bottom up, from the angle of masses rather than elites, with the result that curators have outdone themselves in the pursuit of the raw materials of such inquiries. To take only a couple of examples, the work of Gene Gressley at the American Heritage Center in Wyoming and that of Howard Gotlieb in the Twentieth Century Collection in the Mugar Library of Boston University has centered on acquiring almost exclusively the personal papers of popular authors such as, at Boston, Evan Hunter, author of *The Blackboard Jungle*; Robert Hardy Andrews, author of the radio series, *Big Town*; and Nunnally Johnson, a Warner Bros. and 20th Century-Fox screenwriter.

Parallel to these self-consciously acquired documentations of popular culture were the specialized collections of a more regional, arcane, or political nature that intersected with elements of popular culture studies. For example, movie history may be studied in part through the several university repositories of corporate studio records such as the Warner Archive in the Doheny Library of the University of Southern California, the 20th Century-Fox Archive in the Research Library of UCLA, the Selznick Papers in the Humanities Research Center of the University of Texas, the "Hollywood Ten" papers in the University of Wisconsin. In addition, the historic trajectories of popular culture and national public policy intersect in the records of federal agencies such as the Office of War Information during World War II, or at the state level, the various censor boards that directly affected the substance of movies.

Thus, the issue of quoting publicly archived manuscripts becomes central to the study of popular culture, particularly since all of the records cited above were created by persons active recently enough so that the statutory term of copyright still applies. How else to study the processes of generating popular culture from idea on a page to its reception by an audience? How else to know that the all black, dramatically thin musical, *Stormy Weather* (1943), had started as Hy Kraft's tribute to African American music, only to be diluted by timid producers? How else to know that *Till the End of Time* (1946), Selznick's dramatization of white war veterans' struggles to readjust to civilian life, had begun life as Niven Busch's novel centered in an African American family? How else to know that Salvatore Lobino was persuaded to change his name to Evan Hunter in order to enhance his marketability? More to the point, how else to sharpen the meaning of these intrigues than by directly quoting a few telling fragments that under old scholarly practice would have been considered "fair use" rather than prima facie evidence of copyright infringement?

More than merely wishing to do right by copyright holders, the evolving practice under the recent jurisprudence has obliged authors to pursue heroic lengths in finding letter writers in order to seek permission. Imagine a fan who, in 1946, saw Warners' *It Happened in Springfield*, thought it an eloquent expression of a liberal racial politics, and wished the studio well in making more such movies. How to quote her touching fan letter with its Upper West Side of Manhattan return address? First, gain admission to the Warner Archive at USC; next, pray that the studio's representative grants permission to copy for research purposes; then after several written queries, hope that the studio's legal department will grant permission to publish a few lines (provided you can find the letter writer or her survivors); finally, acting on a reference to her Hoosier upbringing, checking the current telephone directories for Indiana, one finds a retired librarian, asks permission, receives a generous letter, albeit without specifically using the word "permission" that one's publisher requires, thence asking for a rewrite, thereby leading to the eventual published quotation of two lines of type.[1]

Such a lovely outcome is a blessing not often awarded. A major studio, indeed a continuingly powerful one, will deny permission to quote a line or so from a document in its archives, fearing some nameless consequence. Or a widow will have taken on the role of keeper of her late husband's reputation, a calling that obliges her to insist on reading the intended use of her husband's letter and to suggest changes that locate him at the center of the story. In still other cases, the children of powerful immigrants for whom English was a second language have a compelling urge to amend their parents' grammar into a most unlikely standard English. Or worst of all, a story conference might have resulted in pages of corrective marginalia on a script that might have gone through a dozen drafts, each graced by garlands of anonymous, blue-penciled notations whose authorship was impossible to determine and thus equally impossible to quote. The outcome of the resulting negotiations is often so daunting as to give poignantly weightier meaning to the historian Arthur Schlesinger's wry recollection that: "If the law were this way when I wrote the three volumes of *The Age of Roosevelt*, I might be two volumes short" (Kaplan 80).

How did it come to this? "Fair use" law had derived from a handful of nineteenth-century cases, as well as common law itself, augmented by conditions that donors were entitled to impose on archives at the moment of deposit. This loose arrangement by usage and acquiescence had only barely extended the doctrine of "fair use" to the citation of unpublished (thus unmarketed) manuscripts. Then the act of 1976, which had been meant to clarify a few ancillary matters, referred in passing to manuscripts and in so doing awarded them a statutory right that inhered "from the moment an original work of authorship is fixed in a tangible medium of expression." In other words, the manuscript that for generations had been construed as to be *un*published suddenly came to be defined as published from the moment a pen touched paper, an entirely new condition that inadvertently threw into disequilibrium generations of the practice of authorship and citation by extending copyright protection to manuscripts that were never intended for publication (Patterson and Lindberg 214).

Even so, Ray Patterson and Stanley Lindberg in their book, *The Nature of Copyright: A Law of Users' Rights*, insist that this unprecedented principle is "rebuttable" in cases where manuscripts have been donated or sold to publicly accessible archives. Donation or sale, they argue, are by definition evidence of intent to make public and therefore remove the issue of entitlement to privacy as a point of contention, particularly if the donors have received relief from taxes as condition of the donation. Not to grant this point, say Patterson and Lindberg, is to award the power to censor—indeed the power "to manipulate the judgement of posterity"—to survivors who will have contributed nothing creative to the manuscript in question. Moreover, to put the burden of seeking permission upon scholars is to violate the spirit of the first American law of copyright in 1790 which was grounded in the perception of the public's inherent right to knowledge. Without this principle, say Patterson and Lindberg, Americans would be denied access to "the private papers of authors whose works reflect and shape our understanding of life and society" (216-17).

For almost a decade the issues set forth by Patterson and Lindberg passed largely untested in the courts. In fact, in the first such judicial test Supreme Court Justice Sandra Day O'Connor purposely wrote her opinion on the narrowest of grounds so as to avoid inadvertently commenting on "fair use" in a case in which it was not a point of contention. The leftist magazine, *Nation*, had clandestinely acquired and run a fragment of President Gerald R. Ford's memoirs, so that Justice O'Connor in Harper & Row v. *Nation* (1985) could argue that the case turned entirely on the matter of the right of an author to first publication rather than on any ancillary issue of the *Nation*'s right to "fair use" (Margolik 44).[2]

Sadly for the next generation of scholars, one year later Judge Jon O. Walker of the Second U.S. Circuit Court of Appeals invoked Justice O'Connor's opinion and broadened it to embrace a sweeping redefinition of "fair use" of manuscripts. The case was that of the reclusive author, J.D. Salinger, v. Random House, Inc. At issue were a few letters that Salinger's biographer had culled from various archives and from letters he had written to the biographer, Ian Hamilton. Salinger alleged not only violation of copyright when Hamilton ventured to quote from the letters, but also that the market value of the letters had been compromised. Finally, he had argued through counsel that his right to privacy had been invaded.

Judge Pierre N. Leval found against Salinger on the grounds that a serious scholar's work that had cited only 250 words in several snippets clearly constituted "fair use" and most certainly could hardly have preempted Salinger's wish to publish the letters since he had long before forgotten their existence. Salinger had indeed suffered a "Wound," but only to "his wish for privacy," wrote Leval, and copyright law "does not give him protection from that form of injury" (Margolik 44; Kaplan 80; Patterson and Lindberg 171-78). It was on the appeal of this case that Judge Walker seized upon the doctrine of "fair use," drew from Justice

O'Connor's narrow opinion a broad construction, and overturned the lower court's finding, thereby giving Salinger a remedy that all but obliterated the doctrine of "fair use" by giving authors of manuscript materials a nearly unrestricted copyright of such documents *even if deposited in a public archive* in the collection of a third party to whom the letters had been mailed.

Two years later, in the same U.S. Circuit Court of Appeals the court extended its opinion in yet another case involving a biography based upon, as almost all previous biographies had done, manuscript documentation. In this case, the biographer, Russell Miller, had used manuscript materials in writing a sharply critical biography of L. Ron Hubbard, the founder of the Scientology sect and himself a writer of science fiction and pop-theology. In effect, the court found that *any* quotation from unpublished documents constituted infringement and entitled the aggrieved to the remedy of injunction from publishing. Sensing that an ancient practice had been violated, even the popular magazine *Newsweek* reported an immediate "chilling effect" on the enterprise of serious writers, citing as instances James Reston's biography of Governor John Connally of Texas and, astonishingly, Ed Koch's own letters written while Mayor of New York (Kaplan 80).[3]

From that day to this, advocates of an equitable application of the doctrine of "fair use" of manuscripts still search for a broad ground of consensus that recognizes, as Patterson and Lindberg wrote, "the copyright owner's right to economic rewards...and the user's right to employ those copyrighted materials for the advancement of knowledge," an accommodation they hoped would be governed by a classically judicial, "equitable rule of reason." The legal ground not only existed in Section 107 of the 1976 law but, as of November 1992, has been reaffirmed after a long struggle in the Congress to pass a reaffirmation of the openhanded intention of the 1976 law. Both versions offer four tests of whether or not a specific quotation constitutes either "fair use" or infringement. In general, the work in question must have been written for educational purposes or for purposes of offering critical commentary or for the purpose of advancing the frontiers of knowledge and without violating the author's prospective marketplace (Patterson and Lindberg 207, 200, 211). More about the new law later.

Unfortunately for scholars, they remain trapped between the case law established by the Salinger and Hubbard cases and the new law of November 1992 which remains unchallenged and barren of commentary from the bench. Therefore the craft of scholarship remains governed by case law that not only minimizes users' rights to access and quotation but derives its stance from the statutory recognition of manuscripts as entitled to the protection of copyright. Ironically, as Patterson and Lindberg point out, once "publication ceased to be a requirement for U.S. copyright," then the 1976 law that had been intended to recognize the right of "fair use" unwittingly extended the law to embrace manuscripts, thereby suddenly empowering heirs, survivors, and executors with proprietary and literary rights formerly held only by creators (69, 67).[4] In this way, by giving legal standing to both manuscript and printed versions of the same document, the courts had made authors of us all: writers of letters to friends, makers of laundry lists and pocket diaries, supplicants for relief from findings of the Internal Revenue Service, even the keepers of scorecards at a baseball game. All of these "authors" share in common not only the creation of documents but the clear intention *not* to publish their work, and yet each of them enjoys the protection of American copyright law. Indeed, their right under the 1976 law and its precedent-setting cases is probably of considerably greater legal standing than the routinely broadcast announcement during every baseball game that the viewer may not electronically copy a game "without the express written permission of the Commissioner of Baseball."

Clearly, the law of 1976 and its cases had created a new and broadly reaching definition of copyright that all but stifled the advancement of knowledge or its dissemination. "The Salinger case makes copyright a loaded gun aimed at the scholar," wrote Patterson and Lindberg. "The decision's greatest harm is in its *in terrorem* effect, since few publishers are willing to risk the cost of litigation for the cause of learning"—or on behalf of an incautious author (174).

At first, the solution to this conundrum seemed simple, or at least it did so to Congressman Robert Kastenmeier: merely add the phrase, "published or unpublished," to the section of the 1976 law that recognized the right of fair use. In a single stroke, he thought, the rights of archives and their clients would have reached equilibrium with the rights of authors of original works and their estates, and in the bargain the powers of uninterested heirs to coddle the reputations of their forebears, protect the privacy of the dead, or curry favor with posterity would have been diminished (Patterson and Lindberg 176-76; Fields 115).[5]

But such was not to be, at least until the autumn of 1992. Kastenmeier and Senator Paul Simon held hearings in the summer of 1990 as a result of which they hoped to report affirmatively on behalf of revision. They called as witnesses to the need for the restoration of access to manuscripts an array of interested practitioners ranging from Floyd Abrams who represented authors and publishers in copyright cases, to the Pulitzer Prize winners Taylor Branch and J. Anthony Lukas, and even to the judges who had heard the Salinger and Hubbard cases. As Abrams testified, an entire generation of intellectuals had retreated from quoting primary sources, moved by "the gravest concern that even highly limited quotations from letters, diaries or the like will lead to a finding of copyright liability and...injunction against publication." Speaking for the preservation of the rights of literary proprietors, only Jonathan W. Lubell, an attorney for various possessors of unpublished works, spoke as forthrightly of fears that "the First Amendment may be used as a wedge to undermine property rights (Fields 115).[6]

But then Kastenmeier lost his seat in the off-year elections, resulting in, said the publishers' lobbyist Diane Rennert, "a major loss for all of us." In his absence, Senator Simon introduced a bill that he hoped approximated their mutual goal of restoring an "appropriate balance between the interests of scholarship and journalism and the rights of authors," not by means of a narrowly prescriptive bill that would invite yet another generation of litigation, but one that would free the courts to "apply the full fair-use analysis...rather than peremptorily dismissing" all quotations from manuscripts as *a priori* infringements. Only then, Simon said in harmony with the wishes of scholars, could "the specter of historical and literary figures and their heirs exercising an effective censorship power over unflattering portrayals" be exorcised (*Publishers Weekly,* 11 Nov. 1990: 9; 24 May 1990: 91). But in Kastenmeier's absence his old House committee chose not to act in timely fashion and some of its members muddied the issue by proposing the very rigid "guidelines" for authors and "ironclad" definitions for lawyers that Simon and Kastenmeier had been hoping to avoid (*Publishers Weekly,* 18 Oct 1991: 91; Miller Aug. 1991: 10).

To be fair, some members seemed to prefer to wait for the outcome of yet another suit, this one a petition to enjoin Warner Books from releasing Margaret Walker's biography of the African American author Richard Wright. In the suit Wright's widow, Ellen, had already lost in the U.S. Second District Court of Appeals, Judge Walker found no infringement in the quotation of a few lines from Wright's letters. But the case was far from a victory for scholars and other users of manuscript sources. The judge had ruled only on the narrow and slightly absurd ground that Walker had used only "purely factual" material and "minimal quotations" drawn from Wright's journals in the Beineke Library at Yale University, and therefore her book could not have poached upon Wright's prospective marketplace. Far from overturning the Salinger and Hubbard cases, the court had merely asserted that "excerpts from unpublished works did not constitute 'per se' infringement." As a result, Floyd Abrams, who had filed an *amicus curiae* brief on behalf of the Authors' League, reckoned that the "chilling effect" of the judicial opinions could only persist, since the court had merely taken up matters of style—the choice of the "purely factual"—and amounts of quotes rather than the principle of quotation itself (*Publishers Weekly,* 18 Oct. 1991: 13; Reid 8; *New York Times,* 28 Nov. 1991).[7]

By then, after the handing down of the decision that some congressmen had awaited, the picture seemed even worse from a historian's point of view. Congressman William J. Hughes, Kastenmeier's successor in the chair of the Subcommittee on Intellectual Property, having deferred action pending the outcome of the Wright case, could only promise some gesture by the February 1992 session. But Page Putnam Miller, director of the National Coordinating Committee for the Promotion of History and also Washington columnist for the American Historical Association's trade paper, fretted over Hughes's paltering because of his "expressed interest" in using the interim to try yet another rewording after more than a year of hearings and tinkering. "We hope," Miller wrote in January of 1992, "new language will not prolong the effort to clarify the issue" (Miller, Jan. 1992: 12). Finally, late in the session Representative Hughes introduced HR 4412 with the clear intention of making explicit the sense of the Congress when it first passed the law of 1976, a collective frame of mind that took into account the discontinuity and disequilibrium that followed from a half dozen years of rule by court decree. Even then, its departures from the Senate's version required a conference committee to resolve the sticking points (Miller, Apr. 1992: 9).

How simple it all seemed by then. Each of the bills, HR 4412 and S 1035, ran on for only a single sentence, required no budget line, and both referred specifically to the U.S. Circuit Court's stifling decisions. Yet the Senate bill still coyly called for a "balance" between researchers' rights and proprietors' rights while the House apparently denied the need for a "per se" rule against "fair use" but equally coyly evaded its charge by leaving the principle to the courts on a case-basis, thereby finally placing the issue—nowhere (Miller, Oct. 1992: 11).

Finally, during a conference committee negotiation the two houses arrived at a consensus that took several strides toward clarification of the 1976 law while also advising subsequent federal judges on the sense of the Congress. Although the law as passed included words that many scholars might approve, such as the ringing assertion that "the fact that a work is unpublished shall not itself bar a finding of fair use," providing that the finding is made in consideration of the "purpose and character of use" (meaning that it was either scholarly or at least serious in intent), the "amount and substantiality" of the quoted material, the effect on the market value of the quoted work, and only in and with these other factors, "the nature of the copyrighted material" (whether it was published or unpublished). This reading of the law, of course, still left scholars in limbo in that the vagueness of the statutory standards left open to litigation almost any instance of quoting from a manuscript without permission (Miller, Oct. 1992: 11).

In view of this persistent ambiguity, six Senators made a joint statement from the floor, reiterating their dismay over the remaining "chilling uncertainty and serious apprehension" regarding "fair use," an atmosphere of fear that promised "to establish a virtual per se rule against the fair use of any unpublished materials" that would result in "a crippling blow to accurate scholarship and reporting." Moreover, the Senators specifically pointed to the Salinger and Hubbard cases as villains that had brought on "the overly restrictive standards" that the 1992 law was trying to remedy. In closing, the Senators instructed the courts to consider "each of the fair use factors set forth" in the law (Miller, Nov. 1992: 10).

Where does this leave the student of popular culture as we enter the twenty-first century? The good news is implied in the phrasing of the six Senators led by Paul Simon when they call for a loose construction based on several factors rather than the single standard of whether or not a document is published. The bad news is that the Senators' plea does not have standing as part of the law. This means, of course, that the historian in search of a key document may still cleave to his duty to bring it to light and to quote it, not only for the light it sheds on, as Ranke wrote, "wie es eigentlich gewesen war"—how it actually was—but for its flavor, pungency, and aptness of voice. Sadly, the scholar will often stand alone in this struggle, at least until the courts build a body of precedent based upon a more open reading of the law. The reason for his aloneness rests in a standard clause in contracts between authors and publishers, particularly the phrase in which the author "holds harmless from suit" the publisher. In turn repositories themselves remain chilled into inertia behind their own thin armor against hostile litigation. For the moment, at least, the scholar would do well to build a file of letters granting permission to use archives, permission to photocopy documents, permission from the legal staff of corporations to copy and to publish precisely defined small bits, permission from the correspondents who wrote the needed letters, diaries, or scripts—or permission from their heirs or executors.

In other words, the chill clings to scholarship, rendering it timid, altering its voice, threatening it with both conscious and unconscious censors, and denying to a generation of serious readers the voices and flavors of times gone by. Our only hope is that in forthcoming decisions, the federal courts, particularly the Second U.S. Circuit Court of Appeals where so many publishers conduct business, will heed the advice of the Senate, put a loose construction on the law, and free scholars to pursue truth wherever the search carries them and to write their findings for a broad public among whom they will stimulate thought and debate. That is to say, the courts will return to a construction of the law that will encourage an informed, argumentative citizenry that is free to read.

Notes

[1] This account is drawn from Thomas Cripps, *Making Movies Black*.

[2] See also "Letters."

[3] See Patterson and Lindberg, XIV, for citations: Salinger v. Random House, Inc., 811 F2d 90 (1987): New Era Pub. Int. v. Henry Holt & Co, Inc., 873 F2d 576 (1989); Harper & Row, Inc. v. Nation Enterprises, 471 U.S. 539 (1985).

[4] Patterson and Lindberg discuss Justice Story's 1841 opinion finding publication as a *sine qua non* for copyright eligibility.

[5] Fields is also quoted in *Publishers Weekly*, Nov. 11, 1990.

[6] Fields is also quoted in *Publishers Weekly*, Nov. 11, 1990.

[7] See also Michael Les Benedict on "ambiguous" Wright case, made so by the spurious ground that quotes were "short and insignificant," merely "factual points," and had not been meant to "enliven" Walker's book, thus leaving open the entire issue of "fair use" (15).

Works Cited

Benedict, Michael Les. "Noteworthy." *Perspectives* Feb. 1992: 15.

Cripps, Thomas. *Making Movies Black*. New York: Oxford UP, 1993.

Fields, Howard. *Publishers Weekly* 27 July 1990: 115.

Kaplan, David A. "The End of History?" *Newsweek* 25 Dec. 1989: 80.

"Letters." *Nation* 12, 19 Aug. 1991: 178.

Margolik, David. "Whose Words Are They, Anyway." *New York Times Book Review* 1 Nov. 1987: 1, 44.

Miller, Page Putnam. "Capital Commentary." *Perspectives* Aug. 1991: 10.

___. "NCC News." *Perspectives* Jan. 1992: 12; Apr. 1992: 9; Oct. 1992: 11; Nov. 1992: 10.

New York Times 28 Nov. 1991.

Patterson. L. Ray and Stanley W. Lindberg. *The Nature of Copyright: A Law of User's Rights*. Athens: U of Georgia P, 1991.

Publishers Weekly 11 Nov. 1990: 9; 24 May 1990: 91; 18 Oct. 1991: 91.

Reid, Calvin. *Publishers Weekly* 12 Oct. 1990: 8.

Masculine Myths and Feminist Revisions: Some Thoughts on the Future of Popular Genres

John G. Cawelti

I

Since the mid-1960s when Ray Browne founded the serious study of popular culture, the analysis of popular genres has come full circle. The most important work of the 1960s and 1970s was probably that which focussed on two aspects of popular culture: the formal and aesthetic characteristics of popular genres and the way in which popular culture embodied or expressed the basic myths of American culture. These trends reflected the dominant academic literary movements of the time, the New Criticism and American Studies, and both were reactions against the prevailing critique of popular culture as aesthetically and culturally worthless because it expressed only the conventional stereotypes and ideologies of the culture, or worse, simply reduced all cultural and artistic values to the lowest common denominator.

Analysts of the Western during this period were particularly influenced by a few scholars and critics of the 1950s who had suggested that the popular tradition of the Western had a uniquely important cultural position as the expression of basic cultural myths as well as its own distinctive artistic qualities. Henry Nash Smith's *Virgin Land* was the most important of those works linking new trends in American Studies with popular culture, while Robert Warshow's often reprinted essay on the Western which insisted on the serious artistry of films like *High Noon* was perhaps the most important single influence in creating an aesthetic approach to popular genres. Smith's work was continued and expanded in such studies as Richard Slotkin's *Regeneration Through Violence* and *The Fatal Environment*, a large-scale study of the cultural myths embodied in the popular Western tradition, while many studies in the 1960s and 1970s explored the formal and aesthetic values of the Western and other popular genres. These studies resulted in an increasingly widespread recognition of the aesthetic potential of popular genres and, to a considerable extent, in the revision of the literary canon to include a number of writers like Dashiell Hammett and Raymond Chandler and filmmakers like John Ford and Howard Hawks who were not much admired by an earlier generation of critics because their work was largely in popular genres.

It no longer seems necessary to preface analyses of popular genres with an elaborate justification and apology for the "serious" consideration of such material. In fact, when an occasional article does so, one hears the screams of a long-dead horse hovering ghostlike in the air. Yet the very acceptance of the aesthetic and mythical analysis of popular genres has made these approaches, once so innovative, part of the conventional tradition of studies in popular culture. The innovative edge is elsewhere and this has led to a new approach to popular culture on the part of many younger scholars.

This new approach is partly a circling back to something like the more ideology-centered analysis which characterized the critique of the 1940s and 1950s, but it is also very different from the attack on "the vast wasteland" of popular culture which typified that era in three major ways. First of all, the new kind of analysis—let's call it "neo-structuralist" for simplicity's sake, and because I hate the prefix "post" —largely refuses to make the same kind of distinction between high and popular culture that dominated earlier thinking. From this methodological standpoint there is no significant difference between the analysis of the ideology of a work by a major writer and an item of popular culture: they are both seen as cultural or ideological structures which can be "deconstructed." So Barthes has applied the same kind of analysis to the language of fashion as he did to a work of Balzac and Derrida has deconstructed post cards in much the same way as he has Descartes. One consequence of this is that the neo-structuralist critic often really likes the texts he/she is deconstructing. Jane Tompkins, for example, is an avowed fan of Westerns. In spite of the fact that she finds many of the genre's ideological implications deeply disturbing, she is often able to suggest striking insights into why some Western writers, such as Louis L'Amour and Zane Grey, have been so popular and effective with readers.

Second, the neo-structuralists have developed a much more complex method of ideological analysis than that used by the more reductionistic Marxist critics of the 1950s. Though sometimes its practitioners favor an analytic jargon that seems impenetrable to ordinary minds, their basic assumption that all texts have latent as well as overt meanings and that these meanings are frequently in apparent conflict or contradiction with the surface meanings has produced some extremely interesting analysis. There's no doubt but that we can learn a great deal about the layers and levels of meaning in a text from neo-structuralist analysis.

Finally, the neo-structuralists have greatly expanded the traditional Marxian analysis of ideology as an expression of economic and class relationships to deal with other ideological areas, most notably sex, gender and race. Not surprisingly, it's in this latter area that the most striking reinterpretations of popular cultural texts have been taking place and these reinterpretations have begun to suggest some important possible revisions of the history of American culture as well. It's to these reinterpretations and their significance that I wish to turn my attention for the remainder of this paper.

II

My sense of this is that the most important reinterpretation that has resulted thus far from the neo-structuralist approach to popular genres has grown out of a new and more intense attention to those popular genres of the nineteenth and twentieth centuries that have been largely created by and read by women, the traditions of the sentimental novel and the popular romance. It's certainly significant that most of the major popular cultural studies of the 1960s and 1970s (needless to say largely written by men) had little to say about either the sentimental novel or the romance. In these writings, the major popular genres treated were the Western, the detective story, the spy story, the crime or gangster saga, and the best-selling social novel of writers like Harold Robbins, Irving Wallace, James Michener, and Jacqueline Susann. Even in the case of this latter genre, some of the most consistently successful women writers like Danielle Steele or Judith Krantz were largely overlooked. I can myself look back somewhat shamefacedly to the mid-1970s when I called a book *Adventure, Mystery and Romance*, but had almost nothing about romance in it.

Janice Radway's *Reading the Romance* (1984) was one of the first major academic studies of a predominantly female genre and audience, but since that time there have been a large number of important studies of popular genres such as the sentimental novel, the romance and pornography from a variety of approaches concerned with aspects of sex and gender ideology. These studies have made clear in a new way the continuity, the vitality and the cultural significance of predominantly feminine popular traditions. Radway was one of the first to show how the very act of reading romances was in some ways a feminine subversion of patriarchal values in spite of the surface content of most romance novels with its apparent affirmation of the central values of a male-dominated culture. Since then, other critics like Cathy Davidson, Jane Tompkins, and Nina Baym have extended this kind of analysis to the popular sentimental novel of the nineteenth and late eighteenth centuries and have shown quite persuasively that Hawthorne's damned mob of scribbling women were not quite the pussycats they used to seem. These analyses have shown that many earlier women writers like Susannah Rowson, Susan Warner, Augusta Jane Evans, and Harriet Beecher Stowe were far more complex and powerful than earlier analyses would indicate. It's easy to find earlier twentieth-century male scholars who shared Hawthorne's negative, dismissive, and somewhat exasperated view of more successful contemporary female authors. For example in James Hart's 1950 study of *The Popular Book*, one of the earliest academic surveys of popular literature, he remarks of Susan Warner that "one look at her spare equine face distinguished by a pair of eyes set not quite evenly in her head, a thin determined mouth, and hair brushed tightly behind large ears proclaimed her a spinster by nature. She liked to think of herself as another Jane Eyre, though no Rochester ever came her way. All her emotion was channeled into novels" (Hart 95).

The neo-structuralist feminist approach to popular sentimental and romance novels has given us quite a different picture of the ideological and cultural significance of these traditions than their embodiment of spinsterish frustration at not finding an appropriate husband and channeling emotions into domesticity and motherhood. Instead, these analyses present a literature which served as an arena of ideological conflict, a fictional battleground in which the values of evangelical Christianity struggled with an increasingly non-religious capitalistic individualism. As Tompkins puts it, "culturally and politically, the effect of these novels is to establish women at the center of the world's most important work (saving souls) and to assert that in the end spiritual power is always superior to worldly might" (Tompkins 38).

According to this view, the novel of Christian sentiment and domesticity so popular in the mid and late nineteenth century was an expression of the conflict between the traditional Christian ideology of sin and salvation which had become increasingly associated with women and the newer ideology of individualism and monetary success which was becoming in the course of the later nineteenth century increasingly influential in the lives of men. This analysis reflects the concept of the feminization of American culture presented by Ann Douglas and others in that it suggests that one of the major cultural developments of the nineteenth century was the increasingly close association between women, domesticity, and religion which resulted from the increasing importance of business enterprise and the corresponding decline in the social authority of the clergy, whose influence had been so dominant in the seventeenth century. According to Douglas, when the clergy sensed the decline in their status, they turned increasingly to women for the support of the moral and cultural values associated with the Christian evangelical tradition. Thus, for a time, during the later nineteenth century, women gained a moral authority and a cultural and psychological dominance greater than they had possessed before and in some ways different and stronger than they would come to claim even in the twentieth century. The sentimental novel with its powerful and long-suffering female protagonists who usually succeed through their patience and fortitude in bringing about the spiritual reform of an errant male was then the expression of the claim to authority and power.

The modern Western, according to Tompkins, emerged as a moral counterstatement to this ideology of Christian evangelical reform:

> The Western *answers* the domestic novel. It is the antithesis of the cult of domesticity that dominated American Victorian culture. The Western hero, who seems to ride in out of nowhere, in fact comes riding out of the nineteenth century. And every piece of baggage he doesn't have, every word he doesn't say, every creed in which he doesn't believe is absent for a reason. What isn't there in the Western hasn't disappeared by accident; it's been deliberately jettisoned. The surface cleanness and simplicity of the landscape, the story line, and the characters derive from the genre's will to sweep the board clear of encumbrances. And of some encumbrances more than others. If the Western deliberately rejects evangelical Protestantism and pointedly repudiates the cult of domesticity, it is because it seeks to marginalize and suppress the figure who stood for these ideals. (39)

At this point, an obvious objection suggests itself. Actually, the popular Western is much older than the later nineteenth century, going back to James Fenimore Cooper's Leatherstocking who made his debut in 1823, and who multiplied a thousandfold through novels, dime novels, and popular theater after the Civil War. However, this objection doesn't fully apply, for the Western tradition did undergo a radical change just at the turn of the century and this change is reflected in many different forms. There was the rise of the modern adult Western novel as exemplified particularly by Owen Wister's *The Virginian*, but also by other late-nineteenth and early-twentieth-century novelists like Emerson Hough, Harold Bell Wright, and Zane Grey, many of them among the leading best-sellers of the time. In fact, Harold Bell Wright is an interesting case in point since we can see the interplay in his work between the traditional Christian evangelism of *Shepherd of the Hills* and the newer western ethos of *The Winning of Barbara Worth*. There also emerged at this time a new kind of Western art, exemplified by painters and illustrators like Remington and Russell, who left behind the romantic western landscapes of Thomas Moran and Albert Bierstadt to create a visual world of cowboys and Indians, cavalry, cattle and horses: the image of the Wild West as we still know it. This was also the time of the maximum popularity of the Wild West Show and the Rough Riders, and of Theodore Roosevelt's political exploitation of the myth of the cowboy and the Wild West, of the first expression of Frederick Jackson Turner's frontier thesis, and of the first Western films. Such a large number of contemporaneous developments in the imagining of the West are clearly associated with some major cultural changes.

The traditional way of accounting for these changes has been along the lines which Turner himself set forth in his essay on "The Significance of the Frontier in American History." Basically, this argument is that as the frontier experience receded in actuality due to the rapid rise of urbanization and industrialization, it became increasingly important in the imagination of American culture because it established a linkage between the present and the past. The Western, then, was basically a conservative and nostalgic genre seeking to preserve past values which were being increasingly eroded by the social and cultural changes related to industrialization and the rise of the city. It's interesting to note that this was essentially the explanation offered by Wister in his preface to the first edition of *The Virginian* when he says "What is become of the horseman, the cowpuncher, the last romantic figure upon our soil?.... A transition has followed the horseman of the plains: a shapeless state, a condition of men and manners unlovely as that bald moment in the year when winter is gone and spring not come, and the face of Nature is ugly" (x). Yet nine years later when Wister rededicated a new edition, he gave a rather different emphasis to his story by suggesting that it reflects a kind of renaissance of true Americanism rather than a nostalgia for the past:

After nigh half-a-century of shirking and evasion, Americans are beginning to look at themselves and their institutions straight; to perceive that Firecrackers and Orations once a year, and selling your vote or casting it for unknown nobodies, are not enough attention to pay to the Republic. (vii)

Tompkins' explanation of the rise of the modern Western as a reaction against the traditional ideology of sentimental evangelical Christianity does help to account for the substantial differences between the nineteenth- and twentieth-century Westerns and also points to the way in which the ethos promulgated by the westerns of Wister and other twentieth-century filmmakers and writers was related to a whole constellation of new moral and social values which was emerging at this time. With this in mind, we can see that the modern Western represented a new mythology which departed fairly radically from the complex of values characteristic of the earlier western. One sign of this change, as Tompkins indicates in her analysis, is a shift in the treatment of nature from the Edenic Virgin Land of nineteenth-century romanticism to the harsh desert and endless plains more characteristic of the twentieth-century Western. In the modern Western, nature is not a source of fruitfulness and spirituality as it is in Cooper, but an obstacle course through which the protagonists must struggle in their quest for survival.

However, it still remains to be seen how this change in the Western relates to gender issues and why it came about at this particular time. It is certainly true that one of the major characteristics and limitations of the Western genre has been the rigidity of its gender roles. Just as the visual background of the typical Western emphasizes the binary oppositions of desert and mountain, town and wilderness, church and saloon, light and shadow, so the characters divide with equal rigidity along the lines of gender. Men are men and women are women, and attempts to blur this line or to have women playing a man's role have never worked very well. One of the most fascinating and bizarre of Western films, Nicholas Ray's *Johnny Guitar*, is one of the few Westerns in which women enact the rites of conflict and violence which are usually the province of men. In this film, it is a conflict between two women that leads up to the climactic shootout. However, the ambiguity of women playing men's roles is clearly indicated by the strange sequence of costumes worn by Joan Crawford as the female protagonist. When Crawford first appears, near the opening of the film, she is in the elegantly tailored black shirt and pants traditionally associated in Westerns with the gunfighter. Crawford, however, is clearly a gunfighter in drag, for before very long, she changes into the low-cut red dress symbolic of the dance hall girl, and then into a demure white gown and finally into blue jeans. This set of four costumes runs the gamut of the major male and female roles in the Western, but in this case the shifting of costumes seems to symbolize an anxiety of restless shape shifting resulting from the inverted gender roles.

The gender rigidity of the Western tradition becomes even clearer when we compare it to another leading popular genre, that of the detective story. This genre has readily accommodated itself to women protagonists and, in recent years, with the emergence of hard-boiled women detectives in works by writers like Sara Paretsky, Sue Grafton and Linda Barnes, males and females have been virtually inter-changeable in the leading roles in the detective story genre. Even in earlier periods, though the majority of successful detective characters from the later nineteenth and earlier twentieth centuries were men, there were always a few female detectives. This interchangeability of gender has never worked with the Western where women in men's clothing are somehow inappropriate. It may well be that this lack of flexibility in the portrayal of gender roles is one major reason why, after its heyday from the late 1930s to the early 1970s, the Western film and television program has virtually ceased to constitute a significant popular genre. For, in spite of the continued popularity of a few Western writers like Louis L'Amour and an occasionally successful Western film like *Dances with Wolves*, or a mini-series like Larry McMurtry's *Lonesome Dove*, our current interest in the Western seems to be largely a matter of nostalgia. This presentation of the Western hero as a ghost from the past was particularly striking in the recent series of McDonald's television commercials in which aging stars of Western series from the 1950s like Hugh O'Brien and Chuck Connors ride up in spectral black and white to a full-color McDonald's and order the new barbecue sandwich. These nostalgic ghosts are a thin and commercialized echo of the mythical presence which the Lone Range embodied as he rode "out of the past" heralded by the thundering hoofbeats of the great horse Silver.

But why should this particular insistence on the rigidity of gender roles have emerged when it did? Tompkins, as we have seen, thinks that this was primarily a kind of male reaction against the dominant female-centered ideology of evangelical Christianity which gave women and the home the major role in the great life drama of the quest for salvation. However, while the turn of the century did see some major changes in Christianity in America with the rise of the social gospel on one hand and of fundamentalism on the other, I'm inclined to think that there were also other basic social and moral issues which the modern Western was responding to. The most important of these, in my opinion, were the increasing mobility of American life, the beginning of the long-term decline of the home and family and the corresponding emergence of a new ideology of individualism which increasingly de-emphasized the significance of community and family and glorified the virtues of male aggressiveness and competition. This is the same constellation of social changes which, in less popular literary and philosophical form, led to the movement we now refer to as naturalism or social darwinism of which Ernest Hemingway became the most influential literary exemplar. Significantly, the world of Hemingway has many similarities to that of the modern Western.

The modern Western emerged along with the need to mythicize the new values of mobility, competitiveness, and rugged individualism which were replacing the more community and family oriented values of the nineteenth century. The Western glorified and dramatized these values in the struggles of the heroic male Western protagonist, making them the focus of American history as the characteristics responsible for the Winning of the West. The rigidity and separation of gender roles in the Western related more to this, I think, than to the decline of evangelical Christianity, which in fact adapted itself rather effectively to the new circumstances. The male role in the Western symbolized the new world of individual male competition and aggression away from the support of community and family, in other words, the world of modern industrial and business work carried on with increasing separateness from the home. The woman represented the values of the past associated with family, home and community. Typically, in the modern Western, the central female character came to see the necessity of the masculine ethos, and, even, in certain climactic cases, to share in it, as when the pacifist Grace Kelly herself shoots one of the remaining outlaws in *High Noon* when she sees her husband physically threatened. Such moments reverberate throughout the Western to the degree that we can say that there are two archetypal plot structures which dominate the Western tradition: one is the hero's struggle with nature and outlaws, the other is the conversion of the female to the new ethos of violence and rugged individualism. However, this conversion does not mean that the woman becomes interchangeable with the male; on the contrary, in order to affirm the new values of mobility, competition and individualism, the female must remain feminine while at the same time she is forced to recognize that when the chips are down, there is no moral resort beyond the strength and courage of the isolated individual.

III

Now at the beginning of the 1990s, a century after the emergence of the modern Western, another drastic change in popular genres seems to be taking place. It seems to me that the decline of the Western fits together with a number of other tendencies in the development of popular genres to suggest that we are in the middle of another transformation in values and ideologies equivalent to the change which brought about the rise of the modern Western and such related genres as the hard-boiled detective story and the gangster saga. What's happening, I think, is that the erosion of the traditional institutions of community, family, and home which had organized the life of ordinary Americans for generations have reached such a point that many people increasingly reject the modern ideology of individualism. Instead we are rather desperately casting about for ways in which to rebuild new forms of community and family. In terms of popular genres, one of the most significant contemporary trends is precisely this: the dramatization of the process by which new family and community group are created and fostered on a new basis, whether through the interplay of the regulars at a bar or the adventures of a pair of male or female buddies. The isolated individual hero is no longer the archetypal mythical figure which he was in the Western and related genres. Instead, it is the group hero or the ad hoc family that has become the protagonist of the most successful recent popular genres. I will close with two examples which, I think, are indicative. The first is *Dances With Wolves,* virtually the only highly successful Western of the last three years. This film began with the isolated individual hero, but the film was really about his reintegration into a close-knit human community, that of the Sioux. This new myth of the Native American as representing a form of community which the white culture is in danger of losing has been one of the few themes which seem to work with the Western in the last decade or so. Finally, I would point to what happens in the science-fiction movie *Aliens,* which was in many ways the most Western-like film I've seen in recent years. I found the shoot-out between Sigourney Weaver and the alien female in *Aliens* to be the most compelling example of the shoot-out since the Westerns of the 1960s and early 1970s. Significantly, however, the protagonist is a woman and there are no ambiguities about her carrying out a traditionally male action. In fact, Ripley's violence toward the alien creature is a direct outgrowth of the maternal bond she has formed with the young female child she has earlier rescued and not an assertion of her individual courage or an act of revenge—the two primary motives of Western heroism. In *Aliens,* what begins as an adventure into the unknown becomes a desperate struggle to preserve the human family against far more powerful and violent alien forces which seek to destroy it. This seems increasingly to be the mythical adventure on which our hopes and fantasies are centered.

Works Cited

Cawelti, John G. *Adventure, Mystery and Romance: Formula Stories as Art and Popular Culture*. Chicago: U of Chicago P, 1976.

Davidson, Cathy N. *Revolution and the Word: The Rise of the Novel in America*. New York: Oxford UP, 1986.

Hart, James D. *The Popular Book: A History of America's Literary Taste*. Berkeley: U of California P, 1961.

Radway, Janice. *Reading the Romance: Women, Patriarchy, and Popular Literature*. Chapel Hill: U of North Carolina P, 1984.

Slotkin, Richard. *The Fatal Environment: The Myth of the Frontier in the Age of Industrialization, 1800-1890*. New York: Atheneum, 1985.

___. *Regeneration through Violence: The Mythology of the American Frontier, 1600-1860*. Middletown, CT: Wesleyan UP, 1973.

Smith, Henry Nash. *Virgin Land: The American West as Symbol and Myth*. 1950. New York: Vintage, 1957.

Tompkins, Jane. *West of Everything: The Inner Life of Westerns*. New York: Oxford UP, 1992.

___. *Sensational Designs: The Cultural Work of American Fiction, 1790-1860*. New York: Knopf, 1977.

Warshaw, Robert. "Movie Chronicle: The Westerner." *The Immediate Experience*. Garden City, NY: Doubleday, 1962: 135-54.

Wister, Owen. *The Virginian*. 1902. New York: Pocket, 1957.

From Camelot to Graceland:
History and Popular Culture Studies
from the Perspective of the Twenty-First Century

Richard Gid Powers

The Clinton administration—like the Clinton campaign and the Clinton inaugural—seems to be in love with Hollywood...and with MTV and with radio talk shows and with gossip columnists. Not even Reagan romanced show business so lustily.

The Clinton White House is always open house for Beverly Hills' Friends of Hillary and Bill; the First Couple gets the latest hair-dos by celebrity barbers, the President patches into early morning "shock jock" radio shows; never has there been such a synthesis of Washington and Hollywood, such a spill-over of stories from the gossip column to the editorial page (and vice versa).

This is, I suspect, a trend. Clinton is still exploring a discovery that helped him win the election: that the focus of popular interest in current events has migrated from politics to popular culture. And this synthesis of politics and popular culture at the end of the twentieth century is something that historians of American politics are going to have to explore in the twenty-first.

American political historians have not yet, for instance, explored the relation between the rock 'n roll revolution launched by Elvis in 1954 and the civil rights explosion that same year. Martin Luther King and the King of Rock 'n Roll were both—in their own ways—erasing the barrier that had long separated white and black America in society and culture.

There is also an unexplored relationship between the emergence of an adversary culture in the news media during the 1960s (see Moynihan and Garment) and the alienated stance of rock music during the same decade. Before the 1960s the American press had always been partisan in that publishers supported one or the other of the two political parties; since then the press has stood outside the party system in a stance of moral independence from the political process—and even superiority to it. Meanwhile, popular music and popular entertainment were displaying the same hostile relationship toward symbols of national authority.

133

The failure of national leaders since Vietnam to lead—to succeed with "the vision thing"—is another phenomenon that has not yet been seen in relationship to popular culture developments, in this case the increasing ability of celebrities to organize mass movements for social change. Rock music, for example, has mobilized movements for environment, peace, AIDS, even the family farm. Where were politicians when Billy Joel was singing to keep the fishermen of Long Island in their boats?

Historians in other countries have long had to look at popular culture to explain revolutionary upheavals. In America, as Tocqueville predicted, great revolutions have been rare. Nevertheless, America has also undergone enormous changes during this century, though at a glacial pace. It is only within the popular culture that we can detect these slow but essential alterations of public values and attitudes. Historians trying to understand late twentieth-century America will have to know their Elvis, know their Dylan, know their Sex Pistols.

When historians look back at our times, they may conclude that one of the most significant developments during the last half of the twentieth century has been a shift in the power relationship between the state and civil society. The news media, historians, and, naturally, politicians are accustomed to seeing the state as the cockpit of society: the place where the diverse forces of society are resolved into comprehensible programs of action. In other words, the state is the place where leaders lead; society is the place where followers follow.

But less and less is that the case. And not just in America. The collapse of communism has been explained in many ways. But one factor was certainly a rebellion against grandiose and ineffective efforts by the state to control society. Demands for liberal democracy, a market system, and ethnic self-determination were society's declaration of independence from the state—all the more dramatic because of the Soviet-style state's pretensions to unlimited authority over all social institutions.

In America we see the same developments in far less heroic form, since government here has never tried to exercise total authority over society. But within the traditional limits the constitution has placed on government power, Americans *have* looked to Washington for leadership. That tendency increased gradually throughout the nineteenth century, and then rapidly in the twentieth, especially during the New Deal. Under Kennedy, Johnson, and Nixon, presidents were expected to take a stand on every major issue.

But times have changed, and now the public no longer looks so reflexively toward Washington for moral leadership. Within the Beltway,

Washington still seems to be puffed up with a sense of infinite self-importance, but outside the capital, the nation seems interested mainly in itself. Politicians, historians, and reporters lambaste the public for its apathy, reflected (before 1992) in declining numbers of voters, newspaper readers, and ratings for network news. Politicians feel betrayed. They fight, steal, and lie to get to the top of the political heap and then they find that only a rat pack of vicious reporters really cares what they do. And so congressmen resign out of frustration and boredom. (For some discussion of this trend, see Dionne, Slater, Garment, Greider, Leo, and Goodman.)

This decline of politics may be a temporary phenomenon, but I doubt it. Historians who focus on the state and statecraft may be missing some of the most basic forces shaping American society. The traditional theme of political history—power and its uses in society—can now be seen less in the traditional political process, and more within civil society. To an as-yet-unmeasured degree, popular culture has supplanted the political process.

A comparison of two Hollywood films, one from the 1930s, the other from the 1990s, can indicate the dimensions of this shift. James Cagney's *G-Men* premiered in 1935, at the end of five tumultuous years in American political history and the history of popular culture. (This discussion follows the arguments of Bergman and Powers.) Beginning in 1929, crime, always politicized in America, became charged with an even higher level of political significance. Prohibition era gangsters like Legs Diamond, Dutch Schultz, and Al Capone and crimes like the Lindbergh kidnapping came to be regarded as proof of the government's inability to defend national values and to maintain national unity.

Popular culture responded with a wave of gangster pictures, first *Little Caesar* in 1930 and then *The Public Enemy* in 1931. Some of these ended with tacked-on closing epigraphs that crime did not pay, but their real moral was that the law no longer compelled obedience, that the organized underworld was replacing the government as the power center of society. The country had lost confidence that the nation's values could hold the nation together. It was a cultural depression, perhaps as deep as the economic one.

When the Hoover administration failed to take decisive action against an apparent crime wave, the public responded with a grassroots anticrime movement. Beginning as a collection of local crime commissions, by 1932 it had become a loosely organized nationwide network, calling for new federal laws, a new federal police force, and new federal prisons.

The genius of the New Deal was to extract a political program from the cultural depression. The solution to the leadership vacuum was—leadership. It hardly mattered what kind. The Roosevelt program was more a style than a consistent political philosophy: Attorney General Homer Cummings, who would play a key role in the events to follow, called the New Deal "government in action."

The most dramatic symptom of the cultural depression had been the gangster films of 1930 to 1932. The New Deal declared war on the real life counterparts of the movie villains. Adopting the proposals of the grassroots anticrime movement, Attorney General Homer Cummings revamped the image of the FBI to fit the outlines of the public's fantasy of a federal super police force, and unleashed it against the gangsters. The FBI became the symbol of the New Deal style of government, one of the most celebrated of the New Deal's many alphabet agencies.

The New Deal's anticrime crusade began with the Kansas City Massacre of June 17, 1933, when gangsters, trying to free a convict FBI agents were escorting to Leavenworth, killed one agent and wounded two others. Attorney General Cummings branded the attack a declaration of war by the underworld against organized society. As Hoover's men captured or killed Machine Gun Kelly, Pretty Boy Floyd, Baby Face Nelson, Creepy Karpis, and John Dillinger, Cummings shepherded through Congress a package of anticrime laws that vastly increased the authority of the Bureau, which he renamed the FBI, and acquired a military prison at Alcatraz to house the super criminals that the new super police force was capturing.

The public was enchanted, and so was popular entertainment. There were G-Men bubble gum cards, G-Men comics, G-Men radio shows, and G-Men pulp magazines. And there were the G-Men movies. The first, and most successful, of these was *G-Men*, starring the former Public Enemy himself, James Cagney.

Many strands of American popular culture were woven into *G-Men*. There was the rebellious, hyper-energetic action hero played by Cagney. There was the scientific hocus pocus J. Edgar Hoover loved to trot out as the Bureau's infallible arsenal against crime: fingerprinting, crime labs, ballistics, and lots of high-powered weaponry. Most important, *G-Men* took the American detective hero, the private eye, the public's own avenger, and turned him into a government agent. The action detective hero was now a symbol of the federal government fighting to liberate society from the underworld holding it hostage.

G-Men has a documentary look, adhering closely to the public's memory of the gangster wars of 1933 and 1934, but edging that memory into myth: the FBI gets its mandate at a joint session of Congress. The manhunts and gun battles are narrated through newspaper headlines, while eager crowds scan the papers for the latest battle bulletins. The story ties all the big-name gangsters into one gigantic underworld plot against society, a standard plot formula of pulp magazines and pulp-brained politicians. The film ends with Cagney leading the nation to victory over a film stand-in for Dillinger, symbolically defeating all the fears that had constituted the cultural depression.

G-Men's popularity helps explain FDR's political success. The country was looking for unity; the country was looking to Washington to provide this unity. J. Edgar Hoover's G-men gave the country dramatic, even sensational, proof that the country was unified again, that under the leadership of Roosevelt the country had overcome the sense of disintegration that had demoralized it between 1929 and 1933.

G-Men was so successful at the box office, and the FBI was so popular during the 1930s, because there was a vast hunger for reassurance that national unity would survive. In the popular culture of the thirties we can see a vast political pay-off that awaited a political leader able to restore national solidarity through patriotic rituals. In the popular culture of the thirties we can see the country appealing to the national government for such rituals, and the FBI was one of the most effective sources of those rituals of national solidarity.

From 1933, we now jump to December 1991, and another film dealing with the relationship between the national government and civil society. It too was populated with government agents from all the security agencies, FBI agents included; it too was filled with crime laboratory footage, and it too used an initial in its title. This was Oliver Stone's *JFK*, the most controversial popular culture event in many a year.

Both *JFK* and *G-Men* exploit their audiences' anxiety about the role of the government in national life. *G-Men*'s audience was anxious about the government's weakness in the face of big-name gangsters. Stone's starting point is the public's doubts about the truth of the Warren Commission's report on the Kennedy assassination. Both films allege a conspiracy against the nation, but in *G-Men* it was a conspiracy by the organized underworld; in *JFK* it is a government conspiracy against its own people.

JFK begins by reviewing the Warren Commission's most frequently attacked theories, placing them in the most dubious light: the so-called magic bullet that passed through Kennedy's throat, Governor Connally's shoulder, wrist, and knee and then was found, in pristine condition, on an empty stretcher in the hospital emergency wing; the theory that the backward jerk as the second bullet smashed into Kennedy's skull could have been caused by Oswald's shot from the rear; the difficulty of the shots from the Book Depository window.

JFK's semi-documentary scenes bear an uncanny resemblance to the documentary scenes in FBI movies, but *G-Men* presents science as the government's irresistible weapon against crime. *JFK* uses science to expose the government's lies. In the 1930s the government's use of science made government the symbol of the truth in the face of efforts by criminals (like Dillinger) to cover up the facts. In *JFK* the citizenry uses science to defeat government stonewalling.

JFK then argues that if the Warren Commission is wrong, there is no alternative to Stone's own solution, borrowed slavishly from Jim Garrison's *On the Trail of the Assassins*. Garrison had claimed that a right-wing, Cuban exile, homosexual plot against Kennedy he thought he had stumbled on was only the tip of a mind-boggling iceberg: "I believe that what happened at Dealey Plaza in Dallas on November 22, 1963, was a coup d'etat. I believe that it was instigated and planned long in advance by fanatical anticommunists in the United States intelligence community…and that its purpose was to stop Kennedy from seeking detente with the Soviet Union and Cuba and ending the Cold War" (324). And whatever Garrison believed, Stone believed too, and then some.

In *JFK* a network of high-level governmental security operatives, Mardi Gras-costumed homosexuals, radical right-wingers, and anti-Castro nuts plot together to murder Kennedy. And that was just the beginning. The Kennedy assassination fitted into a pattern of secret anticommunist plots during the cold war; the cold war, in turn, grew out of the fascist conspiracy of the 1930s against the left. In *JFK* the Kennedy assassination is treated as a chapter in a century-long plot to use the fear of Communism to protect privilege and repress the left. American anticommunism, Stone charged, was fascism; it had been secretly directing the affairs of the country since the end of World War II.

Twice *JFK* ties its conspiracy theory into that broader sweep of paranoid history. The mysterious Col. X., based on ex-Air Force Col. Fletcher Prouty, tells Garrison that the death of Kennedy was the culmination of a long sequence of similarly motivated crimes: during the forties the plotters had subverted French and Italian labor unions and had overthrown the government of Iran. They had gone on to intervene in national and world politics whenever necessary. The cold war, then, was a hoax concocted by the same plotters who killed Kennedy. (To a certain breed of leftist, an ex-CIA, -FBI, or -military man like Col. X is as persuasive an oracle as ex-communists were to J. Edgar Hoover.) The explanation is that if history had been allowed to take its course without interference, there would have been an accommodation with Stalin in Europe, whether the U.S. liked it or not. (That is, the U.S. would have lost the cold war before it began.) The JFK assassination serves, then, as proof of the far left's conspiratorial history of the cold war.

The second time *JFK* taps into the theory of a fascist plot is during Garrison's summation to the jury. In a remark that must have been as baffling to the film's cast as it would have been to the real Clay Shaw jury, Garrison lets drop the comment that the single bullet theory is the greatest illusion since the Reichstag fire. Although Stone turned the jury into a politically correct demographic slice of the rainbow coalition, no one on the real Clay Shaw jury, probably not Garrison, and certainly not Kevin Costner, would have known the Reichstag fire from a fire sale at Macy's. The only person who would have understood that reference would have been someone (like the scriptwriter who slipped it in) thoroughly indoctrinated in the far left's revisionist history of the twentieth century.

Costner/Garrison was alluding to the international left's most successful propaganda coup of the 1930s. After the fire that destroyed the Reichstag building in February 1933, Hitler tried to frame the German Communist Party and the European branch of the Comintern, but the Communists were acquitted by a not-yet-fully-corrupted German court. The Comintern's leading propagandist, Willi Muenzenberg, was then able to use Hitler's theory of a Communist conspiracy to support a counter-theory in which the fire was a plot by Hitler to discredit the left.

Muenzenberg's instrument for this stroke of propagandistic legerdemain was his *First Brown Book of the Hitler Terror and the Burning of the Reichstag Fire* (Brown and MacDonald 473; *Not Guilty*; Hook 218-47). Stone's allusion to the Reichstag Fire would have conjured up, for those in the know, memories of the precise moment in the 1930s when the left, because of its struggle against Hitler, was at the peak of its popularity in the Western democracies. For example, the ancient Communist culture warrior, Mike Gold, writing in the Communist *Worker* shortly after the Kennedy assassination, worried that "this vile assassination could be turned into our Reichstag fire. The new President's future depends on what he does checking the first big fascist putsch in America. If unchecked, they will strike again" (*Facts* 285).

To dramatize what he thought had really happened at Dealey Plaza, Stone drew on the speculations of Jim Marrs's *Crossfire*: There was another assassin besides Oswald in the School Book Depository, one on the legendary grassy knoll, and perhaps still another somewhere else. Oswald, conveniently a leftist, was the patsy in this scenario, playing the role of the Communists at the Reichstag Fire. (As a film buff Stone could also have gotten the same idea from *The Man Who Shot Liberty Valance.* John Wayne hides in the shadows during James Stewart's showdown with Lee (!) Marvin; when the gun-chary Stewart shoots, so does Wayne, and Wayne's bullet finds its mark [as it usually did.])

With Kennedy and his plans to end the Cold War and withdraw from Vietnam eliminated, and with LBJ in the White House to help with the cover-up, the plotters could escalate the war in Vietnam in order to— well, around here it gets a little murky, but no matter. But for Stone, if JFK had lived, the cold war would have ended during that second term when so many other wonders would have been performed. (J. Edgar Hoover, the Joint Chiefs of Staff and the Southern Senators would all have bitten the dust, for starters.) According to this theory, all the disasters that had afflicted America since 1963 can be traced back to that secret coup d'etat of November 22 (Schlesinger, "Review").

Whenever two paths diverge in the forest of assassination theories, Stone chooses the more sensational. The movie has a mountain climber's logic: by moving ever upward on the pyramid of power, Stone's film carries the audience toward its final revelation, that the conspiracy extended to the government's most commanding heights. In *JFK* Stone has grabbed hold of the most fascinating story in modern American history, tells it well, and dramatizes it with star actors giving bravura performances. So, naturally, people went to see the movie, and since Stone is quite a director, they enjoyed what they saw.

Nearly every newspaper and magazine in the country jumped into the controversy over the movie (See Wicker, Ambrose, Schlesinger, "'JFK,'" "Twisted Truth...," Anson, Lemann, Belin, Raskin, Rogin and Rosenstone, Will, Kempton, and Rafferty). Television networks recycled their old assassination programs.[2] The stars of the conspiracy circuit had their careers revived; Mark Lane hurried a new conspiracy book into print. The books Stone used for the movie shot onto the best-seller lists. Congressmen filmed sound bites calling for new investigations and for releasing the remaining closed files on the killing.

Conspiracy theories like *JFK* evoke passionate responses, and those responses were conditioned by general attitudes toward conspiracy thinking. For *JFK* to have succeeded with the public, that is, for the audience to have been able to suspend disbelief enough to enter Oliver Stone's paranoid world—the American public of the 1990s must have seen itself in an imaginative relationship to the government diametrically opposed to that of the 1930s. Where the 1930s audience searched for ways to identify with Washington and the Roosevelt administration, the audience of the 1990s looked for symbols that expressed its estrangement from the authority structure of the national government. If *G-Men* was a ritual of identification with the state, *JFK* was a ritual of alienation from the government. Stone's film, like *G-Men*, managed to turn the public's deeper attitudes toward the national government into box office.

But that does not mean the public that bought into the *JFK* hype bought the whole bill of goods. If the public felt confirmed in its cynicism about government, it evidently held back from following Stone all the way into the alternative universe of leftist conspiracy theories. Within a few weeks after the film opened, the public had shifted its attention to *Wayne's World* and the general run of escapist entertainment that followed *JFK* into the theaters. And probably for most Americans, *JFK* was simply escapist entertainment for all its semi-documentary and "educational" aspects. Exciting and thought-provoking escapism, but escapism nonetheless.[3]

Stone was showman enough to people the film with a wacky collection of characters played with gusto by some of the best actors in Hollywood, and so the audience could respond to Stone's assassination theory as a wild Hollywood fantasy as entertaining as *Indiana Jones* and with villains who could have wandered out of a *Batman* sequel.

Stone's success in attracting an audience and generating controversy meant that in some part of the national psyche, Americans were as alienated as Stone from national symbols of authority. But only on the far left were there significant numbers willing to take the step from cynicism about politics to full-blown conspiracy theory. The *Nation* filled its pages with analyses of the movie (See "JFK, The Myth," Corn, Cockburn, "Stone's Opening," "Letters," Ephron) and sponsored a Town Hall debate on the film on March 3, 1992. At the Village Gate there was a debate with a crowd of two thousand drinking beer and watching conspiracy theory stars roll their eyes and shake their heads as they listened to their rivals spin heretical theories.[4]

But outside those congenial precincts of the already converted, to ask Americans to reject all of twentieth-century American foreign and domestic policy as a fascist/anticommunist plot, at the very moment when communism was collapsing around the world—that was a very tough sale indeed, and few Americans bought it. They might have their doubts about official reality (the Warren Commission), but they are just as cynical about any alternative theories spun by leftists with a wild cast of eye and a jargon unintelligible outside college campuses and National Public Radio.

Oliver Stone may be totally estranged from American institutions, but in some ways, American popular culture is even *more* alienated. Despite Stone's fury at the direction America has moved since 1963, he still looks to politics to repair the damage. He seems obsessed with the importance of politics and the role of the state in setting national policy. Popular culture, on the other hand, seems to have given up completely on the entire political process.

In some ways Oliver Stone is a throwback to the Camelot days when the (carefully contrived) image of Kennedy's intelligence and vigor created the illusion that no challenge was too great, etc., etc. Whether the issue was segregation in Mississippi, urban decay in New York, soil erosion in the high plains, or starvation in Africa, all that was needed was for the President to make a speech, Congress to pass a law, and Washington to ship out the bucks. Kennedy was confident that politics—government—was where the action was: "The political world is stimulating. It's the most interesting thing you can do. It beats following the dollar." Therefore, government was where the action hero—JFK—should also be.

Why was government where the action was? Not just because it was where the booty was divided up, where men were sent to war or, if you believe Oliver Stone, where conspirators kept them from being brought home. It was because the whole nation sat as an audience watching public dramas being acted out on the stage of state. Norman Mailer, in his study of Kennedy as existential hero (*The Presidential Papers*), was fascinated by JFK because by identifying with Kennedy in self-revelatory action, Mailer could imagine the entire nation learning how to "become itself."

But even at the height of the Kennedy myth, promoted by fellow Harvard grads like Mailer and Teddy White, there was an alternative first family, a blue collar alternative to the Hyannis Port glitterati. This was Elvis, Priscilla, and Lisa Marie. JFK rode PT-109 into the White House, but blue-collar America hated officers, even hero officers, and identified with Elvis as he lost his oiled locks, learned how to clean his M-1, and stood guard duty on the edge of the free world in Germany.

For many Americans, Washington was not where the action was, even in the heady days of the New Frontier. Kennedy was wrong. The action was in Memphis, and the King lived at Graceland. The action was in popular culture, not politics, and as a result, more people visit Elvis's grave at Graceland each year than Camelot's fallen king's at Arlington.[5]

There were signs of this shift from politics to popular culture even during the heady days of the New Frontier. While Kennedy was boasting about politics and its stimulating effects, the women's movement was replying that "the personal is political."⁶ That meant that what a person does in her private life is a critique of the conventional power relationships in society. Private action, then, is political action; civil society is where political reality is most intimately experienced, and it is where reality is changed.

We see this same perception in Billy Joel's "We didn't start the fire," a rap-disco declaration of "our" innocence for the evil of the political order.⁷ When Billy Joel sings "we" he means, "the people of rock 'n roll," the creators and consumers of popular culture, who stand outside the political process, and so are superior to it, not responsible for its crimes.

If the personal *is* political, and if the personal is the antithesis of the political, then there must be something else that is *not* political. By process of elimination, this must be the state and the political process, apolitical in the sense of being irrelevant to the power realities of society. Paradoxically, then, it seems that popular culture is becoming political at the expense of the state, the traditional focus of power. Politics in the traditional sense of the word seems to be losing its centrality in the calculus of power.

Popular culture is filled with signs that many Americans no longer regard the government as the imaginative focus of the nation's energy— that it no longer provides the dramatic action that leads to national self-awareness. In exhorting their constituents to reject apathy and to take part in the political process, professional politicians are coming to sound like ministers preaching to deserted churches.

This suggests another explanation for the rituals of alienation from the state and the political process that have filled politically charged popular culture since the Vietnam/Watergate era. This entertainment justifies the public's indifference to politics—just as critical book reviews seem to reassure people who have no intention of reading a book, any book, that they have made the right decision. Popular culture reassures people who have defected from politics that staying clear of politics makes sense.

Civil society had always produced mass movements that eventually led to government action. What we have at the end of the twentieth century is something different. We now have popular movements that organize themselves into loose institutional forms outside the governmental structure. Political leaders may try to associate themselves with movements like environmentalism or the fight against AIDS, but the government no longer has the money, energy, prestige, or expertise to take them over as it did before Vietnam, Woodstock, and Watergate. Celebrities provide the leadership we once expected from politicians. They supply "the vision thing."

Walt Whitman said somewhere that he did not want to make art that would decide elections; he wanted art that would make them irrelevant. Based on the declining number of eligible voters interested enough in politics to vote, by 1992 popular culture was well on its way to making elections irrelevant. The voter turnout had declined from 63 percent in 1960 to 50 percent in the 1988 election. A straight-line extrapolation using this rate of decline of .5 percent a year would have forecast a 48 percent voter turn-out in the 1992 election; instead 55 percent showed up to vote. Clearly something had happened to reverse a 30-year decline in the voting rate (*New York Times*).

While there is no doubt that concern over the economy gave people more of a reason to vote than during the last few presidential elections, it is reasonable to suppose that the campaigning styles of the two challengers, Clinton and Perot, had something to do with stirring new interest in the political process. And, for the perspective of popular culture studies, what is significant is that Clinton and Perot reinvigorated the tired format of televised speeches and debates by directly borrowing currently popular formats from the world of television and radio entertainment: they both utilized the format perfected by Larry King—the call-in show—and by Oprah Winfrey and Phil Donahue—the audience participation talk show. Clinton also negotiated an agreement to present one of the major debates in a relaxed format that seemed a hybrid of "happy talk" television news and the talk entertainment shows.

Meanwhile, MTV assigned a reporter to the campaign, and presented reports in the short, snappy style made familiar to young listeners by MTV's "video jock" hosts. These MTV reports, which caused a near sensation among high school and college students, had surprising substance, given the temptation—generally resisted—to focus on matters of style. Clinton made an effort—on the Arsenio Hall Show—to break out of the blue-suited politician stereotype by donning sunglasses and grabbing his sax to play "Yackety Yack" with the studio band.

Politics is communication, and communication fails when the prevailing style of political rhetoric grows so stale as to defeat the transfer of information from the (potential) leader to the electorate. Clinton and Perot managed to overcome the hackneyed conventions of political communication by borrowing freely from successful show business formulas. These innovations must have had something to do with Clinton's victory and with Perot's very strong third party showing. In particular, these innovations obviously were successful in luring the previously disaffected youngest voters—the 18- to 29-year-old group that had massively stayed away from the polls in previous elections — into taking an interest in the political process.

Whether the increased voter turnout of 1992 in fact is the beginning of a renewed interest in politics remains to be seen. What does seem sure is that successful politicians are going to have to pay close attention to popular culture to spot show business trends that can be adapted to their purposes. Politicians are going to have to recognize that for most of the public, most of the time, imaginative reality is supplied by popular culture, and not by the political process. The once universal church has had to learn to live as one institution among many in a secular world. Political leaders are going to have to co-exist with a popular culture whose celebrities have greater effect on the public mind than any political leader. And American historians in the twenty-first century are going to have to know their country's popular culture if they want to understand its politics.

Notes

[1]Leftist assassination buffs like Stone love to repeat poll findings that some 60 percent of the public think there was a JFK conspiracy. Since this is one of the rare instances when any significant segment of the American public agrees with the left, the assassination might be used to get a foot in the door for other leftist ideas.

[2]"Nova: Who Shot Kennedy?" was the best. A&E reran its 1986 "The Trial of Lee Harvey Oswald," a five-part dramatization of what the trial might have been like. (It ended with a guilty verdict against Oswald.) James Earl Jones narrated "JFK Conspiracy," a notably inept attempt to tie the assas-sination into the Cuban Missile Crisis, the Bay of Pigs, and even Water-gate.

[3]Which is perhaps why most of the mainstream press took an agnostic position towards Stone's theories, but praised him for "raising issues," thereby indicating skepticism about the government as well as Stone.

[4]There were two Mafia theories (New Orleans mob and Miami mob), a CIA theory, a Secret Service theory, and an insistence by Attorney William Kunstler that whoever dunnit, his former client, Jack Ruby, was innocent. Kunstler angered all of the panelists, since Ruby was essential to all of their theories. For an account, see Evanier.

[5]In a fascinating account of how the Camelot myth was constructed in the days after the assassination, Theodore White tells how he hit upon the metaphor the week after the assassination, based on hints from Jacqueline, while he was under deadline pressure for a byline story for *Life* magazine (511-25).

[6]I was told by Gloria Steinem and Kate Millett in phone interviews on Apr. 29, 1992, that neither of them had originated the phrase, which was "in the

air" in 1970. However, I was later told that a few days after I had talked to her, Kate Millett had begun to stake out a claim to the phrase.

[7]Compare that to a song popular during World War II, "I Don't Want to Set the World on Fire" which is apologetic over the modesty of the lovers' ambitions. Or perhaps it says the same thing.

Works Cited

ADL. *Facts* Mar. 1964: 285.

Ambrose, Stephen E. "Writers on the Grassy Knoll." *New York Times Book Review* 2 Feb. 1992: 1.

Anson, Robert Sam. "The Shooting of JFK." *Esquire* Nov. 1991: 93-102.

Belin, David W. "The 'Lies' of JFK." *New York Magazine.* 17 Feb. 1962: 44-47.

Bergman, Andrew. *We're In the Money.* New York: Harper, 1972.

Brown, Anthony Cave and Charles B. MacDonald. *On a Field of Red.* New York: Putnam's, 1981.

Cockburn, Alexander. "Beat the Devil." *Nation* 6, 13 Jan. 1992: 6-7; 9 Mar. 1992: 294-95, 306.

Corn, David. "X-Men and JFK." *Nation* 27 Jan. 1992: 80.

Dionne, E.J., Jr. *Why Americans Hate Politics.* New York: Simon and Schuster, 1991.

Ephron, Nora. "The Tie that Binds." *Nation* 6 Apr. 1992: 453-55.

Garment, Suzanne. *Scandal: The Crisis of Mistrust in American Politics.* New York: Times Book, 1991.

Garrison, Jim. *On the Trail of the Assassins.* New York: Warner, 1988.

Goodman, Ellen. *San Francisco Chronicle* 5 May 1992: A17.

Greider, William. *Who Will Tell the People: The Betrayal of Democracy.* New York: Simon and Schuster, 1992.

Gross, Babette. *Willi Munzenberg: A Political Biography.* East Lansing: MSU P, 1974.

Hook, Sidney. *Out of Step.* New York: Harper and Row, 1987.

Klawans, Stuart. "Review." *Nation* 20 Jan. 1992: 62-64.

Kopkind, Andrew. "JFK, The Myth." *Nation* 20 Jan. 1992: 40-41.

Leo, John. "Geraldoization of News." *San Francisco Chronicle, This World* 19 Apr. 1992: 2.

"Letters." *Nation* 9 Mar. 1992: 290, 317-20.

Mailer, Norman. *The Presidential Papers.* New York: Putnam, 1963.

Moynihan, Daniel Patrick. "The Presidency and the Press." *Commentary* Mar. 1971: 41-52.

New York Times 5 Nov. 1992: B4.

Not Guilty: the Final Report of the Commission of Inquiry into Charges Made Against Leon Trotsky and Leon Sedoff in the Moscow Trials. New York and London, 1938.

Powers, Richard Gid. *G-Men: Hoover's FBI in American Popular Culture.* Carbondale: Southern Illinois UP, 1983.

Rafferty, Terrence. "Smoke and Mirrors." Review. *New Yorker* 13 Jan. 1992: 73-75.

Raskin, Marcus, Michael Rogin and Robert A. Rosenstone. "Forum." *American Historical Review* Apr. 1992: 487-50.

Schlesinger, Arthur, Jr. "'JFK': Truth and Fiction." *Wall Street Journal* 10 Jan. 1992: A8.

___. "Review" of John M. Newman. *JFK and Vietnam: Deception, Intrigue, and the Struggle for Power.* New York: Warner Books, 1992. *New York Times Book Review* 29 Mar. 1992: 3.

Slater, Philip. *A Dream Deferred: America's Discontent and the Search for a New Democratic Ideal.* Boston: Beacon, 1992.

"Stone's Opening." *Nation* 17 Feb. 1992: 184-85.

"Twisted Truth of 'JFK.'" *Newsweek* 23 Dec. 1991: 46-49.

White, Theodore. *In Search of History.* New York: Harper and Row, 1978: 511-25.

Wicker, Tom. "Does 'JFK' Conspire Against Reason." *New York Times* 15 Dec. 1991: Section 2, 1.

TECHNOLOGY
AND
POPULAR
CULTURE
SCHOLARSHIP

◆

Technology and Popular Culture of the Future

Joseph W. Slade

Economic downturns often increase American hostility toward technology, and the current recession seems to be having that effect. The usually astute Neil Postman has recently published *Technopoly: The Surrender of Culture to Technology* (1992), a book whose insistence that rampant technology undermines the moral foundations of society recalls the gloomy predictions of Jacques Ellul, father of a technophobia that had seemed for a time to be in cultural remission. In other respects, however, thanks to the efforts of organizations like the Society for the History of Technology and popular magazines like *American Heritage of Invention and Technology*, less fearful conceptions of technology have made some gains. If Postman's views are those of a humanist disgruntled by technology, and certain that technology and culture are antithetical, then Samuel Florman's *The Existential Pleasures of Engineering* (1976) and James Adams's *Flying Buttresses, Entropy, and O-Rings: The World of an Engineer* (1991) convey the optimism of engineers convinced that technology will improve the human condition and enrich our culture. The "two cultures"—to refer to C.P. Snow's still current categories— have very different views of the technology that bridges the humanities and the sciences. Despite the moderation of a growing number of centrist critics like O.B. Hardison, Jr., whose *Disappearing Through the Skylight: Culture and Technology in the Twentieth Century* (1989) is a thoughtful effort to synthesize, the debate is unlikely to diminish as we enter the twenty-first century, if only because the rate of technological change, which has been accelerating since the eighteenth century, shows no sign of slackening.

The debate is fueled partly by an inability to agree on what technology *is*. Arguing about technology is like arguing about religion, because hidden assumptions, or at least unexamined premises and attitudes, often color definitions. The real problem, as Bruce Mazlish has pointed out in a famous essay, may be our inability to decide on what it means to be human. According to Mazlish, humans have always resisted ideas that seemed to diminish their centrality in the universe. Humans only gradually accepted a Copernican astronomical system that cast their planet from the center of the universe, a Darwinian evolutionary scheme that denied them a unique place among lifeforms, and a Freudian analysis that undermined the primacy of their conscious human minds. A similar hubris, founded on a dubious conviction that humans will always be superior to machines and systems, says Mazlish, leads humans to deny their kinship with technology (217-20.) We cling to the hope that creators are different from creations, refuse to acknowledge our parenting, and try to define ourselves in opposition to technology, as if technology were somehow an Other that we are not.

As the battle lines of current academic wars indicate, we are just as divided over definitions of culture. We stumble from metaphor to metaphor, most of them inadequate, in our efforts to define both technology and culture, and to describe the connections between them. I want to discuss some of those metaphors, and their assumptions about the relationship between technology and culture, first to sketch conflicting opinions, and second to frame areas that popular culture specialists of the future can properly explore. At the outset, I offer my own definition of technology: it is any means by which a species alters itself or its environment. A bit farther along I wish to propose another metaphor: that culture is itself a technology for sorting information, interpreting messages, assigning values, and establishing meaning. Metaphors are themselves a key technology for the cultural construction of reality; if metaphors do not resolve tensions, they can dramatize and illuminate.

Both technology and culture constantly evolve, which makes their interaction difficult to assess. Indeed, we can only represent this relationship by means of metaphors that themselves become more complex over time. The pull of metaphor is a familiar one, for humans are accustomed to using specific technologies dominant at a particular time to describe cultures of that era. As J. David Bolter points out, potters' wheels and weavers' spindles were the defining technologies of the ancient world, where they not only produced artifacts of enormous utlity but also became symbols of human and cosmic activity. Wheels of fortune and spinning threads served the Greek tragedians as images for human life and fate (15-23). Subsequent periods we call the Age of Bronze, for example, or the Age of Navigation, after the technologies that flourished then. During the latter era, sextants and clocks assumed a cultural importance that lasted well into the eighteenth century, when philosophers and political scientists construed the universe in terms of a clockwork mechanism mirrored in society's own operations, as in the cosmological images Thomas Jefferson scattered throughout the Declaration of Independence. If the computer has become the touchstone of our own era, the metaphor by which we try to comprehend the human mind—as Bolter argues—then one can also point to the still viable metaphorical significance of the principal technological icon of the early Industrial Revolution, which led Sigmund Freud to conceptualize the human psyche as a steam engine, with the id as a boiler and the superego as a flywheel governor. Social analogues of this Freudian psychological model postulated cultural repression periodically released by safety valves, and we still find these steam engine metaphors plausible.

In a sense, such metaphors are just markers in the flow of history. The Industrial Revolution could be represented, as it sometimes is, by a series of labels in which the Age of Steam gives way to the Ages of Steel, Electricity, Chemistry, Transportation, and Communication. The labels imply a definition of technology as the act of *making*. Not so long ago, anthropologists routinely characterized humans as tool-making animals. The shorthand is more sophisticated now. Historians who once thought cultural evolution began with the opposable thumb, which made it possible to construct and hold axes, to build arches, or to machine steel to precise tolerances, are now accustomed to thinking of entire systems as technological constructs.

At this (relatively) simple level, technology is chiefly instrumentality. From this perspective, specific technologies, even at their most complex, are still just tools that humans can choose to employ or not. Adherents of this view are often aware that human intervention may be difficult because technological systems are now so interrelated that action in one sector can have unforeseen consequences in others. Building a mass-transit system in a city, for example, can raise demand for energy, which causes an electric utility to burn more coal, which causes an increase in strip-mining in a neighboring state, which causes an erosion of pasture-land, which boosts the price of milk for schoolchildren in the entire Northeast. Despite the unpredictable effects of decisions, those who believe that only technology can cope with problems generated by other technologies argue that we must nevertheless try to exercise logic, choice, and direction, and that what is required is still greater knowledge about consequences and monitoring by bureaucracies—which are themselves technologies designed to process information. Operationally, technology as instrumentality is a "real-world" approach. Whether the approach works or not, a great deal of government policy is predicated on its validity. Even this practical view of the most practical of endeavors seems constrained by confusion, however.

For many Americans, technology has always been at base *invention*, the crafting of discrete artifacts, usually machines, but also of formulas or processes, the creation of special expertise or knowledge.

The Constitution of the United States singles out only two professions as entitled to special privileges. Because books and inventions contribute to the public good, the framers of Article I of that document permitted writers and inventors to profit through copyright and patent, i.e., through ownership based on originality. Both could license their product for mass manufacture, though somehow the author—as opposed to the inventor—managed to remain untainted by such commerce. Since that time, moreover, writers have invested their craft with high status, insisting on their special role as elegant fabricators of symbols, while inventors until comparatively recently were content to be seen as mechanics who worked with inanimate objects and were not afraid to get their hands dirty. Technological pursuits seemed properly open to the amateur, who might or might not be educated, in a way that serious literary activities were not. The technology of publishing eroded this pretense somewhat, of course, and continues to do so as more and more untalented people write books. Even so, our society still calls a dedicated writer an artist, but cannot agree on what to call a dedicated technologist. Is that person an inventor, a mechanic, an engineer, a scientist, or what? Perhaps because of the fluidity of this occupational category, those Americans who embrace technology, a group large enough to include Jefferson himself and hundreds of innovators from Benjamin Franklin to Steven Jobs, have occupied a special place in popular consciousness.

Both history and popular prejudice have worked against finding an upscale name for the inventor. During the last two centuries, technology has often been conflated with science, and still is, most notably in large institutional efforts like the Manhattan Project, the space race, the building of particle accelerators, or the launching of the Human Genome Project. The linkage has proved ambivalent, since technology has by turns been elevated by the authority and prestige of science and burdened by its alleged soullessness and impersonality. Scientists themselves are apt to regard technology as *applied* science, and often classify technicians as assistants who carry out instructions or construct apparatus that makes genuine experimentation possible. Because so much science has gone into weapons research, scientists may insist on distancing themselves from military engineering as a matter of conviction or ethical convenience. The issues are complicated still further by the increased commercialization of scientific laboratories in recent years, and by the national anxiety over the levels of current American research and development necessary to compete with Japanese and European economies.

Scientists are not above trying to justify huge expenditures by citing the technological byproducts, like the personal computers, advanced weather prediction techniques, medical devices, and consumer goods such as Tang that resulted from the space program. Even so, like humanists, scientists prefer to think that disinterested, "pure" research or labor is more valuable than effort devoted from the outset to a product. While many untutored inventors have intuited the scientific principles that make their devices work, many others have in fact been scientists in every relevant sense. Leaving aside questions of temperament and obsession, what makes inventors successful and different from scientist or humanists is their cultural acumen, their ability to perceive and satisfy social and economic needs. Historians credit Thomas Edison with the invention of electric lighting not so much because he invented a bulb but because he was the first to grasp the social nature of lighting, to conceive of it as a domestic network of illumination (Slade 22). In a sense, then, the inventor resides more comfortably in the larger cultural arena, while his colleagues of the "two cultures"—the humanists on the one hand, the scientists on the other—actually occupy much smaller domains circumscribed by their more exclusive professionalism. Neither the scientist nor the humanist can function without specialized technologies of their own, but they do not see their primary tasks, i.e., the creation of scientific theory, or the fabricating of symbol systems like language, art, or music, as practical.

At the same time, part of the popular, utilitarian American mythos, noted even by Tocqueville, is the conviction that anybody with enough intelligence and grit can fabricate a better mousetrap. The more demotic the origins of an invention, the more authentic it and its inventor seem. We like to think of inventors as neighbors tinkering in their garages, "real" people animated by ingenuity, amateur artisans determined to extend democracy by building devices user-friendly to masses of their fellows. Edison, for example, preferred to think of himself as an inventor rather than a "pure" scientist, perhaps because the posture seemed better suited to his other persona, the public entrepreneur. If technology is instrumentality, then the roles of those who create are important, and a great many popular biographies and essays have been devoted to individuals, especially amateurs—or those pretending to be—who invent new tools or new methods of adapting older ones. The "heroic school" of technology prizes tales of inspiration, emphasizes artifacts that altered the course of events, and dotes on the power they confer on the average person. Probably such devices do empower. Many of us have noticed that the word processors that were supposed to halve the flow of paper have not only doubled the traffic and increased the hours of white collar workers, but also added to the responsibilities and perhaps the understanding of those who operate the systems. Similarly, though studies indicate that the proliferation of household appliances has increased the number of the housewife's chores as much as they have saved her labor (Cowan), surely part of the appeal of domestic hardware is the greater sense of control—illusory or not—that it gives the user.

We like also to think that new inventions break down social, political, and economic barriers by destroying the power of privileged groups. In a famous thesis, Elizabeth Eisenstein noted that the printing press undermined the authority of the priesthood, and by extension the nobility whose servants the priests were, by making possible literacy for the masses. In the long run, according to Eisenstein's argument, the printing press created an informed population, and thus led inevitably to the invention of democracy. Increasingly we assign historical relevance to the pleasures associated with "objects of desire," as the *New York Times* describes the massive collection of chairs, pencil sharpeners, cars, ski boots, typewriters, musical instruments and so on that made up the recent Grand Palais (Paris) exhibit of industrial objects from 1850 to the present (Giovannini, B1). Because they proliferated rapidly in response to popular demand, these thousands of once-utilitarian antiques index their periods as nothing else can. Many of them appealed first to the young, just as their contemporary counterparts do today, because they represented new ways of doing things, and thus seemed revolutionary at the time. That bias still skews acceptance of the new. Today, especially, the young embrace innovation more readily because they have grown up with sophisticated systems, and learned how to operate them, while those born before television, let alone microchips, space flight, and bio-engineering, may still not have come to terms with changes in workplace and home. We all know colleagues who prefer typewriters to word-processors, who cannot learn to program a VCR, or, for that matter, who refuse to pump their own gas at a service station, activities they may think beneath their status.

Celebrations of the heroic inventor foreground legends that usually mask the complex processes by which innovations originate and prosper in the marketplace. Popular culture specialists are familiar with the tropes of these stories, as are historians of technology who must jettison the romantic baggage. John M. Staudenmaier's *Technology's Storytellers* examines narratives in which historians have revised our understanding of artifacts and innovations in a study of a series of articles published in *Technology and Culture*, the journal of the Society for the History of Technology. The historian's task is made easier with the passage of time, as the once revolutionary invention passes out of the marketplace and into the museum, there to be demystified and reappreciated for the beauty of a design that seemed crude at its inception. By contrast, popular culture specialists often prefer to deal with inventions just as they begin to impact on people's daily lives, creating sub-cultures among those who find pleasure and potency in using power tools, repairing automobiles, building model airplanes, communicating via CB radios, playing Nintendo games, or thousands of other activities.

In writing about those activities, we often encounter powerful class prejudices. Behind the arguments of technophobes often lies a distaste for the vulgarity of machinery and popular innovations; behind the optimism of technophiles lurks a delight in their cheapness and availability. The former may see the despair of a consumer society in the hunger for objects of desire; the latter see normal human longing. Again, the distance between technophobes and technophiles has to do with very different conceptions of how technology and culture, both human creations, are related. The nature of that relationship, I think, will occupy us well into the future, and discussion will almost certainly involve issues of age, class, gender, taste, and politics—differences that sharpen the opposition between mandarin notions of culture and those that our discipline calls popular. Although we have grown accustomed to Marxist critiques that identify technology with wealth, privilege, and class oppression, we should also be aware that many attacks on technology are actually attacks on popular culture. Scholars in our field have no special obligation to defend technology, of course, but it will be increasingly difficult to ignore in the twenty-first century. It is not just that a fondness for tools and toys is a hallmark of popular culture, but also that people increasingly cluster around technologies.

One of the factors behind the success of the Industrial Revolution, as Adam Smith predicted in *The Wealth of Nations* (1776), was the specialization of labor that preceded the rise of corporate organizational structures. The cultural analogue of that fragmentation is the specialization of knowledge that leads to bureaucracies of taste and intellect: those bureaucracies are what we indicate by terms like *high* and *popular* culture. Both intellectual disciplines and social groups form around shared information. When scientists professionalized disciplines like physics or chemistry, as Thomas Kuhn has noted in *The Structure of Scientific Revolutions*, they closed ranks against the amateur by establishing systematized bodies of specialized information, using vocabularies unintelligible to and therefore inaccessible to outsiders (17). A similar process governs other sectors of culture as citizens of industrialized countries have tried to define certain kinds of infor- mation—literary, artistic, legal, medical, economic, and so on—as the provinces of professionals, and to arrange them in hierarchies of authority and prestige. "Technical" knowledge has traditionally been way down the list, a ranking whose persistence doubtless led Harvard University to dump its engineering curriculum only a few years after adopting it in the mid-nineteenth century.

The economic application of technical knowledge is another matter. Marxists have long since chronicled the speed with which social and economic elites establish circles of power and influence, the currency of which is insider information, a process that began in this country, as Richard Brown makes clear in his *Knowledge Is Power*, in colonial America. The terms *high culture* and *popular culture* refer in part to the power that access to restricted information confers. Members of elites of course often reject such characterizations by arguing that their groups are merely tastemakers. According to this view, "culture" has to do merely with the preservation of custom and tradition, the promotion of proper standards of behavior, dress, and manners, or the guardianship of sophisticated art and music. From the upper-class perspective, technology either as artifact or power can be separated from more ethereal esthetic and intellectual pursuits; to elites, culture is something substantially different from the mere making of things, as if culture were a realm of ideas rather than endeavors. One need not be a Marxist to spot the self-interest here, although as academics we need not look at every artifact as an expression of the hegemony of one group over another, either.

Considerations of class, based to a degree on the fuzzy distinction between professional and amateur, still carry great weight despite more careful contemporary definitions of technology. Academic critics like Postman are likely to conceptualize technology in broad strokes, as the driving force behind the "military-industrial complex," say, or as the principal support of institutions careless of the fragility of the planet, or as the machinery of a capitalism bent on turning everything into a commodity, or just as a mega-control system that determines our lives and destinies. But enough hints of the demotic nature of invention remain to sharpen their fear that "culture" is being overwhelmed by the socially and intellectually inferior. Although ideology, age, ethnicity, and gender also determine attitudes, class consciousness reverberates in synonyms for technology like "material culture," a term in which one hears the sniff of disdain for "things" as opposed to ideas or values. The prejudice goes a long way back. Even Emerson, who believed that building a better mousetrap was a pretty good route to Transcendence, could still write that "Things are in the saddle, and ride mankind." Marxism inverts categories: in dialectical materialism, technology is an instrument of the ruling class; socialism subordinates it to human labor. The ambivalence is more than just a game of famous quotations, of course: History's verdict may well be that insufficient technology destroyed the Soviet Union.

Complicating associations of class still further are constant revisions of status among specific, undeniably "material" technologies. Over time, economic, social, and political factors reduce some endeavors to lower status at the same time that money and prestige flow to newer, "higher" activities. An electrician is now a blue collar worker, whereas an electronics engineer wears the mantle of a scientist. Steam engines are museum curiosities, the United States no longer makes steel, the chemical industry fabricates bug sprays, and Detroit, by all accounts, has forgotten how to manufacture a decent automobile. The nation's infrastructures, the older transportation, energy, and manufacturing resources of our nation—the roadways, canals, bridges, factories, pipelines, power plants, and electrical grids—still require upkeep. We maintain them—at least those still necessary or cost-efficient (not railroads, for example)—with increasingly high-tech methods, like computerized construction techniques, but they seem less glamorous than robotics, genetic engineering, aerospace, and virtual reality— pursuits that *do* seem less "materialistic" and more dependent on ideas and information.

Some prejudices against technology are moral. Various groups including ecologists, disarmament campaigners, animal-rights activists, "small-is-beautiful" advocates and other devotees of minimalist, lower-case technology implicitly endorse the definition with which I began: that technology is any means by which a species alters itself or its environment. But they often find those means morally suspect. Some, to be sure, object merely to lethal or potentially lethal technologies, like nuclear weapons, recombinant DNA research, or animal experi-mentation, while others are opposed not to technology itself but to the scale of massive industrialized or service-oriented economies. The more extreme, however, consciously or unconsciously blame technology for a spiritual, even ontological break with an alleged natural order. Their metaphysics posits a proto-historical, pre-technological harmony between humans and Nature. For them, technology is not simply *making*; it is a process of *domination*, a deliberate attempt to trifle with the sacred, that taints the enterprise. Technology may thus resemble the poisoned knowledge familiar from the Book of *Genesis*, or take on connotations borrowed from slipshod readings of *Frankenstein*.

The most respectable of these metaphors is that outlined by Max Weber, whose classic *The Protestant Ethic and the Spirit of Capitalism* theorized that humans—Western Protestants, at least—try to *control* rather than co-exist with nature out of fear of nature's teeming chaos.

The real culprit, Weber thought, is a human mind that can not tolerate uncertainty. Using as their tool a destructive logic, Protestants fragment the world with mathematics, develop powerful symbol systems that reconstitute the parts, and establish control over nature's fertility. They strive for dominion by building ever more elaborate social technologies like bureaucracies, secular institutions that displace the reverence due to nature and the moral sensibilities that stem from that awe. The process Weber called *rationalization*, which, once begun, could never be stopped but only deflected (through charismatic movements, for instance). The irony is that the more complex technological systems become, the more *routinized* their operations, the more pervasive and inexorable is the control that they exercise over their creators. Weber's contemporary, Ferdinand Tönnies, pointed out that the process of rationalization transformed social affinities (*gemeinschaft*) into commercial relationships (*gesellschaft*), and thus enshrined capitalism as a mindset and ultimately as a culture. Critics working within this tradition think of technology as replacing the seasonal rhythms of nature with cycles of profit and loss, and thus overlaying the natural landscape with an alien, artificial technological environment. The irreversibility of Weber's process can make for a tragic view of life, since it can only end as the stasis of total, rigid, control. It's a cultural analogue of the Second Law of Thermodynamics.

Humanists have traditionally liked Weber's scheme because it gave them a stick with which to whack science and its alleged bastard, technology, but there are many less elaborate versions, few of them so bleak as Weber's. Some are modest, nostalgic protests against the increasing artifice of the environment. Other variations simply note that at some point technology moved beyond mere tool-making to become systematized into a complexity not susceptible to individual or even collective decision. Victor Ferkiss, for instance, thinks the cusp occurs when machines that did the work of human and animals were superseded by systems that began to do the work of human intelligence. Norbert Wiener settles more precisely on World War II and the pivotal role of radar, from which exfoliate cybernetic systems of command and feedback. Marshall McLuhan champions the advent of electronic media, which become "extensions of man" capable of abridging time and space. And so on. A full-fledged Weberian would say that fixing a historical moment for this shift is irrelevant, for autonomous technology is prefigured in the process of rationalization that created Western culture itself.

The most recent variation on Weber's metaphor, a version of the Fall more applicable to culture than to technology per se, is that promoted by postmodernist schools besotted with the self-reflexivity of language. Like Weber, postmodern theorists understand the power of symbol systems. For them, languages and other symbol systems, because they are arbitrary technologies, ultimately refer only to themselves, not to any "objective" reality. Since humans "know" the world only through their symbol systems, only the mediation itself has any final reality. All other technologies (though postmodernists prefer the word *texts*) are thus determined by the codes that define and describe. Languages in turn interact with the social contexts in which they develop, and are subject to hierarchies of social, political, and economic power. Those classes who hold power, or those social, political, and economic forces dominant within a culture, thus shape language and ultimately construct meaning.

This range of metaphors—in which thinkers as diverse as the German Weber and the French postmodernists insist that technology is both knowledge and instrumentality, i.e., an aggregate of information and a method of doing—can evoke fears of control that are less tangibly and secularly experienced than intellectually apprehended or emotionally intuited. In such scenarios, technology with a capital T is either 1) an ontologically or teleologically deterministic force, beyond human control; or, 2) a social, economic, or political force wielded by economic, social, gender, or racial elites whose symbolic imperialism irresistibly shapes the lives of the masses. The first, that technology is itself deterministic, remains very attractive to critics. But, as James L. Adams asserts,

Historical counterexamples to the philosophy of technological determinism abound, however. Sophisticated technology does not always determine the outcome of war, as shown in Vietnam. Business lore is full of stories of technology-based companies that failed. In general, U.S. industries feel that this country is more technologically advanced than its counterparts around the Pacific rim. Yet the competition from these smaller nations is much fiercer than technological determinism should allow.

China, over the course of its long history, has produced a tremendous amount of technological invention, yet the Chinese have not pursued their innovations for economic gain nearly as vigorously as Western countries have. The Japanese, although they were early innovators in the development of firearms, elected not to use them for 300 years. Something must have been at work in these cultures other than technological determinism. Could it be that societies determine the direction of technology, rather than the other way around? (68-69)

That depends, of course, on how we think of culture and its relationship to technology. Technological determinists may view technological change, usually construed as greater efficiency, as predetermined by immanent necessity. Social constructionists, on the other hand, maintain that technology, however defined, arises in response to cultural—i.e., social, economic, and political—imperatives. One of the leading historians of technology to employ a social construction approach, Donald MacKenzie, nonetheless acknowledges that technology "cannot be simply shaped at will" (412). Marshall J. Bastable, who cites MacKenzie in a brilliant article on weaponry of the last century, extends the point:

Abstract forces of technology and culture, then, are not the only important factors in technological change. Neither science-fiction fantasies nor social, political, or economic "needs" can simply call new technologies into being. It is individual inventors who transform ideas into working hardware. Their motives are neither singular and unchanging nor do they merely express social or biological imperatives.... Individual inventors of the mid-19th century, with their individual motives and abilities, confronted the logic of technological efficiency, struggled with their own rivalries, linked themselves to the shifting social, political, and military interests of the day, and invented modern artillery. (215-16)

It is fashionable to construe everything these days in terms of political power, and paranoia adds urgency to conflicting ideologies. Ultimately, as Langdon Winner suggests, attitudes concerning the uses and effects of technology may best be understood as sets of political "pathologies" (324). We are certainly not going to settle here the question of whether the march of technology enhances the prospects for human freedom and self-realization, dehumanizes individuals and interdicts traditional routes to human community, or alienates and subordinates groups by race, class, or gender. We *can* observe that theories of technological determinism and social constructionism seem equally authoritarian, and that their proponents appear similarly convinced that individual choice is meaningless. Perhaps because popular culture specialists have always explored those margins where mainstream currents seem weakest, they have rarely been sympathetic to these positions (Ray Browne is a veteran of many skirmishes against postmodern autocrats). Even so, contemporary cultural theories offer a great many insights, especially when they focus on informational metaphors, and Mark Poster's *The Mode of Information: Poststructuralism and Social Context* provides an excellent survey.

At this point, looking more closely at some popular technological metaphors of our own time can be helpful. They grow out of terms like the Computer Culture, or the Age of Communication, or the Information Era, tags commonly applied to the latter half of the twentieth century. Because computers and electronic media carry information, and because they demonstrate that information can be stored, processed, transmitted, and disseminated in various forms, they have fostered several metaphors that help us visualize the evolving features of technology and of culture. They are informational, not mechanical, metaphors. Electronic and genetic systems have little in common with cars or turbines; in the second category, physical energy drives wheels or pushes pistons, while in the first communication alters states of being.

Popular as these metaphors are, the ideas they reflect come from thermodynamics, cybernetics, genetics, and information theory. An important and evolving sub-discipline of both communication theory and the history of technology is the diffusion of innovation, which examines the process by which new ideas and new technologies are disseminated throughout a culture. This field of study finesses the distinctions between informational and classic mechanical or materialistic definitions of technology. According to communication theorists, information is defined as a variation in matter-energy that resolves uncertainty in a context in which choices exist as to alternatives. An innovation, provided that it offers a genuine choice, embodies information. The notion is a logical outgrowth of communication theories that represent technology as *stored knowledge*. Reduced to essentials, technology *is* information, whether the technology be a tractor or a library, an organizational strategy, or a genetic code.

Some innovations, such as management techniques or political platforms, are almost entirely informational, but even the most materialistic technologies embody information. As Everett Rogers puts it, using the computer metaphors common to our era, "A *technology* is a design for instrumental action that reduces the uncertainty in the cause-effect relationships involved in achieving a desired outcome. A technology usually has two components: 1) a *hardware* aspect, consisting of the tool that embodies the technology as material or physical objects, and 2) a *software* aspect, consisting of the information base for the tool" (12). The diffusion of any innovation, Rogers has demonstrated, follows patterns that can be identified with great precision. Opinion leaders and agents of influence move information through specific channels of communication at speeds that can be graphed and quantified. The channels fluctuate in hierarchies that vary somewhat from culture to culture, but the model can predict flow from origination to implementation.

Tracing the changes wrought by new technologies is a job for cultural anthropologists and sociologists and, most emphatically, for popular culture specialists, as much as it is a task for historians or communication theorists. Understanding how information moves through a culture requires a familiarity with every channel of communication: face-to-face encounters, mass media, folkways, corporate hierarchies, ethnic, gender, and age cohort pathways, scientific journals, religious structures, governmental and institutional conduits, social organizations, and so on, all of which either promote or resist adoption of new ideas. When innovations are widely adopted, we say that they become popular with one group or another, or with some part of a whole culture. That is where the student of popular culture can make great contributions. The study of technology is properly hers.

But what binds the channels themselves together, and how do messages themselves get assigned to different routes? Here again new metaphors draw on communication disciplines. Those disciplines do not equate concepts like *control* with political terms like *hegemony*. Control is simply one aspect of a process by which a system avoids chaos. All systems, organic or otherwise, are composed of differentiated parts linked in hierarchies whose communication is regulated by command and feedback. In the absence of programming, command, and feedback—without communication, in short—systems cease to function. That these can be neutral terms is difficult for humanists in particular to grasp, especially when they encounter explantions drawn from modern capitalism.

For example, we are just now beginning to understand that the most important achievement of the Industrial Revolution was the corporate bureaucracy, an instrument for the control of production, distribution, and consumption not simply of artifacts but also of information. The principal proponent of that idea is the communication theorist James Beniger, whose *The Control Revolution: Technological and Economic Origins of the Information Society* (1986) is to me the most important book written on technology in the last 20 years. What makes Beniger's thesis convincing is that his discussion of the hierarchies of corporate bureaucracy as the components of an information-processing technology applies just as accurately to the hierarchies of culture.

For Beniger, human brain and human language are what he calls "ambiguous technologies," partly natural, partly invented or environmentally programmed. In this metaphorical configuration, technology is what humans *do*, as production, distribution, and consumption of both material goods and information; technology is the means by which humans alter themselves and their environment, and the patterns of this flow of knowledge and competence are also the means for determining meaning. One of a culture's functions is clearly technological: it programs the individuals who make it up. A culture also changes shape and direction as a consequence of feedback from individuals and institutions in a never-ending cycle of message and response. But specific technologies, instruments or databases or channels, do not determine meaning in isolation; they simply make it possible for the culture itself to do so. We have traditionally accorded to culture tasks like the selective preservation of knowledge, the arbitration of value, the distribution of information, and the assignment of meaning. Technologies by which the culture carried out these tasks have always been there; the advent of new channels and tools has heightened our awareness of their number and presence. The relationship between technology—virtually all forms of human doing and making—and culture—a hierarchical arrangement of those activities—is endlessly reciprocal.

A follower of Mikhail Bakhtin would say that information channels of many sorts—oral, folkloristic, written, printed, electronic, institutional, and so on—occupy "niches" that structure the culture hierarchically, in strata that constantly shift according to agendas that are self-reflexively social, political, and economic. These hierarchies are similar in both corporations and cultures; their function is to facilitate the flow of information up and down and horizontally. Both corporations and cultures stabilize themselves by programming; command and feedback are as essential to one as to the other. Like a corporation, then, a culture as a consequence *itself becomes an information processor* for sorting messages, assigning value, and generating interpretation, operations that acknowledge the ambiguity, probability, and redundancy of those messages. Media, for instance, do function as instruments of control, in the sense of agents of order and stability—rather than, or not simply as, instruments of domination and oppression—in an arena increasingly public and increasingly diverse, as different groups advance their concerns toward the center of the larger arena. The metaphor suggests that in an information age technology can empower the individual as much as it alienates masses; that it can encourage sharing as much as it divides; that it redistributes control as much as it enclusters privilege; that it alters the conception of property by converting everything—artifact as well as idea, "high culture" or "low"—into commodities to be consumed.

The implications of this metaphor—and of the history leading up to it—for popular culture studies are profound. This model suggests that the relationship between technology and culture is not simply far more intimate than previously thought, but that it transcends divisions between high and low strata of culture. At the very least, technology continuously reconstitutes culture by empowering different classes, ethnic groups, and special interest clusters—what we dimly apprehend by the term *multiculturalism*. It does so in a variety of ways whose operations are beyond the scope of this paper, though we can mention as one example the argument of Joshua Meyrowitz, whose *No Sense of Place: The Impact of Electronic Media on Social Behavior* (1985) contends that media destroy barriers between public and private space, alter patterns of behavior that are traditionally site-specific, enfranchise larger numbers of people with information previously shared by the few, and continuously erode distinctions between high and low culture.

No one would claim that the information-processing is efficient. Moreover, the sheer volume of information that our culture generates and transmits carries dangers. In another recent attempt to label our era, Bill McKibben, in *The Age of Missing Information* (1992), maintains that the flood of information unleashed by television actually separates people from meaningful sources of knowledge. Worse, the mass of information, because it defies interpretation, may further disenfranchise the uneducated. Class assumptions about the quality of ideas and the nature of meaning are everywhere apparent in this reading of the 1700 hours of messages carried by a Fairfax, Virginia cable system in a single day. But the threat—that we will be overwhelmed by the redundant, the misleading, the trivial—is something we nonetheless feel keenly, and such warnings, along with those of other critics, are welcome. Moreover, McKibben's book points up a most important fact: in our culture, information is increasingly packaged in visual form.

Already there is some indication that the techniques of "visual literacy" that McLuhan and his followers insisted would emerge are beginning to cope with the potentially menacing flow of information. Books like the cult classics *The Visual Display of Quantitative Information* (1983) and *Envisioning Information* (1990), both by Edward Tufte, and *Mapping the Next Millenium: The Discovery of New Geographies* (1992), by Stephen S. Hall, assert that the volume of information is now so great that it can be apprehended, at least at first, as a form of pre-processing, as visual aggregates of data whose contours can be read at a glance. (For a whimsical example, we might point to Spock's console on the *Enterprise* in *Star Trek*.) In such displays, nuances register in cartographic patterns and color or pattern codes, as in charts of sub-atomic particle showers or maps of the human genome or screens of far more "vulgar" material. In future, being able to read the structures of culture from aggregates of data may be more important than content analysis of individual messages. In fact, says Joshua Meyrowitz, analyzing media messages as a way of understanding technology is like trying to understand the early Industrial Revolution by focusing on the colors of the textiles that the then-novel power looms turned out (15).

What does all this mean for the twenty-first-century student of popular culture interested in technology? First, the metaphors we use to conceptualize both technology and culture are just that. Metaphors, as Thomas Pynchon says in *The Crying of Lot 49*, "are a thrust at truth and a lie" (95). They have limited utility, and the ones that seem most useful now will probably be superseded even more quickly than others we have briefly surveyed. Even so, the growing intimacy between humans and information technologies like cybernetics, artificial intelligence, genetic engineering, and virtual reality will probably occupy us well into the next century. Since the next generation of scholars will have been raised on computers, they should be comfortable with informational metaphors.

Second, both technology and culture are human creations. Technological systems and cultural hierarchies may have reached levels of complexity that mimic organic processes, but if so they can be understood by the same tools that scientists use to explore physical and biological realms. And there will always be smaller domains to explore. One of the assumptions of popular culture has long been that embracing or rejecting a particular technology is a matter of individual choice, taste, enthusiasm, and love. At the quotidian level, technology is entertainment—passive or active, fun or magic. Making, doing, inventing, playing, learning: these are technological activities, and they define—for me, at least—what it means to be human. No culture can exist without them.

Third, whether we map them one on the other or not, technology and culture constitute reciprocally-intertwined environments in which humans must live. As technological animals, humans adapt. Scholars of popular culture have always sought out public and private spaces, discovered the communities that cluster there, and charted the experiences they share. Those experiences, it also seems to me, are no less "authentic" for taking place in "artificial" environments.

Fourth, scholars will need continuously to invent new tools for accomplishing these tasks. I have no doubt that they will do so.

Works Cited

Adams, James L. *Flying Buttresses, Entropy, and O-Rings: The World of an Engineer.* Cambridge: Harvard UP, 1991.

Bastable, Marshall J. "The Invention of Modern Artillery, 1854-1880." *Technology and Culture* 33 (1992): 213-47.

Beniger, James. *The Control Revolution: Technological and Economic Origins of the Information Society.* Cambridge: Harvard UP, 1986.

Bolter, J. David. *Turing's Man: Western Culture in the Computer Age.* Chapel Hill: U of North Carolina P, 1984.

Brown, Richard. *Knowledge Is Power: The Diffusion of Information in Early America, 1770-1869.* New York: Oxford UP, 1989.

Cowan, Ruth Schwartz. *More Work For Mother: The Ironies of Household Technology From the Open Hearth to the Microwave.* New York: Basic Books, 1983.

Eisenstein, Elizabeth. *The Printing Press as an Agent of Change: Communications and Cultural Transformations in Early-modern Europe.* 2 vols. Cambridge, England: Cambridge UP, 1979.

Ferkiss, Victor. *Technological Man: The Myth and the Reality.* New York: New American Library, 1969.

Florman, Samuel. *The Existential Pleasures of Engineering.* New York: St. Martin's, 1976.

Giovannini, Joseph. "The Objects of Desire That Defined Their Eras." *New York Times* 4 June 1993: BI, B5.

Hall, Stephen S. *Mapping the Next Millenium: The Discovery of New Geographies.* New York: Random House, 1992.

Hardison, O.B., Jr. *Disappearing Through the Skylight: Culture and Technology in the Twentieth Century.* New York: Viking, 1989.

Kuhn, Thomas S. *The Structure of Scientific Revolutions.* 2nd ed. Chicago: U of Chicago P, 1970.

MacKenzie, Donald. *Inventing Accuracy: A Historical Sociology of Nuclear Missile Guidance.* Cambridge: MIT P, 1990.

Mazlish, Bruce. "The Fourth Discontinuity." *Technology and Culture.* Eds. Melvin Kranzberg and William Davenport. New York: New American Library, 1972: 216-32.

McKibben, Bill. *The Age of Missing Information.* New York: Random House, 1992.

McLuhan, Marshall. *Understanding Media: The Extensions of Man.* New York: McGraw-Hill, 1964.

Meyrowitz, Joshua. *No Sense of Place: The Impact of Electronic Media on Social Behavior.* New York: Oxford UP, 1985.

Poster, Mark. *The Mode of Information: Poststructuralism and Social Context.* Chicago: U of Chicago P, 1990.

Postman, Neil. *Technopoly: The Surrender of Culture to Technology*. New York: Knopf, 1992.

Pynchon, Thomas. *The Crying of Lot 49*. New York: Bantam, 1967.

Rogers, Everett M. *Diffusion of Innovations*. 3rd ed. New York: Free, 1983.

Slade, Joseph W. "The Man Behind the Killing Machine." *American Heritage of Invention and Technology* 2:2 (Fall 1986): 22-26.

Staudenmaier, John M. *Technology's Storytellers: Reweaving the Human Fabric*. Cambridge: MIT P and SHOT, 1985.

Tufte, Edward. *Envisioning Information*. Cheshire, CT: Graphics P, 1990.

___. *The Visual Display of Quantitative Information*. Cheshire, CT: Graphics P, 1983.

Wiener, Norbert. *The Human Use of Human Beings: Cybernetics and Society*. New York: Avon, 1967.

Winner, Langdon. *Autonomous Technology: Technics-Out-of-Control as a Theme in Political Thought*. Cambridge: MIT P, 1977.

The Rhetoric of Media and Popular Culture as the Basis of Culture Studies: A Postmodern Critique

Carl Bryan Holmberg

Few interdisciplinary culture studies ever mention the rhetorical tradition as formative of Western culture as do Donald Clark and Jacqueline DeRomilly. Perhaps this situation is understandable since there are so many views on rhetoric. For some theorists the term applies only to persuasion, while for others "rhetoric" means the exercise of compositional style or rhetoric's epistemic and metaphysical characteristics (Bitzer & Black). In the Durants' multivolume *The Story of Civilization*, rhetoric is merely a cultural trend to be mentioned along with other trends; in itself, rhetoric does not shape culture. Few interdisciplinary textbooks on the history of Western culture mention the term "rhetoric" at all.[1] Postman's *Amusing Ourselves to Death* mentions rhetoric periodically but the monograph is mostly limited to North American culture and does not really dig into cultural periods between the ancient Greeks and "the age of show business." While the rhetorical tradition has been in large part a male-dominated discipline, surprisingly very few have come close to seriously factoring rhetoric and communication into the cultural mix which captures the spirit of an age or which drives humans from one age to the next—which presents us with a curious dilemma. The rhetorical tradition has been employed at almost every turn of Western culture (McKeon "Methods") and yet remains almost invisible in studies which discuss culture.

The traditional ways of describing an historical period or zeitgeist are frequently philosophical, focusing on the predominant definitions within a particular age for the terms "being," "human being," "human activity" and "human spirit." Artifacts are then discussed for their congruence to the predominant definitions for a particular age. One need only look at Fleming's *Arts and Ideas,* Burckhardt's *The Civilization of the Renaissance in Italy*, McKeon's "Rhetoric in the Middle Ages," Lovejoy's *The Great Chain of Being* and the works of many others to find this pattern for presenting cultural information. Let us now then also factor into Western interdisciplinary and cultural history *the predominant media from particular Western epochs as well as the corresponding predominant media formats.*[2] As we perform this activity, let us recognize it as a rhetorical act of invention.

The New Architectonic Factors:
Commonplaces of Media

The customary defining factors for describing an age or zeitgeist are philosophical in leaning and include a) the predominant definition of *what is* (reality, cosmos, being), b) the predominant definition of *human being*, c) the predominant definition of *knowledge* for figuring the interaction of humans and what is and d) the *correct action* for living in what is. The emphasis upon definition and particularly upon themes of knowledge is a clear sign of the customary philosophic underpinnings of data selection and analysis in interdisciplinary culture studies. The four defining factors additionally require sets of data drawn from each age in order that the era may be described adequately. Each characteristic set of like data—e.g., sculpture, architecture or literature—may then be tracked or typified for comparison and contrast from time period to time period.

The traditional four sets of data to be interrelated to describe any age comprise a fairly simple commonplace or rhetorical system. Commonplaces are terms which have a general meaning but which, when interfaced with other general terms, begin to acquire systemic and quite specific meaning (McKeon "Creativity and the Commonplace"). Commonplace methods have a longstanding rhetorical tradition in the West (Lechner) and it is the intention here to add two additional sets of commonplaces to the traditional four used to describe cultural ages. The two new sets are added since the original four have been found wanting in that, while they very well discuss male and elite viewpoints of culture, they do not promote or actively allow other viewpoints to emerge which also adequately describe particular ages or the progression of time periods.

The first set of commonplaces to be added are the *predominant media* which emerge anew in a particular age. "What is" is poignantly irrelevant if it is not communicated. The second set of commonplaces to be added are the *predominant media formats* which were developed during each time period, particularly the ones which depend upon the common coinage of the newly predominant media of that time period.

The "Event Matrix of Media and Western Culture" (174-75) combines the four original means for identifying Western cultural ages with the two new means, forming a matrix of rhetorical signification. The matrix is rhetorical in that each discrete entry is a commonplace or touchstone for generating meaning which may be discussed and interpreted in the manner of free invention. The best invention upon the matrix however is not mere whim, but would have as its goal to confirm some of the kinds of observations available under the older, fourfold system of descriptive cultural invention as well as to demonstrate new observations—equally true, depending on the perspective chosen— which were not available or noticeable under the older system of cultural invention.

The matrix is organized in the following manner: Column 1 presents the traditional name or names applied to historic ages or time periods. The top row names the columns. The predominant media column (column 2) is placed immediately next to the time period's name as a kind of enthymeme. Normatively one of the four traditional defining factors is associated with the name of the age. I would maintain that the main defining feature of an age is its predominant medium for communication, not a received definition of what is, not the activities of males and not the material inventions of humans except as they function as media for communication. Therefore it is more appropriate to associate the name of an age with its predominant medium or media of communication. The most specific data is placed in column 7 at the far right since Western eye movement leads to and rests at the right. It also places data immediately next to the correct action column, which is important. Communicating is *a kind of action* and thus the predominant media formats may be experienced as a performance of correct action. In sum, the cultural norms for each age are not set merely by its traditional definitions of being, humanness, knowledge and action, but are also highly influenced by the predominant media and the forms which are most congruent with them.

Before I run through a new version of Western culture, two final, general observations seem to be in order. Knowledge is consistently described in the matrix in a rhetorical fashion, as placement. Philosophical grounds for knowledge change with the ontological fashions of each age. However, the common procedure for determining knowledge or passing it on never really changes its rhetorical, communicative form. A commonplace is what nowadays we would call data as opposed to information. Literally, "data" are something done, but apart from other things done they are difficult to ascertain as to their meaning. Therefore, *placing* data in relation to other data is the perennial and imaginary fascination of humans. A "place" (*topos, -oi* in Attic Greek) may be a physical place, like the memory device described by Cicero—memorizing information by assigning data to the rooms or decor of a villa (465-71). Or, a place may be nonphysical, in the realm of ideas or symbols, like Quintilian's "thesis or passage dealing with some

An Event Matrix of Media and Western Culture

1 Age/Time Period	2 Predominant Media	3 "Being" Is	4 Humans Are	5 Knowledge Is	6 Correct Action Is	7 Predominant Media Formats
Archaic, PreSocratic, Prehistoric	Oral	Spirit World	Spirit[s]	Placement in Spirit or the Spirit World	Spirit Seeking Spirit	Prayer, Song, Storytelling, Spells, Poetry, Epic, Speech Dance, Rhythm
Classical, Ancient	Oral & Early Written	Plural Phenomena	Spiritual/ Physical/ Actional/ Symbolic	Placement in the Pantheon of Alternative Phenomena	Consistency with One's Choice of Phenomena	Oratory, Poetry, Prose
Late Classical & Medieval	Middle Written & Oral	The Quick & the Dead	Spirit with a Temporary Body	From God; Placement in God's Design	Thanking God for Being	Preaching, Letter Writing, Bureaucracy
Renaissance	Written	Physical	Body with a Temporary Spirit	Placement in Space	Figuring Human Movement in Space	Mechanical Methods

Enlightenment, Neo-Classical & Revolution	Mid-Written	Physically Productive	Body as a Means of Production	Placement in Plentitude	Calculating & Planning Maximization	How-to Manuals, Newspapers, Pamphlets, Novels
Romantic & Victorian	Late Written & Early Electric	Nationhood Preservation	Body as Drives	Placement in Observation	Reduction to Least Parts & Effort	Science, Periodicals, Shipping, Telegraphy
Late Victorian, Early to Mid-20th Century or "Modern"	Electric/Electronic	Experience	Sensorium	Placement in Relationship to Anything One Can Experience	Action in the Form of Action	Radio, TV, Film, Recorded Music, "Live" Journalism & Public Relations, Includes Partying
Late 20th Century, Late Modern, Postmodern or Fusion	Computer	Events of Deep Structure	Genetic Consciousness	Placement in Bit Maps; Placement Is the Event of Events, or, Programming	Exploring Matrices of Data Bits *and* Balanced Fusion with Them	Horror, Fusion & International Genres, Simulations, Including Computer Programming and Virtual Reality Technologies

general principle or theme" (Vol. 2.9). But whatever the metaphor for place, placing commonplaces together is the act of making sense, of understanding, of generating knowledge.

Second, notice there are no dates assigned to each age. Historic dates are not irrelevant—but they are misleading. For instance, Italy enjoyed a Renaissance for approximately one hundred years before rebirth hit other locales; it would be incorrect to say that the Renaissance began at the same time in Britain. Likewise, many media formats do not disappear with the advent of a new age or its new predominant media. Thus it would be artificial to maintain that orality disappeared once and for all in Western culture as writing became predominant. Orality did change however and simultaneously early writing sometimes had strong oral/aural characteristics. In other words, both on the culturally descriptive level and on the artifactual level, ages overlap. Tidiness is a scholar's dream.

The Invention of Western Culture
by Its Media

The Archaic, presocratic or prehistoric period is commonly acknowledged as an oral period. Most recently Joseph Campbell and a host of researchers on shamanism in various cultures have demonstrated that fact along with other features of the archaic worldview, that from the perspective of archaic experience, everything that is, is spirit—that humans are spirits, knowledge is placement in the spirit world and correct action is the balance of spirit seeking spirit. The predominant media formats like prayer and storytelling are quite revealing of the norms of archaic peoples, even some still contemporaneous with ourselves. The predominant media formats exist orally or they have oral, rhythmic qualities. Rhythm is itself an important archaic factor of orality (Mickunas). When confronted with a problem, archaic peoples consult a shaman or medicine person who acquired his or her expertise from visiting the otherworld, talking to the spirits of plants, ingesting them, etc. (Harner). Even learning the art of drumming may at times be the mythic enactment of one's cultural norms; the specific rhythms are taught in the form of a prayer; playing the rhythm is prayer (Diallo and Hall). Carpenter also suggests that the signal media characteristic of archaic culture is the polysynthetic quality of orality—that all words merge into one saying, that there is often no separation of meaning into discrete words as in the modern, Western custom (162).

Writing was so new a medium of communication in the Classical period that Aristotle did not have an adequate word for what we call prose (*Poetics* 1447b). One of the early examples of writing in Greek shows curious signs of archaic orality. Sometimes manuscripts render words in the form of "boustrophedon" or plowing. The writing begins in the customary left to right manner to which we are accustomed but when the end of the line is reached the writing moves from right to left, like this:

Furthermore, words are squeezed together polysynthetically with no regard to discrete, separate words. This is perhaps the earliest example of a new medium preserving the form of an older medium, covering up its radical newness by masquerading in the form of the old. Walter Ong has specialized in formulating observations about the change from orality to writing and would maintain that eventually writing took on its own hegemony in the thought patterns it promoted; meanwhile, orality became embedded and hence disguised in the growing number of written formats (*Presence* 17-110).

Perhaps in part because the means of communication were now plural, the fundamental definition of being was no longer unified as spirit. Richard McKeon well documents the new competing philosophies of what is, now encapsulated in columns 3 and 4 ("A Philosopher Meditates"; see also Buckley).

Despite the new medium of writing, two of the new predominant media formats were oral, *viz.*, oratory and poetry. Because oratory worked through speaking, we have inherited the Greek term for speaking as an ancient and specialized term variously denoting persuasion, bilk and bombast, *viz.*, rhetoric. However, both Aristotle and Plato applied the term to oral and written communication, admittedly with a preference for oral rhetoric, as did the later Romans.[3] As it did for the ancients, so should it also do for us: "Rhetoric" *means communication and* its *formative qualities* in *any* medium of communication—and not just in oral communication.

Jacqueline DeRomilly maintains that Gorgianic oratory was disguised, magical spellmaking, the first self-conscious masking of the oral tradition's spiritual assumptions in the new media format of oratory.

Orality also loosens up meanings and frees us from orthodoxy, giving us "doxa" or seeming. This is a particularly significant observation since rhetoric is often also disparaged as mere relativism. Plato's greatest scorn was heaped not just upon sophists and orators; it was also generously poured upon poets, playwrights and musicians—and all of them utilized oral media. Orality in its media aspects was thus given a bad press, as it were, early in Western culture because it could only give alternative viewpoints of seeming truth (*doxa*) when Plato was most intent on the one, correct viewpoint.

As culture turned from Plato it often included Plato's exclusionary viewpoint through writing as much as through ideas. Orthodoxy of various kinds may have been difficult to promote without writing—and without writing in the control of the late Roman Empire and later of the Roman Church. It is no accident that Augustine's major work on communication is named *On Christian Doctrine*. The work is concerned with language skills, correct interpretation of scriptures and then, last of all, preaching. The major defining features in this row in the matrix are derived from LeClerq's *Love of Learning and the Desire for God*, except for the final entries in column 7, preaching and letter writing, format terms which are derived equally from Augustine and Baldwin's work *Medieval Rhetoric and Poetic*. Literacy was by no means universal but was mostly a privilege controlled by the Church. The Church assumed the bureaucratic mantle of the Roman scribal system and transformed it into a new media system which focussed upon preaching and letter writing.

What is most significant for our purposes was how preaching, an oral activity, took on characteristics of book writing. In the Medieval period, as now, a preacher could literally speak with *author*ity, just as Carpenter maintains about book culture (163). The congregation was placed in a passive role, much like the reader of a book who must follow the path written by an author. Most importantly, the preacher, guided by Augustine's *On Christian Doctrine*, no doubt, sought to deliver correct doctrine, the mostly dictated party line of the Church or at least, the local church. Preaching was thus *oral writing* and set the later norm in the West of finding correct, particular ideas as opposed to the diverse means of addressing any situation. In other words the conjuncture of writing, orality and Church doctrine began a 1500-year hegemony of written media patterns of thinking which encouraged and eventually led to self-evident norms of clarity in the Enlightenment or Neoclassical period. Even today scientific and social scientific norms of correctness insist on words defined with one and only one meaning as well as systems of presentation and analysis with unambiguous procedures.

The Renaissance proved to be the first era of growing literacy among the secular sectors of Western society. The return to classical norms in architecture, painting, sculpture and even music created a situation in which the norms established for each community's arts were no longer always determined by aristocrats and the Church. Competitions like the one awarding Ghiberti the right to finish Florence's Bapistry doors were public and were adjudicated by fellow artists and townspeople. While artists like Vasari, Brunelleschi, Michelangelo and others were certainly heavily subscribed by Church and nobles, not all their work was commissioned, nor did they always deliver the norms requested. The fact that numerous artists were also what we today might call engineers (architects), chemists (painters) and metallurgists (sculptors in bronze) and that many of these persons kept notes of their methods as well as documented Classical methods (Palladio, Cellini, and others) demonstrates both their literacy and their zeal for the newly rediscovered, replicable methods of mechanics which had been jealously kept secret among the aristocracy, guilds and Church for almost a thousand years. The publication of their own methods and innovations assured that knowledge of placement in space—mechanical methods—could not easily be held any longer as a privilege of the few.

Naturally this led to the how-to manuals and the popularization of knowledge and ideas in the Enlightenment and Revolutionary periods. Diderot's *Encyclopedie* had as its goal the accessibility of information for anyone literate in French. Growing literacy among the middle classes of Europe and the Americas not only aided the subscription of such works but also encouraged works like Johnson's dictionary, cookbooks and the Gothic novel. Voltaire's *Candide* did as much to popularize skepticism of religion, monarchy and received philosophy as any political pamphlet.

Newspapers also emerged during these time periods but were not necessarily as culturally dominant as paper artifacts like handbills, broadsides and pamphlets which, in the North American colonies, could more readily be passed from person to person as well as hidden, disposed of or burned at need. Carpenter observes that the new print media of and like newspapers put readers in a new role, an active role of deciding which information to read first, and this observation pinpoints a significant media factor in the history of Western culture (163-64), one which Carpenter does not mention however: that the new and active reader role helped to stir revolution. It is difficult to imagine revolution in the American colonies without "Common Sense" and other easily passed subversive handbills as well as newspapers, all of which by their media format required readers to make their own decisions. Readers became their own *authority* for determinining truth as empowered by the new media format.

The concept of commoners voting was much disparaged by royalists and those of a conservative bent, *except* as tied to the people's literacy, which was why literacy and schooling were an important thrust of the Founders' political and electoral schemes. Literacy was thus plausibly tied to Montesquieu's political scheme for organizing a democratic government which was in turn based on Aristotle's *Art of Rhetoric* and the three kinds of communication: epideictic (Executive Branch), deliberative (Congress) and judicial (Supreme Court). However, most commentators miss the fact that left to their own devices on the eastern shore of North America, early settlers turned to the native peoples for survival skills and insights about organization that works in the wilderness. Adams, Franklin and others most admired the Iroquois Confederacy—a system of government almost identical to the later Continental Congress's plan, except for the fact that the Iroquois Confederacy had already worked as an oral tradition for hundreds of years (Mander 230-45). Most of the oral characteristics were deleted by Europeans, which perhaps begins to explain the exclusion by American history textbooks and works of political science of Native American mentorship—there is no value given to orality in mainstream scholarship. The predominant preference for written media among European-Americans is an antiquated, myopic norm which must no longer limit scholarly investigation when it favors the truth capabilities of one medium of communication over another.

The Enlightenment and Revolutionary time periods in European-American culture also foresaw the growth potential of science applied to natural resources, but fell short of an industrial revolution because the technologies available for the exploitation of nature were not fully invented nor mechanized. Renaissance reports from explorers in the New World had fired the imagination not just of aristocrats but of ill-fed commoners. Thus, colonization accompanied by slavery, indentured servitude and penal colonization aided the planning of maximized economic and political power for the more centralized European powers while removing adventurous aristocratic sons and common malcontents from the European scene. The growing literacy however short-circuited some of their maximization. Continued European exploitation of the North American colonies was made additionally difficult by the distance and the dearth of communication controlled by European party lines and capital. Oral communication and letters of correspondence were still popular means of subverting the wishes of owners some 2,000 miles away.

Even then, the seeds of change were already extant in Britain. The first real popular publishing phenomenon was the advent of the Gothic novel which sold to the literate women of the growing middle class; themes of sexual discomfort and domestic imprisonment abounded, even in the early, preromantic examples like Walpole's *The Castle of Otranto.*⁴ Even Joshua Reynolds' orations delivered at The Royal Academy of Painting's commencement exercises were quickly published and subsequently sold well despite the fact that Reynolds' politics and views were not the King's views.

The Romantic and Victorian periods witnessed the early dehumanization of workers in the Industrial Revolution at the same time many writers began to glorify the genius and importance of the common person. The Romantic and Victorian time periods also witnessed the subjugation of nature and also saw the rise of environmentally oriented poetry and prose which included themes glorifying commoner status, like Shelley's "Ode to the West Wind," Emerson's "On Nature," Long-fellow's "Song of Hiawatha," Thoreau's *Walden* and Cooper's novels. Science gained ascendency as the major means for collecting data, analyzing it and then working up the means of production in accordance with its methods and findings, from agriculture to the human body. While observation had always been acknowledged as an important means of knowledge, now observation coupled with experimentation as a way of building new methods applied to tasks never before attempted became the hallmark of the period. Science was still largely a venue open mostly to the rich, aristocratic and well-educated, but scientific ideas, among others, were disseminated by means of faster moving shipping like steamboats and trains as well as early telegraphy.

Most cultural studies do not include shipping as formative of a time period's spirit, let alone as a form of media. The need to move materials and information more quickly to serve growing markets, particularly with perishable products and ephemeral news, takes second place to the fact that shipping and telegraphy changed the shape of human consciousness. McLuhan unquestionably regards telegraphy in this manner (*Understanding Media* 217-27), but steamboat shipping and trains also allowed for life to move more quickly, trends and fashions to spread more avidly and for a growing number of peoples of the world to expect information and goods more quickly from each other and on a fairly regular basis. Incipient mass culture, national culture and international economics were—and are—media systems. They are media systems not just because of the obvious communication media which they employ but also because of the *material media* of transportation which communicate products and the products' styles which in turn are indicative of cultural values. Mail order periodicals still serve as icons for an age in which large department stores were geographically distant, and thus the presence of mail order catalogues in later "period" aesthetic artifacts like movies and television shows provides opportunities for giving a sense of the Romantic and Victorian time periods.

The modern advent of local, regional and national radio programing immersed humans in a new media environment, one which was prepared by the earlier flowering of film. With radio, a renewed emphasis was placed upon the direct experience of hearing the human voice in one's home as well as music broadcast from afar. The new orality of radio allowed people to experience new information almost instantaneously; it also allowed listeners the luxury of getting caught up in an illusion of storytelling. Experience itself became the watchword of the new radio medium with its new focus on producing thrills by broadcasting ball games, drama, horror stories, the news, gossip about media stars and the latest music and comedy. Unquestionably, a trip to the movie theatre produced the same direct massaging of the human sensorium with the added pleasure of immense spectacle. However, radio was available on a daily basis with the added illusion of being free.

Film also set a new cultural norm—that the best art is acted and is in the form of effortlessly performed action. Many arts thus began to promote themselves as if they were film; radio gave the illusion it was direct storytelling and not electronically mediated while it was clearly acted with high and low theatrical effects. Citing Adorno, Middleton calls this media phenomenon a "pseudo-individualized effect," the ability of one media format to masquerade as another (36). In addition, as action and movement rapidly became cultural norms via cinema, art deco streamlining was increasingly used to show violent or graceful movement and became part of the vocabulary of the industrial design of locomotives, automobiles, phonographs, cameras and other products as well as the design of war posters, advertising ephemera and comic books, among other twentieth-century media formats, and not just part of "high" or fine arts.

While advertising was not in itself a twentieth-century invention, it emerged from its late Victorian, public relations forerunners of calling on friends and neighbors as well as socializing among fellow workers; these practices were clearly linked to the middle class's upward mobility in the attempt to mimic the upper crust (Braden 65). Porches and verandas were designed for socializing just as carefully as fund raisers for politicians. The diverse societies of North America were not alone in this regard, as similar opportunities were planned and attended both in Europe and South America. Philanthropic events also undergirded the first welfare system in democratically-minded countries and thus fundraising events rose in importance for most professions. Church festivals, apartment parties and travel also presented similar venues both for raising funds and for meeting new and potential clients or workers. These and many events like them were opportunities to get to know people outside of work as well as to work the crowd with whatever interests one may have. The prohibition of alcohol in the United States was therefore an incredibly important public relations and media event. It served to inhibit newly immigrated—or liberated—ethnic groups who were interested in maintaining their solidarity as well as gaining access to political power through their traditional means of associating publicly and privately while drinking—and even making—wine, beer and liquor. In essence, prohibition was a law which suppressed the freedom of assembly for those communities which still preferred a heavy dose of orality to their public concourse. Prohibition was not just about alcohol; it was a gag order on unwelcome ethnic groups and a denial of the First Amendment—no small media event, but usually glossed as anything but a media event.

Television brought a new rhetoric to the people. Touted by some as a door which would open discourse, public and private, it provided the means for disintegrating traditional values (Mander 96-119) as well as undermining the planned, face-to-face, interactive communication involved in electing the House of Representatives every two years (Holmberg "Stray the Course"). The television medium tends to render audiences passive with its largely unidirectional format. The rhetoric implicit in television presents itself in its illusion of access to information with the reality of that information controlled mostly by monied interests, especially in the United States, but not exclusively there.

The Late Modern period with its hyperreal, synthesized pastiches of intercultural fervor is the age of computer simulation. Computer simulation is instantaneously systemic in that doing one thing in the hyperspace of a computer program affects the rest of the program, sometimes in a major way, sometimes minimally. So too is the architectonic influence of information released in global communication networks. The power to influence is the power to read and manipulate media situations architectonically, as if they were computer programs (Holmberg "Rhetorical Terrorism")—even media not formerly regarded as having computerlike qualities. Computer programming is matrical in its organizational formats and is well-suited for the fractal description of human reality—as opposed to linear, statistical models. Now, newly emerging late modern media have already assumed matrical, fractal and computerlike characteristics.

Horror narratives in various media have become a predominant media format since the vagaries of intercultural friction as well as accomodation have sunk into the ethnic and racial consciousness of interacting peoples, touching the deep structures of human existence: life, death, joy and fear. Our central nervous system has been externalized and exposed to the contending media previously unavailable in kind, magnitude or influence. The dreariness of work pales when hack and slash video games invite some of us into a temporary vacation in hyperspace, a world similar to our own imaginary experience. Horror literature and movies also revivify while they comfort (King). Even media formats which do not exclusively focus upon terror, like adventure stories and fairy tales, still include vignettes of horror (Tolkien 75-83). Horror has been with us since the Archaic period but only now in the Postmodern period is it placed so copiously before us and in such distilled and heady formats. Horror is yourself as the only real media while other media insist you are to pay attention to them (Holmberg "Clive Barker's Poetics"). Horror is the exploration of one's own deep structures of consciousness, the ultimate medium.

A Postmodern Critique:
The Future of Popular Culture Studies

The "Event Matrix of Media and Western Culture" is itself an example of the Postmodern period. Its knowledge potential is accomplished by the placement of data into a bit map, a matrix. It calls for the reader to fuse his or her consciousness with the format and find verity or incongruity on his or her own. The matrix need not be read or presented in the chronological manner just suggested. For instance a particular media format can be selected and then tracked through the time periods, perhaps to verify the matrix's claims about the nature of a time period or instead to demonstrate changes and variations by era. Similarly, a researcher may sidestep the issue of historical development and look for the poetic characteristics of artifacts from different ages. This approach is particularly helpful when attempting interdisciplinary culture study which includes nonwestern artifacts. Other cultures have not encountered the same progression of media developments and yet their artifacts sometimes clearly illuminate similar structures, trends, motifs and themes. The treatment of media from culture to culture is itself a worthy area for investigation since each culture may be characterized by its customary media practices and expectations.

The Event Matrix presents itself as a new fusion of cultural data, a synthesis of popular culture and media phenomena drawn from numerous Western subcultures and historical periods. Yet as it stands on paper it is a montage of rhetorical invention in the new media format of systemic or architectonic simulation (McKeon "The Uses of Rhetoric").

As a critique the Event Matrix is both descriptive and evaluative. It is descriptive of Western cultural history with the new inclusion of media yet it may also be used to evaluate prior or future cultural histories which do or do not include media in the explanatory mix for understanding culture. Without the accompanying essay the Event Matrix also returns to the rhetoric of display as a form of demonstration, but in a new way. If the matrical artifact is true and useful it attains those values only through its display ability, just like performance art which convinces of its authenticity through observer experience—and yet is self-referential and can also just stand for itself.

The Event Matrix, however, is also a simulation and is an example of the hyperreal possibilities of rhetorical invention which masquerades in matrical, computer programing format. It reminds us that *all media are hyperreal,* not just late-twentieth-century, North American television, film and artifacts (Baudrillard). *All media simulate human experience.* All media create norms of preference for personal value as well as social necessity. All media may replicate themselves in whatever holographic norms are prevalent as guided by the contemporary zeitgeist's predominant media. It is shortsighted of many postmodernist writers to find hyperreality only in late twentieth century aesthetic events when the spoken word thousands of years ago as well as today conjures images which speak to our sensory experience—as do music, painting, comic books, video games, concerts, the theatre and so many other arts. All communication employs symbol systems which may evoke nonpresent realities or fantasies.

We should thus expect more scholarship which draws upon matrical formats for presenting data and findings—as well as presentations of research which are mimetic of fractal organizations of knowledge. Poststructural forms—a contradiction of words but not necessarily of facticity—will soon begin to report information in nonrepetitive, repetitive media formats—or, in fractally rhetorical media.

One of the ways this will be accomplished will shadow forth in media formats for presenting research which are themselves entertaining. The media formats for communicating are now already legion, but some of the formats—like scholarly writing—are not always as pleasurable to experience. There is no reason artists and media moguls should have exclusive rights to delightfully entertaining presentational modes. There is no reason wisdom cannot be communicated by means of the eloquence of pleasurable media. The restricted conception of rhetoric as it appears in scholarship is most remarkable since wisdom and eloquence are not limited to symbol systems which only employ words. Scholars are still mostly wrapped up in the Ancient, Medieval and Renaissance written formulas of books.

For example, research about horror will at times take on the look and feel of horror narratives. Research about music will be performed as music, etc. In some senses this is already being done at some popular culture conferences, particularly those panels in which research is presented in the form of performance art. Media form is the content of the new popular culture research. It presents in the manner of the subject it discusses. Soon research will also be presented and marketed as videos and floppy disks. Interactive means of presenting research are already available, but are still little used and undervalued for promotion, tenure and merit raises compared to hard-copy media printed on paper— interactive means like CD-ROM systems, on-line journals, network bulletin boards, e-mail groups and other formats yet to be invented. Soon the norms for presenting research will not be limited to style sheets but will be liberated by the entrepreneurial elan of researchers producing artistic presentations of arts and ideas. The authority of the written word may yet yield to the authenticity of aesthetic experience as a primary avenue to truth—and understanding and sharing the human lot.

Popular culture not only has a future, it has a past. The past of popular culture is hidden in the elitist assumptions of defining cultural ages by being, human being, knowledge and correct action—which excludes popular culture from the study of the history of ideas. The more complete past of popular culture is revealed when communication or rhetorical media are included in the description and evaluation of culture. The future of popular culture studies is thus revealed in the tolerant inclusion of media studies as rhetorical and as the primary basis for culture study.

The future of popular culture studies will live in the simulations of the media and media formats which people, communities and cultures employ to communicate their insights, joys and fears to each other. The simulation of media and culture is not appropriate merely for the study of Western culture; it is appropriate for the study of any culture. The future of popular culture studies is the freedom to study culture without being limited to the received, value-laden norms of written media and to present the studies in as appealing a manner as the artifacts, events, personalities and symbols studied.

Notes

[1]For example, Harold Spencer describes continuity and change, but not the change brought about by new communication media; instead he discusses social factors in *The Image Maker: Man and His Art* (25-57). Phrases like "tide of worldliness" and "development of individuality" are mentioned prominently with regard to the rise of humanism and its consequent Renaissance in Bernard S. Myers' *Art and Civilization* (363). E.H. Gombrich's *The Story of Art* suggests that the change from the Medieval period to the early Renaissance was marked by the burghers' challenge to the power of the Church and the feudal lords, mentioning nothing of media or cathedrals as media (149). Rather, he discusses the technical advances of roofing and vaulting (119ff).

[2]A notable exception is Lancelot Hogben's *From Cave Painting to Comic Strip, A Kaleidoscope of Human Communication* which discusses cultural history in terms of communication. However, it does not link media as a defining, formative feature of an age with the causal nexus of change from one time period to another.

[3]Walter J. Ong maintains rhetoric only applied to orality, not writing in *Rhetoric, Romance and Technology: Studies in the Interaction of Expression and Culture* (2), which is certainly debatable.

[4]See Kate Ferguson, *The Contested Castle, Gothic Novels and the Subversion of Domestic Ideology*, Juliann E. Fleenor, ed., *The Female Gothic* and Les Daniels, *Living in Fear, A History of Horror in the Mass Media*.

Works Cited

Augustine, Bishop of Hippo. *On Christian Doctrine*. Trans. D.W. Robertson, Jr. New York: Liberal Arts P, 1958.

Baldwin, Charles Sears. *Medieval Rhetoric and Poetic*. New York: MacMillan, 1928.

Baudrillard, Jean. *America*. Trans. Chris Turner. New York: Routledge, Chapman and Hall [Verso], 1989.

Bitzer, Lloyd F. and Edwin Black, eds. *The Prospect of Rhetoric*. Englewood Cliffs, NJ: Prentice-Hall, 1971.

Braden, Donna R. *Leisure and Entertainment in America*. Detroit: Wayne State UP, 1988.

Buckley, Michael. *Motion and Motion's God, Thematic Variations in Aristotle, Cicero, Newton and Hegel*. Princeton, NJ: Princeton UP, 1971.

Burckhardt, Jacob. *The Civilization of the Renaissance in Italy*. 2 vols. Trans. S.G.C. Middlemore. New York: Harper and Row, 1958.

Campbell, Joseph. *The Hero with a Thousand Faces*. New York: Pantheon, 1949.

Carpenter, Edmund. "The New Languages." *Explorations in Communication.* Eds. Edmund Carpenter and Marshall McLuhan. Boston: Beacon, 1960. 162-79.

Cicero. *De Oratore.* Trans. E.W. Sutton and H. Rackham. London: William Heinemann, 1967.

Clark, Donald Lemen. *Rhetoric in Greco-Roman Education.* Westport, CT: Greenwood, 1977.

Daniels, Les. *Living in Fear, A History of Horror in the Mass Media.* New York: Charles Scribner's Sons, 1975.

DeRomilly, Jacqueline. *Magic and Rhetoric in Ancient Greece.* Cambridge, MA: Harvard UP, 1975.

Diallo, Yaya and Mitchell Hall. *The Healing Drum: African Wisdom Teachings.* Rochester, VT: Inner Tradition, Destiny, 1989.

Durant, Will and Ariel Durant. *The Story of Civilization.* 10 vols. New York: Simon and Schuster, 1935-67.

Ferguson, Kate. *The Contested Castle, Gothic Novels and the Subversion of Domestic Ideology.* Urbana, IL: U of Illinois P, 1989.

Fleenor, Juliann E., ed. *The Female Gothic.* Montreal: Eden P, 1983.

Fleming, William. *Arts and Ideas.* New York: Holt, Rinehart and Winston, 1974.

Gombrich, E.H. *The Story of Art.* London: The Phaidon P, 1964.

Harner, Michael. *The Way of the Shaman.* New York: Bantam, 1986.

Hogben, Lancelot. *From Cave Painting to Comic Strip, A Kaleidoscope of Human Communication.* New York: Chanticleer P, 1949.

Holmberg, Carl Bryan. "Clive Barker's Poetics: The Rhetorical Nature of Horror and Human Experience." *Studies in Popular Culture* 14 (1992): 85-95.

___. "Rhetorical Terrorism and the Torture Shift." *The Ohio Speech Journal, Golden Anniversary Edition* 21 (1983): 57-64.

___. "Stray the Course: Technology's Impact upon the Representative-Elector Artifact." *Communication Quarterly* 32 (1984): 84-90.

King, Stephen. *Danse Macabre.* New York: Berkley, 1983.

Lechner, Joan Marie. *Renaissance Concepts of the Commonplaces.* New York: Pageant P, 1962.

Leclercq, Jean. *The Love of Learning and the Desire for God, a Study of Monastic Culture.* Trans. Catharine Misrahi. New York: Fordham UP, 1974.

Lovejoy, Arthur O. *The Great Chain of Being.* Cambridge, MA: Harvard UP, 1936.

Mander, Jerry. *In the Absence of the Sacred: The Failure of Technology and the Survival of the Indian Nations.* San Francisco: Sierra Club Books, 1991.

McLuhan, Marshall. *Understanding Media: the Extensions of Man.* New York: McGraw-Hill, 1964.

McKeon, Richard P. "Creativity and the Commonplace." *Philosophy and Rhetoric* 6 (1973): 199-210.

___. "The Methods of Rhetoric and Philosophy: Invention and Judgment." *The Classical Tradition, Literary and Historical Studies in Honor of Harry Caplan.* Ed. Luitpold Wallach. Ithaca, NY: Cornell UP, 1966. 365-73.

___. "A Philosopher Meditates on Discovery." *Moments of Personal Discovery.* Ed. R.M. MacIver. New York: Harper, 1952. 105-32.

___. "Rhetoric in the Middle Ages." *Speculum* 17 (1942): 1-32.

___. "The Uses of Rhetoric in a Technological Age: Architectonic Productive Arts." *The Prospect of Rhetoric.* Eds. Lloyd F. Bitzer and Edwin Black. Englewood Cliffs, NJ: Prentice-Hall, 1971. 44-63.

Mickunas, Algis. "Civilizations as Structures of Consciousness." *Main Currents of Modern Thought* 29 (1973): 179-85.

Middleton, Richard. *Studying Popular Music.* Buckingham, Great Britain: Open UP, 1990.

Myers, Bernard S. *Art and Civilization.* New York: McGraw-Hill, 1957.

Ong, Walter J. *The Presence of the Word: Some Prologomena for Cultural and Religious History.* New York: Simon and Schuster, 1970.

___. *Rhetoric, Romance and Technology: Studies in the Interaction of Expression and Culture.* Ithaca, NY: Cornell UP, 1971.

Postman, Neil. *Amusing Ourselves to Death: Public Discourse in the Age of Show Business.* New York: Penguin, 1988.

Quintilian, Marcus Fabius. *The Institutio Oratoria of Quintilian.* Trans. H.E. Butler. 4 vols. London: William Heinemann, 1921.

Spencer, Harold. *The Image Maker: Man and His Art.* New York: Charles Scribner's Sons, 1975.

Tolkien, John Ronald Reuel. *The Tolkien Reader.* New York: Ballantine, 1991.

Works Cited Entries:
Books, Periodicals and Beyond

John S. Lawrence
Tim Orwig
Marty S. Knepper

Documenting and Citing in the New Humanities

During the 1980s many Americans believed that thousands of children were being abducted from school grounds, shopping centers, street corners, and even from their own back yards. Businesses and community organizations publicized "stranger danger" and sought to rescue the captive children. Missing children appeared on billboards, comic book pages, and on the advertising panels of buses and subways. Their faces were printed on inserts for utility bills. Children were fingerprinted en masse, some even registering their "video portraits" with service groups. Mass mailers for commercial products included missing children displays along with their merchandise and price information. America's dairies and supermarkets were recruited. They offered printed panels with missing child mug shots on shopping bags and milk cartons. Eventually, jokes about having your face on a milk carton became a standard part of political humor.

In a precise, documented discussion of this phenomenon, how would you cite a milk carton or a billboard? Or a flyer for an electronic bug repeller that contained an abducted child inset? This complex of artifacts and popular beliefs is but one example of the difficulties in documentation that we encounter when we move beyond the safety of books and journals. Bumper stickers, billboards, political buttons, T-shirts all convey messages that are important to their creators and consumers. Does documentation really matter? Do we really want to bother with documenting the ephemeral and idiosyncratic aspects of material culture?

We suggest that developing consistent and understandable indexing categories and citation methods is a significant challenge to popular culture methodology. Unless we can refer to the objects of our discussion without ambiguity, it seems unlikely that we can establish popular culture studies as a discipline among "the new humanities." It

191

also seems imperative that we teach students how to respect, recognize, and describe the objects so that they can share their discoveries in a public discourse.

In what follows, we offer guidelines that have evolved at Morningside College for undergraduate instruction in popular culture. We believe they are also suitable for use by scholars in their publications. We grant permission for others to copy these guidelines for use in their teaching or scholarship. Finally, we invite additions and corrections to what we have done. We hope that the guidelines will eventually be available as an appendix in popular culture texts or in pamphlet form.

I. General Principles

In the most recent change of MLA citation practice, the suggested title for the references page was changed from "Bibliography" to "Works Cited." This recognizes the need to document sources beyond traditional book or periodical categories. Since the study of popular culture often involves material culture—toys, cards, maps, etc.—even broader principles and models of citation are desirable. We have developed here forms and examples of citations for a variety of media or artifacts you might deal with in a research paper or survey project. The citation formulas are arranged to show required information (when available) for each entry, and suggested additional information [in brackets]. These forms extend and illustrate the principles of Chapter 4, Section 8 of the third edition of the *MLA Handbook for Writers of Research Papers* by Joseph Gibaldi and Walter S. Achtert (New York, MLA, 1988). Consult the handbook for further information.

A final innovation in Section VI deals with the results of bibliographical research done with online electronic or CD-ROM databases.

When you are puzzled about issues of form and how to fully document your item, remember that the principal functions of a citation are:

1) to help readers locate the source/item (or something exactly like it) for their own review/OR,
2) to help them understand the unique identity of the item you encountered.

Before we illustrate documentation for somewhat exotic popular culture artifacts, we will remind you of the basic forms for standard written sources in an MLA style "Works Cited" list.

One final recommendation not reflected in these examples: *always double-space Works Cited entries in a manuscript*. Also, titles that we show in italics would be underlined in a manuscript.

II. Standard Sources and Citations

1. **Book:** Author's name (reversed). Title (underlined). Place of publication: Publisher, Date.

Braudy, Susan. *What the Movies Made Me Do*. New York: Knopf, 1985.

2. **Article in an Anthology:** Author's name (reversed). Title of article (in quotes). Title of anthology (underlined). Editor(s) of anthology. Place of publication: Publisher, Date. Page range for article.

Lasch, Christopher. "The Great Experiment: Where Did It Go Wrong?" *Beyond Cheering and Bashing: New Perspectives on the Closing of the American Mind*. Ed. James Seaton and William K. Buckley. Bowling Green, OH: Bowling Green State U Popular P, 1992. 8-18.

3. **Article in Popular Magazine:** Author's name (reversed). Title of article (in quotes). Magazine name (underlined) Date: page range. Note the different treatment of the date for monthly vs. weekly magazines.

Schudson, Michael. "Natural Urges." *Utne Reader* Jan./Feb. 1992: 73-76.
Bonfante, Jordan. "Everybody's Fall Guy." *Time* 10 June 1991: 22-23.

4. **Article in Scholarly Journal:** Author's name (reversed). Article title (in quotes). Name of periodical (underlined) Volume Number.Issue number (date of publication in parentheses): page range.

Rathgeb, Douglas L. "Bogeyman From the Id: Nightmare and Reality in *Halloween* and *Nightmare on Elm Street*." *Journal of Popular Film and Television* 19.1 (1991): 36-43.

Moving away from these standard forms requires both inventiveness and common sense.

III. Variability of Item Arrangement

Remember that the order of the elements may change, depending on your emphasis. An entry is alphabetized by the item of information most important to your paper. For example, if your principal focus is movies, list titles first; if your subject is the director's work, you would list the director first; if you are studying an acting performance, you would list the actor's name first. Here's an array of possible entries for a film, *The Year of Living Dangerously*:

The Year of Living Dangerously. Dir. Peter Weir. With Mel Gibson, Sigourney Weaver, and Linda Hunt. United Artists, 1982.

Hunt, Linda, actor. *The Year of Living Dangerously*. Dir. Peter Weir. With Mel Gibson and Sigourney Weaver. United Artists, 1982.

Jarre, Maurice, composer. *The Year of Living Dangerously*. Dir. Peter Weir. With Mel Gibson, Linda Hunt, and Sigourney Weaver. United Artists, 1982.

Weir, Peter, dir. *The Year of Living Dangerously*. With Mel Gibson, Linda Hunt, and Sigourney Weaver. United Artists, 1982.

Williamson, David, Peter Weir, and C. J. Koch, screenwriters. *The Year of Living Dangerously*. Dir. Peter Weir. Based on the novel by C. J. Koch. With Mel Gibson, Linda Hunt, and Sigourney Weaver. United Artists, 1982.

IV. Inventing Citation Forms

If you are citing something that doesn't fit any of the following categories, you'll have to make up your own form. Write down any specific information you have about the item, then decide what's most important, and alphabetize by that. For example, say you want to cite a toy. From what is printed on the toy itself, you could construct acceptable entries:

"Mini-Bus." Toy. Fisher-Price Toys, 1969.

"Hanna-Barbera's Peter Potamus Frame Tray Puzzle." Puzzle. Whitman Publishing, 4512, 1964.

Quotes around the toy title will separate it from the descriptive label that follows.

Maybe you need to cite a post card. This would be an acceptable entry:

"The Capture of Rickett's and Griffin's Union Batteries at First Manassas." Plastichrome post card. Manassas National Battlefield Park, Manassas, VA, series. Colourpicture. Boston, n.d.

You should always cite the date or year of an item. If none is given, but you can make a good approximation of the date, write "c." and the year (for example, c. 1986); otherwise, write "n.d."

If the item you cite has a regional character, you should provide information that would help you or a reader reconstruct some of the local history:

"Tie-Liter." Cigarette lighter in the form of a bolo tie. Sioux City, Iowa, Box 1025, n.d.

V. Some Special Citation Forms

1. **Computer Software**: Author (when given). Title (underlined). "Computer software" designation. Distributor, Year. [Computer, Memory, Operating system, Diskette format].

Appleworks. Computer software. Apple, 1983. Apple IIe, 128K, ProDOS, 5.25" or 3.5" diskette.

2. **Newspaper Articles, Columns, Editorials**: Author (if given). Title in quotes (if none, descriptive label). [Editorial (if applicable)]. Newspaper (underlined) and Date: Page.

"Little Sioux Farm Will Become State Forest." *Sioux City Journal* 13 May 1987: A5.
"Pulling Back on Farm Safety." Editorial. *Des Moines Register* 31 May 1992: C1.
Greene, Bob. "Red Ryder Lives, Kind of." Column. *Sioux City Journal* 13 May 1987: A4.

3. **Pamphlets**: Author (if given). Title (underlined). City: Publisher. Year.

Gary Hart: Leadership with Courage. Denver: Friends of Gary Hart 1988 [Presidential campaign year], c. 1986.
Progress? Cambridge, MA: Cultural Survival, n.d.

4. **Radio or Television Program**: Episode title (when available) in quotes. Program title (underlined). [Writer. Director, Narrator, Actor, Producer, etc., if important]. Network. Broadcast station, City. Broadcast date.

A Prairie Home Companion. With Garrison Keillor. National Public Radio. KWIT, Sioux City, IA. 9 May 1987.
"City on the Edge of Forever." Writ. Harlan Ellison. *Star Trek.* Created by Gene Roddenberry. Dir. Joseph Pevney. With William Shatner, Leonard Nimoy, and Joan Collins. NBC. KVFD, Fort Dodge, IA. 6 April 1967.

5. **Recordings:**
    A. Classical: Composer. Selection title (in quotes). Artist. Recording title (if different from selection). Manufacturer, Catalog number, Year.
    B. Contemporary: Artist. Selection title (in quotes). Recording title (underlined). Manufacturer, Catalog number, Year.

Weill, Kurt. "Youkali Tango." Armadillo String Quartet. *Lost in the Stars.* Prod. Hal Willner and Paul M. Young. A & M Records, SP 9-5104, 1985.
The Mothers of Invention. "Who Are the Brain Police?" *Freak Out.* With Frank Zappa. Verve, V6-5005-2, 1966.

6. **Films, Film strips, Videotapes:** Title (underlined). Medium. Director. [Actor, Writer, Producer]. Distributor, Year. [Length (for videotapes)]. See III. above for examples of films.

Drink, Drank, Drunk. Videocassette. Dir. Jack Kuney. PBS Video, n.d. 60 min.
Doing Something. Videocassette. Writ. and Dir. Lee R. Bobker. Video Outreach, 1984. 22 min.

7. **Performances:** Title (underlined). Author. Director. Theater, City. Date.

Cat on a Hot Tin Roof. By Tennessee Williams. Dir. Tim Case. Klinger-Neal Theater, Sioux City, IA, 25 Apr. 1987.

8. **Musical Compositions:** Composer. Work (underlined). [If referring to a published score, give publication information last].

Weill, Kurt, and Bertolt Brecht. *Die Dreigroschenoper [The Threepenny Opera].*

9. **Works of Art:** Artist. Work (underlined). Date. Location, City. [If referring to a photograph of the work, give publication information last; also, provide any information about the history of an item that would help someone trace it.]

Wood, Grant. *Corn Room Mural.* c. 1926. Martin Hotel Ballroom, Sioux City, IA. Rediscovered and conserved 1983-1985. Sioux City Art Center, 513 Nebraska, Sioux City, IA 51101-1305.
Rembrandt van Rijn. *The Return of the Prodigal Son.* Hermitage, Leningrad. Plate 127 of *Rembrandt: Paintings, Drawings, and Etchings.* By Ludwig Goldscheider. London: Phaidon P, 1960.

10. **Letters**: Author. Recipient. Date. Location, if accessible to researchers.

Carver, Raymond. Post card to the author. 7 Aug 1985.
Carlyle, Thomas. Letter to Mr. Dowie. 10 July 1868. Morningside College
   Archives, Sioux City, IA 51106.

11. **Interviews**: Interviewee. [Role.] Descriptive label. Date.

Scholten, Jim. Baseball coach. Personal interview. 13 May 1987.
Miller, Mary. Nursing supervisor. Telephone interview. 12 May 1987.

12. **Maps, Charts, Blueprints**: Name (underlined). Descriptive label. City: Publisher, Year.

Iowa. Map. Des Moines: Iowa State Development Commission, 1985.
Iowa Topography. Des Moines: Geological map. State Surveyor's Office, 1982.
Star Wars Blueprints. Blueprints. New York: Ballantine, 1977.

13. **Cartoons, Illustrations**: Cartoonist or Illustrator. Title (in quotes). Descriptive label. Publication information.

Breathed, Berke. "Bloom County." Cartoon. *Des Moines Register* 13 May
   1987: 3T.
Bishofs, Maris. Illustration. *Atlantic* March 1987: 83.

14. **Lectures, Speeches, and Addresses**: Speaker. Title (underlined) or descriptive label. Meeting. Location, Date.

Knepper, Marty, and John Lawrence. Lecture. American Popular Culture
   Seminar. Morningside College, Sioux City, IA, 11 May 1987.

15. **Manuscripts and Typescripts**: Author. Title (underlined or in quotes). Descriptive label. Location of ms. or ts., if accessible to researchers.

McCallum, Paul. "Explication of 'To A Young Ass.'" Unpublished essay, 1986.
Lewis, C. *Rev. George C. Haddock, A Brave Prohibitionist, Murdered at Sioux
   City, Iowa, August 3, 1886*. Bound collection of newspaper clippings.
   Morningside College Archives, Sioux City, IA 51106.

16. **Comic Books**: Story (in quotes). Author. Artist. Magazine (underlined). Date: Pages.

"Mr. Monster's Vacation." Script Greg Georgas. Art Michael T. Gilbert and Gerald Forton. *Doc Stearn...Mr. Monster* Apr. 1987: 1-16.

17. **Catalog Advertisements:** Product name (in quotes). Description. [Price.] Catalog Name (underlined). Date: page. Location of Vendor.

"Mission Accomplished." Pocket knife. $59.95. *The Sportsman's Guide.* 1992: 15. Golden Valley, MN 55427-4398.
"Safe Sex—Sleep With An American Soldier." T-Shirt. $9.98. *Originaltees* (flyer). Nd. Tinley Park, IL 60477.

18. **Magazine Advertisements.** Product name. Product type. Magazine title (underlined). Date: page.

"Mazda Navaho." Truck. *Time* 10 June 1991: 24.

19. **Stamps**: Title. Face Value. [Postal reference number.] Date of issue.

"Honoring Those Who Served—Desert Shield/Desert Storm." 29 cents. 4495. 4 July 1991.

VI. Bibliographic Reports from Online or CD-ROM Databases
Bibliographic information is increasingly available, sometimes exclusively, in online or CD-ROM databases. For example, flagship popular culture publications such as *Journal of Popular Culture, Journal of American Culture, Journal of Popular Film and Television, American Quarterly*, and *American Studies* are currently indexed in the Wilsonline Humanities Index, which is also available on Wilsondisc CD-ROM [H.W. Wilson Co., 950 University Ave., Bronx, NY 10452/1-800-367-6770]. Several reasons favor disclosing search strategies and general results of a search. Electronic search options present a greater variety of ways of "casting the net" for references. Different combinations of search terms can yield radically different results. Since access to online databases can be expensive, you can assist others by "citing" your database. Depending on the information in your citation, you may make it unnecessary for someone else to perform a similar search. A citation of the kind that follows in example 20 would be relevant in discussing when the mainstream newspapers lost interest in reporting on the civilian hostages of the Persian Gulf conflict.

20. **Database Citations**. Database. [Vendor]. Date of search. Search terms, relevant findings ("hits").

National News Index. DIALOG/Knowledge Index. May 29, 1992. Search parameters were 'Persian Gulf' and 'Hostages,' yielding 141 hits. The latest entries were in January (1 hit) and March (4 hits).

VII. Final Thoughts
Don't forget to have fun with your research and documentation. You can make an interesting game of figuring out how to cite accurately items you have studied. Taking the time to do it thoroughly and consistently will increase the value of the research to yourself when you return to the topic later. Good documentation also allows others to share in and to respect the care and accuracy of your research.

CASTING HIS HOPE WITH THE PEOPLE

✦

Casting His Hope with the People
Selected Articles by Ray B. Browne

Introduction

John G. Nachbar

My master's degree work in English in the mid-1960s was typical of the time. It was understood that students served as apprentices to published scholars whose suggestions we were to slavishly follow. If we did this successfully and thoroughly learned all the past scholarship on given topics, after several years we ourselves might aspire to attend professional conferences to hear revered colleagues and after that, perhaps, experience the thrill of scholarly publication. In the fall of 1970 I began my doctoral studies in English at Bowling Green State University and on the Monday evening of my first week of class I spent three hours in Ray Browne's "Introduction to Popular Culture" graduate class. My perspectives on education would never be the same. Ray asked opinions continuously and he listened to what students had to say with respect. What's more, when he told us about our course papers, he said that we should do work that would be published. After a lengthy discussion about how traditional critical approaches were not adequate for the study of popular materials, I saw Ray after class and asked to do a short paper other than the one that had been assigned. After a few clarifying questions, he smiled and told me "Why not?" Later that semester, he invited all of us to come and participate in the first national meeting of the Popular Culture Association at East Lansing—in the spring a number of the 20 students in the course did just that, taking advantage of the free housing Ray had arranged for students. And three years later, when I knew Ray better, it came as no real surprise to me that the paper I had written in that course had become the basis for my dissertation.

Ray's faith in his students to do their best work if left free to work on what interested them, his respect for graduate students as scholarly colleagues now rather than in some mystical future and his refusal to set some hierarchical pecking order as he planned the first national meeting of the PCA were mind boggling for me in 1970. What I have to come to understand in the nearly quarter century since that wonderful Monday night, however, is how typical that evening was in a Ray Browne course and, indeed, how typical his attitudes in that course were and are in all of his professional writings. In a publishing career that includes scores of books and articles written over more than 40 years, three values dominate Ray's perspectives, no matter what the audience or subject matter.

The first of these values is an immense faith in American democracy. It is perhaps Ray's rural Alabama upbringing in near poverty during the 1930s, his respect for the poor people he grew up with, their neighborliness and Ray's personal rise to success from these beginnings that explain his continuing faith in democratic values, a faith that to too many academics seems old-fashioned and naive in light of current cultural theories. Naive or not, however, Ray's enthusiasm for the nobility of common people and their cultures has directed his professional life from his graduate training as a folklorist to his accomplishments as a founding father of the academic study of popular culture. As he says of Melville in his article on *Billy Budd*, Ray Browne "cast his lot with the people" and, if his prolific career as a publishing scholar bears testimony to his choice, the people have never disappointed him.

The other two values that define Ray's work are extensions of his faith in democracy. The first is a general sense of optimism, especially for the potential of the future. In article after article, Ray preaches that we must learn to respect the past but never to worship it. The old masters, he insists, have some things to teach us, but their voices do not signal the end of the opera. The past should be used as background for the future which promises to be richer and more exciting, and, hopefully, wiser than either the past or the present. It is this optimism, I suspect, that gives Ray such faith in graduate students and new scholars. At conferences he organizes and in the publications he edits, there is a place at the table for anyone who is enthusiastic and has something fresh to say, no matter what their academic status.

The other value is the flip side of Ray's faith in the common person. Quite simply, Ray is deeply suspicious of bureaucratic authority and he is actively contemptuous of the arrogant and the snobbish. It is for this reason that so many of his writings during the 1980s and 1990s have been polemics against traditionalist academics who claim that they have the answer to "the best that has been thought and said." And the same perspective has led Ray to strike out against many of the practitioners of contemporary cultural theory because he believes they have created a new academic elite defined by trendy, esoteric jargon that purposely excludes the vast majority of intelligent readers. Even at the conference in honor of his retirement, Ray, in his remarks to the assembled scholars, warned of arrogantly becoming too distant from common readers and deflated some of those present by referring to much of current critical theory as "the critic's jabberwock."

The following five articles were selected from a group of essays that Ray Browne includes as among his favorites. They are meant to reflect the consistency in Ray's thought about popular culture and at the same time show the development of his ideas from his earliest publications in the 1950s about folklore and American literature to the end of the 1980s when he was jousting with the academic reactionaries of the Reagan era. The first two essays, published early in Ray's career, reflect Ray's bedrock faith in American democracy. Hawthorne, in the first essay, is loved not as the creator of immortal art, as he is in much standard analysis, but as the purveyor of commonly told stories, some of them thousands of years old. In his well-known essay on *Billy Budd*, Ray interprets the story as an allegory positing the triumph of Tom Paine's democracy over the anti-democratic arguments of Edmund Burke. The essay ends with Ray's typical optimism as he views this story from the traditional American literature canon with new eyes as an "attestation of the power and future of democracy."

The third article, "Popular Culture: Notes Toward a Definition," is one of the famous essays from the era when such scholars as Russel B. Nye and John G. Cawelti were outlining the assumptions and boundaries of popular culture studies. In the article Ray once again embraces the common as an exciting new area for future study. He also reveals his early distaste for elitism by making elite culture the one area of culture that clearly does not belong under the popular culture umbrella.

The final two articles argue for a future academe that embraces popular culture as both appropriate for a democratic society and an answer for some serious educational ills. The future of the humanities, if they are to truly humanize, must include popular culture, and literacy now and in the future must be redefined to include all of the mass media. Both articles skewer educational traditionalists who insist on a narrow canon of readings, mostly from the distant past. Instead of training the members of our democracy for a mass-mediated future, Ray argues, the traditionalists are snobs who voice "poisonous nonsense" trying to "clone" themselves and "relive" the past. Despite his condemnation of academic ostriches, Ray, as usual, remains optimistic. The last essay concludes with an affirmation of the American dream.

Readers should note in all five essays the democratic clarity of Ray Browne's writing. Ray has always written with accessible prose, with a zest for homely metaphor and with genuine feelings for what he is writing about. It's good conversation, albeit intellectual, around America's pot-bellied stove. Pedants, martinets and pompous boors in Ray's pieces all have to stay outside on the leaky porch of the past. That is why, finally, it is so appropriate to honor Ray Browne with a book of essays about the future of popular culture. His writings in their disarming simplicity invite all of us, *all of us*, to embrace our popular culture and walk toward the light of the next generations. It was like that for me that first night in Ray's class. And for much more than a quarter century, for hundreds of us who have been influenced by Ray Browne, that has never changed.

The Oft-Told *Twice-Told Tales*:
Their Folklore Motifs

Ray B. Browne

Critics agree that much of Hawthorne's greatness derives from his probing "human nature in the mass," or, as he said in the Preface to "The Snow-Image," "the depths of our common nature."[1] But commentators have failed to recognize one aspect of the direction and extent—and the significance—of this probing: that aspect which makes the stories read like artful folktales.

This folkloristic quality does not result from the author's use of the Puritan past and of New England legends as bases for some stories, nor from his inclusion of superstitions, although this superficial dress does unavoidably add a certain folk atmosphere when it is used. But Hawthorne ranged much more widely and deeply. He was nationalist or regionalist, as critics insist, only superficially. He was rather internationalist, for, having restricted himself geographically to the little lump of New England soil which was, he said, all his heart could "take in," he bored through the crust of life until he tapped the underlying ocean of story, which is fed by all lands, and he drank deeply of this continuum of human experience; knowingly or unknowingly he was the major American voice of a part of what Jung later called the collective unconscious: through him welled up the international folklore motifs— the themes—of life.

For folktales of all kinds, regardless of provenience or surface features, treat the fundamentals of life, those aspects common to all mankind: hates, loves, desires, ambitions, frailties, the evil of the human heart. Hawthorne's development of his stories in parallels to these motifs made him transcend regional and national boundaries and become thoroughly internationalized and universalized. And this broad folklore quality enriches the allegory and symbolism in the stories.

Further evidence of the closeness of Hawthorne's works to the true nature of folklore is that some of his tales, with little or no variation, have in fact become authentic folktales of New England.

Reprinted with permission from *Southern Folklore Quarterly* XXII (June 1958): 69-85.

Most of his stories which are more than mere sketches contain these international parallels and could be used to illustrate my thesis. But for this discussion I have chosen the *Twice-Told Tales*. These stories, as far as sources are concerned, are of three kinds: (1) those based on historical events; (2) those not based on historical events; (3) those which are a combination of these two types. We shall examine them under these three categories.

I

One of the most universal motifs in all folklore is that of the champion who returns to succor his people in time of crisis. The oldest known record of such an event is an Assyrian papyrus text of about 420 B.C., which tells the story of Achikar, the wise minister of the ruler Asarhaddon. Achikar is condemned to death, but manages to escape and hide; when the land is in great danger, he appears and saves his people.[2]

In Western Europe the most famous of the champions who will return are Frederick Barbarossa, who is asleep in the Kyffhauser, a mountain in Thuringa; Arthur, who is waiting in Avalon; Fionn, of the pre-Celtic people, who is now asleep on an island or in a mountain,[3] waiting; Marko, famous Serbian hero; and Holger the Dane.[4] Such legends are widespread also among the North American Indians. The most famous is that of Hiawatha (real name, Monabozho), in whose going west there is at least a hint of an eventual return to succor his people.[5]

Hawthorne's "The Gray Champion" (1828-29),[6] which was based on an historical event that became a well-known legend, follows the pattern for such a story: New England "groaned" under the "tyranny" of its Governor, Sir Edmund Andros. One afternoon the people assembled on the streets. Andros, hoping to avoid trouble by dispersing the people, marched on them. "'Oh Lord of Hosts,' cried a voice among the crowd, 'provide a Champion (sic) for the people'." At this point a "gray patriarch," "whom the oppressor's drum had summoned from his grave" demands that Andros give way, explaining, "'I am, here, Sir Governor, because the cry of an oppressed people hath disturbed me in my secret place'." After forcing the Governor to back up before his wrath, the old man mysteriously disappears. "His house is one of darkness, and adversity, and peril. But should domestic tyranny oppress us, or the invader's step pollute our soil, still may the Gray Champion come...." In writing this story, Hawthorne could hardly not have had in mind folklore parallels. His development is too close to them for coincidence.[7]

"The Maypole of Merry Mount" (1828-39), though occurring on Midsummer Eve, actually centers on May-Day and May-Pole revelries and Puritan opposition to such activities. For, as Hawthorne said, though "Midsummer eve had come," "May, or her mirthful spirit, dwelt all the year round at Merry Mount," and, as he knew, traditionally May Day is observed any time during May or on Midsummer Eve. Hawthorne based his story on the historical account of Mount Wollaston or Merry Mount, run by Thomas Morton in the first days of the Massachusetts Colony. For details of the May-Day and May-Pole activities he used Joseph Strutt's *Sports and Pastimes of the People of England.*[8]

The festivities at Merry Mount are paralleled with slight variations throughout Western Europe, where they appear to be already traditional in documents as old as the thirteenth century.[9] In England the first mention is made of the Maypole, at Cornhill, in an anonymous poem called "Chaunce of the Dice." A brief account of May-Day activity is given in the old Romance *The Death of Arthur.* In 1611 Beaumont and Fletcher celebrated the season in their *Knight of the Burning Pestle.* Earlier, during the sixteenth century or before, May-Day revellers had begun imitating Robin Hood and his Merry Men. Henry Eighth at least once made himself into a kind of May-Day Robin Hood. Garrick in his *Collection of Old Plays* includes one called "A New Playe of Robyn Hood, for to be played in the May-Games, very pleasant and full of Pastyme."[10]

After this high water mark, however, the tide of enthusiasm went out, at least in England, and only waves of interest sporadically returned. The Puritans hated the institution and preached harshly against it. During Elizabeth's reign all poles were chopped down and May Day outlawed. Raised again by James' *Book of Sports* they were again pulled down during the Commonwealth, only to be raised after the Restoration.[11] Since then interest has faded, though we still have our May baskets and exhibition dances. Hitler revived all May-Day festivities in a play for nationalism. And the importance of the day for Socialists and Communists and in the USSR is well known.[12]

"The Ambitious Guest" (1832-33), perhaps more characteristically Hawthorne's than the preceding two stories, tells how the happy family in the Notch of the White Hills and their young guest are destroyed by a mountain slide. This tale was based on a true incident, which has subsequently grown into one of the most popular of New England folktales.[13] There are three kinds of folklore represented in this story,[14] but the most important is the motif. Obviously the theme is not only the futility of personal ambition (for a parallel to which see "The Ambitious Chandala Maiden," below); rather it is the larger theme of man's weakness in the hands of indifferent fate and the impossibility of avoiding disaster.[15] This theme—"what is to be will be"—is prevalent in folktales, and without being forced Hawthorne's story is a close parallel. A good example of such a story is "Sleeping Beauty," one of the best known märchen in Western Europe.

Except in detail all versions of "Sleeping Beauty" are the same: A childless King and Queen want a child more than anything else in the world. Finally a beautiful girl child is born. In the christening ceremonies (or celebration of some kind), a wicked fairy (Uglyane) prophesies that Aurora (or Briar-Rose) on her fifteenth birthday will prick her hand with a spindle and die. The good fairy Hippolyta (who has not yet given her gift) cannot completely avert the evil prophecy, but she mitigates the doom to a hundred years sleep, with the promise that at that time a Prince will kiss Aurora and waken her. Despite all precautions taken by the King and Queen, Aurora does prick her finger and fall asleep. But after a hundred years, during which time many Princes have lost their lives trying to reach Aurora, the appointed Prince comes by, easily walks through the giant hedge, enters the castle, and kisses and rescues Aurora—just as had been predicted.[16] The parallel between this story and Hawthorne's is close.

In several other *Twice-Told Tales* Hawthorne caught beautifully the quintessence of the folktale although actual parallels cannot be found. In such stories as "The Wedding Knell" (1834), "The Minister's Black Veil" (1835), and "The Prophetic Pictures" (1835-36) the reader feels very strongly the folklore quality. These stories are now printed in collections of New England folktales—again indicating their similarity to folktales.[17]

"The Wedding Knell" is one of the stronger folktale-like stories. At the beginning Hawthorne says that the event which he tells really happened in his grandmother's youth in a "certain church in the City of New York." Skinner, in his collection of tales,[18] identifies the church as St. Paul's, Broadway, New York City. Both Hawthorne's and Skinner's versions are the same with one exception: Hawthorne has the bride cry "Cruel, cruel" at the groom's masquerade; Skinner puts the single word "Cruel" in the mouths of the spectators. It is impossible at this time to determine whether Skinner had access to the same source as Hawthorne or whether he simply rewrote Hawthorne's story. There are no obvious parallels to this story in other folktale collections, though the final triumph of true love over all obstacles (the overlying theme of Hawthorne's story) is of course the very stuff that folktales are made of.

"The Minister's Black Veil" likewise has no parallels in folktales for the main theme, but for the symbol of the veil there are many. Historically the veil has been widely used, especially by women, particularly in the East, as a symbol of separation and protection from the world. It is a symbol of purity, and as such has always been denied to harlots and traveling girls. It likewise has always been a symbol of good breeding and gentility.[19] Furthermore, there are stories which tell how the spirit is veiled to separate it from the world. Mr. Hooper is not, therefore, vastly different from folklore usage when he drapes his face in black as a symbol of his sinful heart. This story derived from a true incident, and Hawthorne apparently altered it very little from the version he took it from.[20]

The idea for "The Prophetic Pictures," according to Hawthorne's headnote, came from an anecdote in Dunlap's *History of the Art of Design* which tells how Lord Mulgrave employed Gilbert Stuart to paint a portrait of his brother, General Phipps, only to discover that the artist had prophetically painted the brother as insane. "It is thus," Dunlap's account concludes, "that the real portrait painter dives into the recesses of his sitters' minds and displays strength or weakness upon the surface of his canvas."[21] Here is the beginning of Hawthorne's moral—that even if people could see into the future, they would discount their foreknowledge and continue their ways as blindly as if they had not been given the warning. Few if any parallels for this particular development exist in folklore. But there is one parallel to the story of Stuart's power of perception: Leonardo da Vinci caught the presentiment of early death and painted it into his portrait of Beatrice d'Este.[22] Hawthorne may or may not have known of this instance. Although no direct parallels to "The Prophetic Pictures" exist, this kind of story is treated in folktales. And, as we shall see later, the power of the portrait or statue to respond sympathetically and actively to the affairs of life is a widely used motif (see "Edward Randolph's Portrait," below).

II

In the stories not based on historical events, Hawthorne perhaps did not plumb human nature more deeply than he did in those anchored in historical fact, but his themes are more widely paralleled in international folklore. Seemingly, when he was free to let his imagination work he turned intuitively to the folklore motif and method to deepen his studies.

"Sights from a Steeple," though only a sketch, borrows from international folklore. In addition to several classical references. Hawthorne mentions two interesting allusions: the "Limping Devil of Le Sage" and the speaking chimneys of Madrid. The Limping Devil refers to Le Sage's *The Devil on Two Sticks*, based on the Spanish *El Diablo Cojuelo* (*The Limping Devil*, 1646) by Luiz Velez de Guevara. The theme of both stories is the common Faust-motif—Satan on earth seducing man. In Le Sage's version, Cleafas (a wanton student) finds

Asmadeus (the Devil) imprisoned in a bottle in the room of an absent astrologer. Cleafas releases the spirit, and in return Asmadeus takes the student to the highest steeple in Madrid (idea probably from the Bible— Satan tempting Christ on the pinnacle of the temple). There Asmadeus seemingly removes the roofs from the buildings and reveals the inmost thoughts and most secret acts of the people of the city.[23]

The reference to the speaking chimneys is more elusive. It is hard to tell how much familiarity Hawthorne had with Spanish literature. He read it, we know, and was fond of Cervantes.[24] Hawthorne's reference is probably literary. It is somewhat in line with a saying common among the people of Spain, and Madrid in particular, and prevalent in Spanish literature for several centuries. It derives from Madrid's being a city of cliques so small and intimate that everyone knew everyone else's business. This intimacy resulted in the Spanish proverb: "Todo se sabe en Madrid"—everything is known in Madrid.

"Peter Goldthwaite's Treasure" (1837) enriches its atmosphere with folkloristic references to alchemy, black art, Aladdin's lamp, love-tokens and the Faust-theme of man's entering a contract with Satan for earthly gain. But beyond these superficial references no folklore motifs can be found, though the reader feels sure they exist. The story of the eccentric and individualistic monomaniac who is so sure that his great-granduncle's treasure is about to be found that he tears down plank by plank the house he is living in is folkloristic in tone and outcome.

"The Seven Vagabonds" (1830), too, has several references to folklore: magicians, a pretty girl minstrel, and "the words of an old song"—"Where are you going, my pretty maid?"—which could be almost any old song. The motif also is folklore. The casual meeting of the seven different kinds of persons, who, it develops, all have one goal in mind (the camp-meeting at Stamford) brings it mind immediately *The Canterbury Tales* and other frame-stories.

"Mr. Higginbotham's Catastrophe" (1832), in design at least, is a full-scale folktale. Hawthorne even toyed with the idea of telling the story as a modern wandering jongleur. There are no exact folktale parallels to Hawthorne's tale, but the three main elements are conventional: the suspense element in Mr. Higginbotham's murder being reported on two successive days by different men; the merchant or pedlar being the spreader of news; and the fairy tale ending of the pedlar's marriage to the daughter of the rich man, inheriting his fortune, and living happily ever after.

The suspense element is decidedly Eastern in flavor. The second element, merchants and pedlars as spreaders of news, is universal among trading peoples, and was widespread in such old Romances as *Girart de*

Roussillon (1160-70), *Doon de Maience* (after 1250), *Cleomades*, by Adenet (1274-82), *The Erl of Tolous* (15th century), and in *The Canterbury Tales*. Traditionally a fair is the place where misunderstandings are cleared up (see *Decameron*, II, 9); in Hawthorne's story it is the piazza of a tavern and later the orchard where Mr. Higginbotham was almost hanged. The happy ending (the third element in the story) is a key note of fairy tales: a real Prince or one in disguise (or a poor man who deserves to be Prince) undergoes various troubles but eventually marries the Princess (real, disguised, or girl deserving to be one). The Parallel to "Mr. Higginbotham's Catastrophe" is obvious.

"The Great Carbuncle" (1832-33) is one of the most widespread of New England legends. Hawthorne's idea came from an Indian story. Another Indian parallel illustrates how other versions run: A great carbuncle burned on the eastern face of Mount Monroe in the White Mountains. (New Englanders called these the Crystal Mountains because of the glass-like objects found on them.) The Indians believed it was guarded by the spirit of a dead chief. They looked upon the gem as an evil eye. Among the white men who were out to find the jewel, there was one grown old in seeking. One day his rivals (here the rivals are mentioned in general, not in particular, as in Hawthorne) saw the old timer reach a spot where the carbuncle was within reach. He sank to the ground. They called him but got no answer. He was dead. The carbuncle rolled into the Lake of the Clouds at the base, where it still is today.[25]

The legend of a great carbuncle or of jewels of one kind or another is very old and world wide. Sometimes it is based on the story from the rabbis of the diamonds and other precious stones that Noah used to light the ark, or of the basin of jewels that Abraham used for lighting the enchanted city that he had built for his wives with walls so high they shut out the sun.[26] Sometimes it is of a magic stone or jewel in the head of a serpent, of a dog, or in the face of a mountain; sometimes the story of mountains formed of jewels, crystals, etc., prevalent in Medieval allegories.[27] Sometimes of the Book of Morman, where a prehistoric submarine was lighted with stones. Clearly Hawthorne added his story to a widely used motif.

Hawthorne felt strongly that a person's life is a part of such a finely adjusted system that once he disturbs the mechanism he is likely to change everything forever and to become an "Outcast of the Universe." In "Wakefield" (1834) he wrote of a man who is so curious about what kind of life he leads and how important he is to his little circle that in a thoughtless moment he separates himself from his group and, as it were, views himself and his life from a detached point of view. To a certain extent, "Wakefield" is, as Matthiessen called it, a "modern Rip Van

Winkle," building on the folklore motif of the long sleep. But beyond this, the story illustrates a kind of anti-feminism found in all folklore and develops, furthermore, the almost universal desire of mankind to re-experience the freedom of yesterday and yesteryear; this wish fulfillment is the core of all märchen.

Hawthorne apparently used no sources for his story, but similar tales, true or legendary, were extant around him. Melville, for instance, in the summer after he finished *Pierre* (1852), on a visit to Nantucket, learned a tale about a woman named Agatha who had been abandoned by her husband under conditions somewhat similar to those in "Wakefield." Melville sent this story to Hawthorne,[28] who did nothing about it since he had already published his own version (written probably 1834, published May 1835). Further evidence that such a story probably existed lies in the recorded versions of folk stories similar though not exactly in the same vein. One, "Bringing In The Log," has Sam Slick tell how a boy sent out to bring in the back-log was away eight years, then one night calmly walked in and said: "I've brought you in the back-log, sir, you sent me out for."[29]

One outstanding characteristic of folktales, and märchen in particular, is vividness of detail and singleness of purpose. Frequently, however, as time separates the tale from its original *raison d'etre* the motif loses its sharpness of outline, and several themes can merge into one story. Such is the case with Hawthorne's "White Old Maid" (1834). This story is a loose heap of suggestions tied up with the strings of three motifs: Pride shall be humbled; the Token and the meeting in the future; and the dead shall not rest quiet until justice prevails. In the story, Pride is humbled[30] when the haughty maiden, now an old woman, prostrates herself at the gentle one's feet; the Token, a lock of hair once sable but now green with mold, is brought back to the meeting; and apparently the ghost has now been laid, for it entered the room to meet the two women, justice prevailed, and the ghost is no longer present in the chamber.

Perhaps it was inevitable that Hawthorne should write a story about how people would act if they were miraculously given the right to relive their lives. This he did in "Dr. Heidegger's Experiment" (1835-36). This theme of the return to youth is old and widespread. The most popular conception has always been the fabulous Water of Life—usually found after a long quest and always powerful against both death and disease.[31]

In the East the idea dates back to the Babylonian worship of Ishtar, where she (the goddess of love and fertility) descends to Hades to get the Water to restore her husband, Tammuz, to life.[32] In Eastern Hindustan there has long been the belief that the Water of Life actually exists in everyone's little finger and could be drawn out at will if one but knew the key.[33] Interesting variations of belief in the Water exist around the world. In Western Europe since the 8th century, alchemists have tried to mix the elixir of life. In America there were eleven Indian tribes with their own versions of the presence of the Water,[34] and the famous Fountain of Youth set Ponce de Leon and his brother Luis Ponce on their fruitless quest.[35]

Hawthorne used the Fountain of Youth for his story, but, according to Skinner, there was one closer to him: in 1720 a Salem chemist tried to brew the elixir of life, but failed, and fell dead after drinking the incomplete potion.[36]

The famed Water of Life is the motif, throughout the world, for creation myths,[37] restoration to life,[38] fulfillment of happiness,[39] magic wisdom,[40] and long-passage-of-time myths.[41] Recorded versions,[42] in addition to those already cited, are found in the märchen of Esthonia, Finland, Lapland, Norway, Sicily, Czechoslovakia, and Russia.[43]

"The Three-Fold Destiny" subtitled "A Fairy Legend" (1838) sums up very well Hawthorne's closeness to folklore motifs. In the introduction the author states his purpose of telling an allegory "such as the writers of the last century would have expressed in the shape of an Eastern tale," but one clothed in more human warmth. The story in development is in fact straight from folkland: A man becomes aware (by one means or another) of his future greatness. He goes on his quest in search of three things: Love—the maiden of his heart will be wearing a token, and they will speak to each other in a way immediately recognizable to both: Fortune—he is to find a rich treasure ready for his taking, marked by the Latin word "Effode"—Dig; Honor—he is to be honored by other men.

The dream of future greatness and the resulting quest (usually to the other world) is widely known and old. One such tale, popular with both priests and rabbis of the Middle Ages, is that of the Boy who Learned Many Things. Understanding the language of birds, this boy hears them prophesy that his parents will humble themselves before him. When he repeats this prophecy, his parents drive him away. He returns after many adventures a great man, and the prophecy is fulfilled. This story has been collected at least once in the folktales of every country in Europe. It is primarily literary, probably stemming from the biblical story of Joseph. In other accounts, unlike Joseph's, the hero does not reveal his dream. After many adventures—solving riddles, performing difficult tasks, etc.—he overcomes his enemies and wins the Princess. This version likewise is old and has been popular, particularly in Western Europe, Hungary and the Baltic States.[44]

Perhaps slightly less popular though still widespread in folktales are stories of searches for treasure. From the treasure guarded by Fafnir (the guardian of the Nibelungs' treasure) or the fire-drake in Beowulf to that of Captain Kidd, the search has gone on. As in the case of Hawthorne's wanderer, frequently there is a hand with the finger pointing to the spot and the words "Dig here" to help the searcher find his goal.[45]

Stories of the search for the person with the right token are too numerous to itemize. Sometimes the searcher looks for a person wearing the right token and/or with the right answer; less frequently he looks for a person with the corresponding other half of the token or saying. The important thing is that the two persons always recognize each other readily.

The moral of Hawthorne's story is that one should first look around him before he goes off looking for greater things just over the next hill. Tales exemplifying the futility of this search are plentiful, though because of man's love of the romance of travel they are not so numerous as are those which show how much is to be gained by travel and adventure. One entertaining example of the futility of searching comes from the *Ocean of Story* (V, 85-86) and is called "The Ambitious Chandala Maiden" (this story should be read in connection with Hawthorne's "Ambitious Guest"): An ambitious Chandala maiden determines to marry the monarch because she thinks him the greatest man in the world. She follows the king, but abandons him when he bows to a hermit. She follows the hermit but likewise abandons him when he worships Siva. She changes to Siva, but deserts him in favor of the dog that urinates on him. She follows the dog until he rolls at the feet of his master, a young Chandala man. The maiden thus decides that her caste is good enough for her and chooses this young man for her husband.

III

The "Legends of the Province House" fall somewhere between those stories based on actual events and those of the imagination. Three of the four clearly are in folklore tradition.

"Howe's Masquerade" (1838), with its ghostly review of the old governors of the Colony passing before the company at the ball, the rear being brought up by the ghost of the last and then living governor, finds its counterpart at least as far back as the legend of the handwriting on the wall before Belshazzar (538 B.C.)[46] and probably before. This is the dream of doom that runs through folktales of most countries and much literature. How much Hawthorne's idea came from his reading about Province House is hard to determine. There is an account of a great festivity that took place just before Howe left for England.[47]

"Edward Randolph's Portrait" (1838) is more provably folkloristic. Here the faded portrait of Randolph reassumes its brilliancy for a moment to warn Lt. Governor Hutchinson against making the same kind of dreadful mistake that he (Randolph) had made earlier. This sympathy of portraits and statues, especially the latter, and their interference in ordinary affairs of life is an old motif. Stories of this kind were particularly popular in Medieval Saints' Legends, in which statues shed tears out of sympathy and sometimes came to life to perform deeds for their worshippers.[48] In the New World at least twenty-two Indian tribes told such stories.[49]

There are also analogues in New England legends. Not all are as sinister as Hawthorne's. One, for instance, tells how, during an evening of drinking and fun at Buxton Inn, a jolly old gentlemen, dressed in rich but antiquated clothes, enters. He drinks with the bumpkins and wins all their money in an all-night game. As dawn breaks, the maid enters to clean up the debris and recognizes the old gentleman as the one on the picture before the inn, that of the original owner, long dead. In their amazement all the people rush to the window to confirm her statement. It is still too dark for them to discern the picture on the sign, but when they turn back to the room, the jolly old man is gone.[50]

In "Lady Eleanore's Mantle" (1838) drawn from Lady Knox, Hawthorne dealt with one of the most universal themes in all folklore: Pride must fall.[51] In the *Ocean of Story* (II, 106 n3) Pride is listed among the Six Faults that are enemies of man. From all over Europe, India, and in Aesop, there are recorded tales of Pride's fall. Such stories are found among the märchen of Esthonia, Finland, Denmark, Czechoslovakia, and in Finnish-Swedish tales and in Grimm's.[52]

Among the American Indians Pride never went unpunished.[53] Skinner tells how a proud old Indian witch, Mother Kway, would not allow her beautiful blond daughter, Sun Locks, to marry anyone less than a chief. In punishment for the mother's pride, Sun Locks lost her beauty, no man would have her, and the old mother had no one to provide for her old age. In another widespread story (prevalent among the Tsimshian, Tlingit, Haida, Chehalis, and with remote analogies among the Crow and Hopi),[54] a proud Indian Princess demands that her cousin slash his face and cut his beautiful hair to prove that he loves her. After he has done these things, she scorns his affection. The Prince is then made beautiful by Chief Pestilence.[55] When the proud Princess now falls in love with the Prince, he scorns her and makes her inflict the same disfigurement on herself, and then rejects her. Chief Pestilence will not restore her to her original beauty, and she soon dies of shame.

Readers of the *Twice-Told Tales* consciously or unconsciously hear the echo of other stories they have heard or read. This oft-told, folkloristic quality makes Hawthorne's subjects and treatment more familiar and enriches the stories. From this characteristic comes much of the tales' total effectiveness.

Notes

[1] The most penetrating study of this aspect of Hawthorne is still that by F.O. Matthiessen in *American Renaissance* (New York, 1941). But especially sensitive and seminal is *The Power of Blackness*, by Harry Levin (New York, 1958), which studies Hawthorne at least partially from a comparative literature point of view.

[2] Stith Thompson, *The Folktale* (New York, 1946), p. 277.

[3] Almost always connected with the legends of the returning champion is the explanation of how he spends the long period of waiting, and where. In nearly every case in Western Europe and with North American Indians, the champion is waiting in a mountain. Sometimes he is asleep. Often he goes about life as usual, but in a magic land where time means nothing, where one year or 100 or 1000 are as our day. Such conditions obtain in the fairy stories of all lands. In the *Thousand Nights and a Night* there is the amusing story of a young Vizier who at a sorceror's bidding plunges into a magic cauldron. Immediately he finds himself in the sea and discovers that he is a woman. "She" becomes in time the mother of seven children, finally gets tired of this life, plunges back into the sea, discovers herself back in the magic cauldron (this time again a man) and learns that only a few seconds have elapsed since he left.

[4] Marko Kralyevic, Serbian hero, was a son of the Serbian King, or Prince, Vukasin (d. 1371). Because he did not succeed his father he led a revolt against the new ruler. He was killed in battle in the service of the sultan about 1394. Subsequently stories of strength and wonder have gathered about his name. He lived 300 years, rode a horse 150 years old. He figures in Serbian epic poetry and also in epic poems of the Rumanians and Bulgarians. (See *Marko, der Konigssohn*, Vienna, 1883.) Holger Dansk—Olgier the Dane. Hero of romance. Identified with the Frankish warrior Autchor (Autgarius, Auctorius, Otgarius, Oggerius). With Desiderius, king of the Lombards, he marched against Rome in 772. In 773 he submitted to Charles of Verone, and finally entered the cloister of St. Foto at Meaux. In the Carolingian romances he is placed in the family of Doon de Mayence because of his revolt against Charlemagne. (See H.L. Ward, *Catalogue of Romances*, I, 604-610).

[5] Thompson, *The Folktale*, p. 308.

⁶Dates for stories are as given in E.L. Chandler, *Sources of Tales and Romances Written by Hawthorne before 1853 (Smith College Studies in Modern Languages*, VII, No. 4, July, 1926).

⁷To show another aspect of the university of these motifs, I am citing in footnotes the works of literature in which the themes occur. The legend of the Angel of Hadley has been used eight times—by Increase Mather in *Brief History of the War with the Indians* (1676); by Cooper in the *Wept of Wish-ton Wish* (1829); by Scott in *Peveril of the Peak* (1823); by James McHenry in *Spectre of the Forest* (1823); by Delia Salter Bacon in *Tales of the Puritans* (1831); by W.L. Stone in *Mercy Disborough: A Tale of the Witches* (1834); by R.L. Underhill in *The Witches: A Tale of New England* (1837); and by Southey in an unfinished poem called "Oliver Newman" (1829). See G. Harrison Orians, "The Angel of Hadley in Fiction," *American Literature*, IV, 257-69 (Nov. 1932); and S.A. Drake, *Book of New England Legends and Folklore* (Boston, 1894), p. 449.

⁸May Day originated in 242 B.C., in celebration of the famed courtesan Flora who gave her fortune to the people of Rome if they would yearly celebrate her memory in dancing, singing and drinking. After some years the Senate exalted Flora to be goddess of flowers, and May-Day festivities were regularly observed thereafter.

⁹See Wilhelm Mannhardt, *Walt- und Feldkulte* (Berlin, 1904), I, 160.

¹⁰See John Brand, *Popular Antiquities* (London, 1777), I, 241.

¹¹Since Hawthorne's time there have been other accounts of this colony: the two novels by John Lothrop Motley, *Morton's Hope* (1839) and *Merry Mount* (1849), and the opera *Merrymount* (1934), by Robert L. Stokes and Howard Hanson.

¹²See *Encyclopedia Britannica*, 14th ed.

¹³Legend likes to romanticize the story by adding details. B.A. Botkin, *A Treasury of New England Folklore* (New York, 1947) gives a version in which the grandmother escapes on that fateful night. She was crippled and could not leave the house. During the slide she rocked back and forth in her chair. C.M. Skinner's version, *Myths and Legends of Our Own Land* (Philadelphia, 1896), has a version apparently rewritten from Hawthorne. Here the young man has been wandering through the mountains enjoying the beauty.

¹⁴There is widespread belief that both animals and people have a sixth sense which makes them aware of coming doom. This accounts for the unusual nervousness in all the residents the night of the slide. Another old belief is that of the grandmother, who knows that her corpse will not rest easy in the grave unless it has been laid away with all clothes exactly right. Hence she wants someone to hold a mirror before the face of her corpse so that she can check her shroud.

¹⁵Note Hawthorne's references to fate: "The whole family rose up...as if about to welcome some one who belonged to them, and whose fate was linked with theirs." And "Is not the kindred of a common fate a closer tie than that of

birth?" The family cannot avoid fate though they have taken every precaution against it. Hawthorne shows the futility of ambition by showing that everybody is a pawn on the board of indifferent and unalterable Fate.

[16]A.T. Quiller-Couch, *Sleeping Beauty* (New York, 1910).

[17]"Endicott and the Red Cross" is usually printed in these collections. But it is more historical anecdote than folktale.

[18]Skinner, *Myths and Legends*, I, 112. Skinner's "folklore" must be viewed with dubiety. Collecting with a commercial market in mind, he sometimes includes rewritten versions of literary works.

[19]For fuller discussions on uses of veils, see T.F. Elworthy, *The Evil Eye* (London, 1895); S. Seligmann, *Der Böse Blick und Verwandtes* (Berlin, 1910); Schell, *Bergishe Sagen* (Elberfeld, 1922).

[20]See the *Col. of Maine Historical Society* (1891).

[21]See Bayley and Goodspeed (eds.), Dunlap's *A History of the Rise and Progress of the Arts of Design in the United States* (Boston, 1918).

[22]See Walter Pater, *Renaissance* (Mod. Library edit., p. 92).

[23]There have been many imitations of this novel: Marcel Schwab and Andre Gide in France, and in England Richard Garnett's *Twilight of the Gods* (1988) are perhaps the most famous. See Le Sage, *The Devil on Two Sticks* (London, 1927), Intro. by Arthur Symons.

[24]Cervantes was included in Hawthorne's great authors in his "Hall of Fantasy." Ernest Hemingway says, in *The Fifth Column* (1938; III.iv.): "In Madrid everybody knows everything often before occurrence of same."

[25]See Skinner, *op. cit.*, II, 222. For another version see S.A. Drake, *New England Legends and Folk-Lore* (Boston, 1894), p. 461.

[26]The Arabian version is undoubtedly based on this idea. See W.A. Clouston, *Tales From a Persian Garden* (London, 1890), p. 196.

[27]Such mountains are the Otherworld. They are hard to ascend. The Gods live on them. The idea appears in 14th century German Minneburg. (Alain Chartier's *Hospital d'Amours*, jeweled). The Grail castle in Arthurian Romance is on a mountain (underwater, but that does not matter); Mountain of Venus in Tannhauser legend; Faustus goes to the hill Caucasus, highest in Scythia. For a complete treatment of this subject of mountains, see Howard Rollin Patch, "Medieval Descriptions of the Otherworld," *PMLA*, XXXIII. (1918), 607-642.

[28]Melville's letter is dated August 13, 1852. See *New England Quarterly*, II (April 1929), 296-307.

[29]See Botkin, *Treasury of New England Folklore*, p. 110. There are no parallels between this story and other works of literature, but enough similarity between it and George Crabbe's "Parting Hour" exists to suggest possible borrowing. A.A. Procter's "Homeward Bound" parallels Tennyson's "Enoch 'Arden," but both came out too late to have influenced Hawthorne.

[30]For a full discussion of Pride see under "Lady Eleanore's Mantle" below. For the Token, see under "The Three-Fold Destiny."

[31]Thompson, *The Folktale*, p. 255.

[32]Lewis Spence, *Myths and Legends of Babylonia and Assyria* (London, 1916), p. 129.

[33]C.H. Tawney, *The Ocean of Story* (Translation of Somadeva's *Katha Sarit Sagera*, London, 1924-28), III, 253, n.l.

[34]Stith Thompson, *The Folktale Among the North American Indians* (Cambridge, Mass., 1929), pp. 284, n. 50a; 354; 330; 355 n. 279a.

[35]See T.W. Higginson, *Tales of the Enchanted Islands of the Atlantic* (New York, 1899).

[36]Skinner, *op. cit.*, I, 296.

[37]For a complete discussion of Creation Myths, see Thompson, *Folktales Among the Indians*, pp. 303ff.

[38]Tawney, *op. cit.*, IV, 145. References are made to a fountain that restored a fish to life, and one that made one of Alexander's daughters immortal.

[39]See Andrew Lang, *The Pink Fairy Book* (New York, 1897), for a story from *Cuentos Populars Catalans*, per lo Dr. D. Francisco de S. Maspous Y. Labros (Barcelona, 1885), which tells how three brothers and one sister need the Water of Life, a branch from the Tree of Beauty, and the Talking Bird to complete their happiness. In the Quest all are enchanted but the sister. She reaches the top of the mountain, gets the three articles, disenchants her brothers and many other persons, marries the Prince, and all live happily ever after.

[40]J.A. MacCulloch, *Mythology of All Races* (Boston, 1931) III, 120.

[41]See Jeremiah Curtin, *Myths and Folk-lore of Ireland* (Boston, 1890), p. 327.

[42]For a complete listing of types of marchen and their distribution see Stith Thompson, *The Types of the Folk-Tale, FFC* 74 (Helsinki, 1928).

[43]In literature the idea has not caught on. Dumas borrowed it for his *Memoirs of a Physician*, but that is the only example.

[44]Thompson, *The Folktale*, p. 139.

[45]Thompson, *The Folktale*, p. 262.

[46]The story of Belshazzar is an old Jewish legend. Belshazzar was a general of the Babylonian army, not the last king of that city, as reported in the *Book of Daniel*.

[47]This affair took place in Philadelphia, and the similarity is only coincidental or hinted at.

[48]In many beliefs power is received from pictures by a person's kissing or otherwise coming in contact with them. In some legends, pictures turn pale and die as the original dies. In Cloister Marie Kirkheim in Reis, the picture of the Virgin Mary cries whenever a high abbess dies. People claim they have witnessed her crying. See Sabine Baring-Gould, *Lives of the Saints* (Edinburgh,

1914); C. Grant Loomis, *White Magic* (Cambridge, Mass., 1948); Anton Birlinger, *Volksthümliches aus Schwaben* (Freiburg, 1861). See also O.W. Holmes, *The Guardian Angel* (1868), in which a portrait issues a strong influence on a person.

[49]Thompson, *Folktales Among the Indians*, p. 357 n. 287 i.

[50]Botkin, *New England Folklore*, p. 347. In literature there are at least two parallels: Wilde's *Picture of Dorian Gray*, and Gogol's *The Portrait*.

[51]Examples of Pride being the worst sin are almost too numerous in literature to itemize. It is in Dante, Milton, Spenser, Edwards, to mention only four. For Continental works treating Pride, see *MLN* XXXIV, p. 16. See also the *Oxford Dictionary of Proverbs*.

[52]For further treatment of Pride see the following: *FFC* LXXIV, 84, 141, 126, 136; W.H.D. Rouse, *The Talking Thrush* (London, 1899), p. 156; J. Jacobs, *Indian Fairy Tales* (New York, n.d.), P. 160; F.A. Steele, *Tales of the Punjab*, p. 144.

[53]C.M. Skinner, *American Myths and Legends* (Philadelphia, 1903), II, 72. For another version see II, 134.

[54]Thompson, *Folktales Among the Indians*, p. 394.

[55]The Prince is beautified by being boiled in a kettle until all the flesh is off his skeleton. The bones are then rearranged, a girl jumps over them, and the man is alive again.

Billy Budd:
Gospel of Democracy

Ray B. Browne

That *Billy Budd, Foretopman* must be given on one level a political interpretation is generally recognized. Among other philosophical-political messages, critics see the "doctrine of worldly accommodation" in action,[1] the "sacrifice of self to the historical moment,"[2] exemplification of the "utilitarian principle of social expediency,"[3] and evidence that a "judicious combination of instinct and reason can...eventually [produce] a new set of objective conditions which require less repressive forms for man's governance."[4]

Such critics generally agree that in the struggle between Claggart and Budd Captain Vere stands ground between the two, forced by the power of evil to destroy that which he loves, a Lincolnesque figure of great tragic proportions: the spokesman for Melville. Other critics, however, find in Melville's treatment of Vere an irony which turns all forms of "acceptance" into "resistance," and makes of the Captain a caricature of what he appears to be.[5] These readers are, it seems to me, much nearer Melville's meaning. Instead of being the voice of the author, Vere is in fact Melville's antagonist.[6]

On a strictly political level *Billy Budd* is a search for the best form of government—autocratic vs democratic—a question on which Melville worried all of his mature life and on which he had especially agonized during the writing of *Clarel*. On this level, as Noone has shown, Claggart can be equated with the Hobbesian primitive man and Budd with the Rousseauvian "noble savage," with Vere as a spokesman or apologist for and manipulator of Hobbesian despotism as compromise. But Melville had more immediate political references. As he makes abundantly clear, his concern is with reform and liberalism (as illustrated in the original impulse of the French Revolution, before its excesses) and with its archenemy, status quo and conservatism (as exemplified in the British government). Melville naturally chose as

Reprinted from *Nineteenth-Century Fiction*, March, 1962, pp. 321-337. Used by permission.

223

spokesman for these opposing ideologies those authors and their books that were contemporary with the setting of the story: Edmund Burke and his *Reflections on the Revolution in France* (1790); and Thomas Paine and his answer in the *Rights of Man*, Part I (1791) and Part II (1792). For around these authors and works had generally polarized the basic views in the struggle between conservatism and liberalism, political expediency and principle, down to Melville's day. At that time, in fact, the battle was especially violent.

The novel becomes, then, a study in the conflict between these opposing ideologies. In this context the struggle is not between Claggart and Budd, but between Captain Vere as spokesman and apologist for authority (with Claggart serving only as prime mover) and Billy, who is on this level, Melville takes great pains to point out, the common, ordinary sailor. Billy is, in other words, the voice of the people in their insistence on their rights. Vere is the opponent of these rights. He represents Edmund Burke. In his conflict with and ultimate triumph over Vere, Melville uses two voices, that of Billy the common sailor, and his own as author, both of which—or the sum total of which—represent Thomas Paine.

My thesis is, then, that the novel instead of demonstrating the irresistible triumph of political evil, of conservatism, insists on the opposite; that the Veres (and Claggarts) prevail only in the short run, never in the long; that though the Budds seem to lose and are even destroyed personally, they ultimately conquer, not in themselves but in the political philosophy and in the people they represent. In the struggle for power Melville casts his hope with the people. They will outlast all other persons. And they will inevitably inherit the earth.

In this study five aspects of the novel must be considered: 1) the form; 2) the role of Vere; 3) the relationship of this work to Burke and Paine and their political philosophies, and the relevance of this controversy in Melville's time; 4) the role of Billy as common sailor; 5) the use of songs to strengthen the common-man theme. We will correlate these five as we work through the novel.

In *Billy Budd* form is of paramount importance. Though Melville wrote several digressions here, as in his other works, he included no irrelevancies. The Preface is therefore significant: "The year 1797, the year of this narrative belongs to a period which as every thinker now feels, involved a crisis for Christendom not exceeded in its undetermined momentousness at the time by any other era whereof there is record."[7] The key word here is *now*: that is, in Melville's America the conflict between conservatism and liberalism, it was generally agreed, involved a momentous crisis.

The assumption that Melville was anchoring his novel on contemporary political philosophy is not far-fetched. Such a thinker and worrier as he was could hardly have been alive in the time and not be aware of the currents and cross-currents of political upheaval around him. Henry George's *Progress and Poverty*, for example, published in 1879, was creating great agitation among both conservatives and liberals. Edward Bellamy's *Looking Backward*, with its picture of a communistic-socialistic state, came from the press while Melville was working on his novel. Economically and politically the West was rebelling against the East and the rich. Anarchists, foreign and domestic, were terrifying the land with their potential threat.

Thomas Paine was also very much in the air. Two books on him had recently appeared.[8] Elihu B. Washburn, the U.S. Minister to France, had published in 1880 in *Scribner's Magazine* his study of Paine and the French Revolution. The firebrand Robert Ingersoll had recently (1879) brought out his "Vindication of Thomas Paine," and his "Mistakes" had been corrected by James B. McClure (1880). Ingersoll's "atheism," everybody knew, derived from Voltaire and Paine. The biggest bombshell of all had been Theodore Roosevelt's denomination (1887) of Paine as "the filthy little atheist," which words cost him in subsequent years "many moments of explanation and vexation."[9] The 151st anniversary of the birth of Paine was commemorated in Chicago in 1888. The centennial of the publication of Paine's *Rights*, as well as of Burke's *Reflections*, came as Melville was writing his novel.

Burke, too, was on the minds of Americans, and was influential. Increasingly from 1850 to the end of the century he "became the symbol of wise and heroic statesmanship" in America, as well as in England. His love of rhetoric and his pronouncements on the sublime had in the past influenced and still affected American oratory and literature. Men of letters such as Holmes and Emerson, although narrowly read in political classics, never tired of praising Burke.[10] His works had recently been published twice in Boston (1861-1871, 1881).

The Gilded Age was, then, quite conscious of and concerned with the writings and philosophies of Paine and Burke.

Melville, too, was aware of these two antagonists before he discussed them in this particular work. His "Fragments from a Writing Desk," Sealts says, for example, "imply his youthful familiarity" with Burke. He also apparently owned *The Philosophical Inquiry into the Origin of our Ideas on the Sublime and Beautiful.*[11] But more important evidence is to be found in *Clarel*, Melville's last major work before *Billy Budd*, which he probably meditated on after his return from the Mediterranean in 1857 and began actively to write in 1870. A philosophical poem probing the conflict between "heart" and "head," it also vividly reflects Melville's interest in politics, in the French Revolution, and in Thomas Paine. The doors of the walls around Jerusalem, for example, "as dingy were / As Bastille gates."[12] Are "Mammon and Democracy" inseparably linked? he asks (Part II, canto V). The "holy and right reverend" abbot denounces change and those people who espouse it as being worse than Paine. But the abbot is "stone-blind and old" and longs to retain "that toy, / Dear to the old— authority" (Part III, canto XXIII). Even more revealing is a conversation between Ungar, the part-Indian American, and Derwent and Rolfe, with Vine and Clarel listening in. Ungar, thoroughly disillusioned with materialistic America, writes off the country as a total loss: without the Past, with no regard for its value, the New World will end up in the "Dark Ages of Democracy." Derwent, in answering, bases his hope for America's future on reform:

> Through all methinks I see
> The object clear: belief revised,
> *Men liberated—equalised*
> *In happiness.*
>   …
> *…True reform goes on*
> *By nature; doing, never done.*
> Mark the advance: creeds drop the hate;
> *Events still liberalised the state.*

Even Ungar admits that there was justice initially in the French Revolution:

> The mob,
> The Paris mob of 'Eighty-nine,
> Haggard and bleeding, with a throb
> Burst the long Tuileries. In shrine
> Of chapel there, they saw the Cross
> And Him thereon. Ah, bleeding Man,
> *The people's friend*, thou bled'st for us
> Who here bleed, too!
>   (Part IV, cantos XX-XXI; emphasis mine)

Though *Clarel* is a series of questions without answers, it vividly reveals Melville's continued interest in the best government for man.

In *Billy Budd* the second sentence carries on Melville's purpose of highlighting the political significance: "The opening proposition made by the Spirit of that Age involved the rectification of the Old World's hereditary wrongs" (p. 131). This "Spirit" is the same as that which motivated the *Rights of Man*, Part I, which had as its main purpose disproving Burke's contention that Englishmen in 1688 had entered into an agreement that bound them and their descendants to a particular form of government "forever." This eternal maintenance of status quo is for Melville the "Old World's hereditary wrongs." He points out that the spirit of rectification "became a wrongdoer" in the French Revolution when under the Directory and Napoleon it became "more oppressive than the king['s]" rule. But the end result of this paroxysm, although temporarily aborted, was good, was "a political advance along nearly the whole line for Europeans," or as a variant version read, "along the whole line for man." Melville further particularized that from the spirit of the Revolution came the successful resistance to "real abuses" in the English navy at Spithead and Nore, and their eventual amelioration.

Melville was not here condemning this "Spirit of that Age." He was against tyranny of either the left or the right. But it was *excesses* he opposed, not change. The Great Mutiny was a "demonstration more menacing to England than the contemporary manifestoes and conquering and proselyting armies of the French Directory" (p. 151). In the Nore Mutiny *"Reasonable* discontent...had been ignited into irrational combustion" (p. 151, emphasis mine), which could have been prevented had the English been willing to grant reasonable corrections to the status quo. In other words, Melville saw the alternatives as change or chaos.

Even more unequivocally political was Melville's conclusion about these two mutinies. "Final suppression...there was," he said, then added a moment later: "To some extent the Nore Mutiny may be regarded as analogous to the distempering irruption of contagious fever in a frame constitutionally sound, and which anon throws it off" (p. 153). Here is dramatically mirrored one of the great arguments between Burke and Paine. Burke insisted that the English had a constitution tacitly recognized by all—and followed by the king and the lawmakers. But Paine claimed that there was no English Constitution—no inviolable document—unless it could be seen in writing. The French, on the contrary, had a Constitution. This written agreement guaranteed protection of the people. It assured soundness to the body politic. Melville, then, was agreeing with Paine that within the framework of a sound constitution mankind could be assured of progress, but without such a guarantee nothing could be certain.

The political theme of the novel continues in the first chapter, the beginning of the narrative, which is a general statement focusing on the Handsome Sailor. This Handsome Sailor is the universal hero type, the savior. Bastard that he is—and apparently of "noble" parentage—Billy stands with other heroes of uncertain paternity like King Arthur, Roland, Abraham Lincoln,[13] Galahad, Christ, and many others—as well as Mortmain in *Clarel*, and others in Melville's later works. Thus the superhuman Billy and Claggart—who is also a bastard of apparent noble descent—are paired off as antagonists in an elemental struggle. Billy is not therefore in any wise the illegitimate son of Captain Vere, although Melville points out that as far as their ages are concerned he might have been. But there is grim irony in that "might have been." Vere is sterile, incapable of producing anything, even his own kind. A loner in life, unmarried, uninterested in women, he dies with no progeny and no reputation, in fact nameless.

But Billy is also a political figure. He is, as Melville says, primarily the Handsome Sailor "of the military and merchant navies" (p. 133). He is, in other words, the navy man's idealization of the sailor pictured in sea songs, and in navy life as Melville would have remembered it from his own days on the sea. Though this sailor is "some superior figure of their own class," he is *of their own class*. Furthermore he is more than the conventional, white man's Christ. He is every race's savior—black, white and in between. In fact the black Handsome Sailor is more remarkable than the white, and more nearly represents mankind of the Revolution, as Melville's mention of Anacharsis Cloots demonstrates: Cloots appeared at the Bar of the French Assembly at the head of thirty-six foreigners of all colors and for this "embassy of the human race"[14] declared that the world insisted on the Rights of Man and of the Citizen.

Billy, like other saviors, stands forth with his disciples, the sailors, clustered around him on the beach—on land, that is. Here we have a joining of the land and sea, which, as we shall see, develops into an important theme in the novel.

Another political point worthy of notice is that Billy is taken from a merchant vessel. Why not some other kind of ship? Or why is he not simply impressed while on shore? Because Melville is here echoing the philosophy of Thomas Paine, who felt that commerce is the proper business between nations: people who trade do not fight; in this commercial intercourse there is great exchange of ideas from which proper alterations in political and social structure will grow.[15]

Not content with having drawn a close parallel with the Burke-Paine controversy, Melville actually labors his point by spending several sentences stating that Captain Graveling named his merchantman *Rights of Man* in honor of Paine, "whose book in rejoinder to Burke's arraignment of the French Revolution had been published for some time and had gone everywhere." This Captain, Melville adds, was in company with "Stephen Girard of Philadelphia, whose sympathies, alike with his native land and its liberal philosophers, he evinced by naming his ships after Voltaire, Diderot, and so forth" (p. 141).

The political aspect of the novel is continued as Billy is selected from the crew of the merchantman to be taken aboard the man-of-war. Billy's fellow sailors, who have known what their rights are and have enjoyed them, all "turned a surprised glance of silent reproach" at him (p. 137) for leaving his ship without resistance. They cannot understand his not fighting for his rights. Furthermore, as Lieutenant Ratcliffe and his crew—with Billy—are leaving the *Rights of Man* and passing under the stern, "officers and oarsmen were noting—some bitterly and others with a grin—the name emblazoned there" (p. 142). Here is a split reaction to Paine. Some of these sailors have not enjoyed their rights, but they know that they have been deprived of them, and are bitter; others, however, forswear their natural rights easily, and are in fact merely amused by hints—or promises—of them. These people ally themselves with the lieutenant—one of the robots of the King and of Established Authority—who "with difficulty" represses a smile when Billy salutes his former ship. But all is not well with Authority on board the *Indomitable* that the small boat returns to. Though "very little would have suggested to an ordinary observer that the Great Mutiny was a recent event," the key words here are *very little* and *ordinary observer*. Rebellion has not been strangled forever. The common man has not been given his rights. But Democracy will continue to fight for its deserts.

The irony in the portrait of Vere which Melville soon presents proves the author's hostility to him. It also makes the Captain blood brother to Burke. Vere does not owe *all* his advancement to his "influences." Neither did Burke; he was very capable, but his rise resulted from his alliance with the Rockingham Whigs, and throughout life he had to cling to powerful political leaders. Vere and Burke are similar intellectually. Vere's "bias was towards those books to which every serious mind of superior order *occupying any active post of authority in the world*, naturally inclines; books treating of *actual men and events* no matter of what era—history, biography and unconventional writers, who, free from cant and convention, like Montaigne, honestly and in the spirit of common sense *philosophize upon realities*" (emphasis mine). And

His settled convictions were as a dyke against those invading waters of novel opinion social political and otherwise, which carried away as in a torrent no few minds in those days, minds not by nature inferior to his own (p. 164).

Burke's political opinions, even when he was justifying the American Revolution, were always practical, expedient. Like Vere, again, he had grown more and more "intellectual" through the years, profoundly learned and superb as a reasoner. But as man in authority, or supporting authority, he became more and more politically illiberal. He would entertain only those notions which supported his own point of view, would read only those books which confirmed his feeling that he was correct.

Burke was in Melville's mind when he said the following of Vere:

While other members of that aristocracy...were incensed at the innovators mainly because their theories were inimical to the privileged classes, not alone Captain Vere disinterestedly opposed them because they seemed to him incapable of embodiment in lasting institutions, but at war with the peace of the world and the true welfare of mankind (p. 164).

Burke, if narrow and conservative, was the sincerest man alive. He always felt that his views were held only in the best interests of mankind.

There is another strong similarity between Burke and Vere. The former's companions in Commons, like the latter's fellow officers, found him, in Melville's words about Vere, "lacking in companionable quality, a dry and bookish gentleman," rather "pedantic." Again, it could be said of Burke, as it was said of Vere, he was likely to "cite some historic character or incident of antiquity," some "remote allusion" (p. 165) without bothering to remember that most of his auditors were his inferiors in knowledge. So boring did Burke become, in fact, that he was called the "Dinner Bell": when he started to speak many of the members of Commons went to dinner.[16]

More of Melville's political slant is seen in his effort to explain why Billy is completely innocent. He does not know of evil intuitively. But, then, Melville points out, "as a class, sailors are in character a juvenile race....Every sailor, too, is accustomed to obey orders without debating them; *his life* afloat *is externally ruled for him*" (p. 206; emphasis mine). In thus pointing out the universal naivete of sailors Melville is echoing the usual belief[17] of the time, but his real purpose is to contrast sailors with landsmen. The common sailor, he says, is in every way less prepared to combat life than is the common landsman. "The sailor is frankness, the landsman is finesse. Life is not a game with the sailor, demanding the long head" (p. 206), as it is with his counterpart on land. Thus he is easily imposed upon and advantage taken of him. What is the cure for this gullibility? asks Melville: "promiscuous commerce with mankind," which will sophisticate him.

This re-introduction of the comparison of sea men with land men here is extremely important in the development of Melville's political purpose. Both kinds together make up the common man; only when both—*all men*—live together are they complete and prepared to combat evil, especially political evil. The pen is Melville's, but the sentiments are Tom Paine's.[18]

All the above is, of course, background to the drama of the accusation of Billy, the consequences and the *denouement*. In this drama the action is rapid, the air electric. The circumstances surrounding the affair must be remembered.

The climax begins in a supercharged atmosphere. Vere's ship has just encountered a frigate, a sure prize, but the smaller ship has outrun the *Indomitable*. Then "ere the excitement incident thereto had altogether waned away" (p. 213), Claggart, choosing his moment wisely, approaches the Captain with his suspicions of Budd. Vere, "absorbed in his reflections" is caught off guard and off balance; he does not ever regain his equilibrium. Through the next few minutes the tension is intensified. Vere gets more taut, more nervous, less reliable. Claggart, on the contrary, remains always cold and calculating. After Claggart is killed, Vere's mind and nerve crack. He tries to be the strict "military disciplinarian" but cannot. He becomes more and more excited. His actions thereafter are always erratic. Melville spends three paragraphs analyzing the Captain to determine if he is truly mad. The Surgeon surely thinks he is. Melville, speaking in his own person, implies that he is. In this breakup of Vere Melville invalidates the Captain's credentials as a political philosopher. Vere has become, in fact, capable of great evil, of much destructiveness.

In his madness Vere can think only of self-protection. He wants to "guard as much as possible against publicity" by "confining all knowledge [of the event]to the place where the homicide had occurred" (p. 235). Does Melville approve of this action by Vere? Hardly! In being so secretive Vere "may or may not have erred," but surely "there lurked some resemblance" to the tyrannical policies "which have occurred more than once in the capital founded by Peter the Barbarian" (p. 235). In this denial of news to the general public—and its being equated with tyranny—there lie general political overtones and a striking similarity to the efforts of the British Government to strangle the *Rights of Man* by confiscation of the book and prosecution of the author.

The trial scene further highlights the political overtones. Throughout it Vere demonstrates his hatred of democracy. The Captain of the marines was reluctantly appointed to the drumhead court because he was too much a man of "heart" rather than of "head." Furthermore Vere constantly condescends to the court as "men not intellectually mature." But even more important, Melville, speaking in his own person, says, "Similar impatience as to talking is perhaps one reason that deters some minds from addressing any popular assemblies" (p. 243)—in other words, impatience with the speed with which the common people learn, and therefore contempt for their intelligence and for their rights. Vere's real feelings burst forth a few moments later when the junior lieutenant asks if the court might not "convict and yet mitigate the penalty?" Vere answers: "The people (meaning the ship's company [and thus the common man in general]) have native sense." They will "ruminate," will think the clemency "pusillanimous," will believe that Authority is "afraid of them—afraid of practicing a lawful rigor singularly demanded at this juncture.... You see then, whither prompted by duty and the law I steadfastly drive" (p. 248). Melville could hardly have drawn a more precise picture of Burke even if he had called the Captain by Burke's name.

With Vere's statement to the sailors about the coming execution of Billy, Melville begins to emphasize the theme which has been present though somewhat subdued all along: the overriding significance of the reaction of the common man. To their Captain's announcement the sailors listened "in a dumbness like that of a seated congregation of believers in hell listening to the clergyman's announcement of his Calvinistic text" ("Jonathan Edwards" was written in the margin of the text). As Vere ended "A confused murmur went up. It began to wax." It might have grown into mutiny then had it not been quelled by the boatswain's whistle. The importance of the passage lies in the fact that the people were beginning to react strongly to events. Just as most people had earlier found intolerable Edwards' unyielding doctrine of predestination and had forced it to be modified, so most were finding unbearable the iron-bound conservatism—and despotism—of Vere (and Burke) and were beginning to insist that it be altered.

At the actual hanging the people's incipient rebellion begins to run at a higher tide. Though they echo Billy's "conventional felon's benediction" ("God bless Captain Vere!"[19]) they do not mean it. At the moment the sailors say these words, "Billy alone must have been in their hearts, even as he was in their eyes" (p. 265).

The absolute silence attending the hanging is followed almost immediately by a murmur which is scarcely audible at the beginning but which gains volume until it clearly emanates from the sailors on the deck. Melville continues, meaningfully: "Being inarticulate, it was dubious in significance further than it seemed to indicate some capricious revulsion of thought or feeling such as mobs ashore are liable to in the present instance possibly implying a sullen revocation on the men's part of their involuntary echoing of Billy's benediction" (p. 269). Melville's political message here is that the masses are inarticulate, and therefore their intentions and actions are often misunderstood, their compliance misread. But he ties together the commoners of the sea and of the land and indicates that this total humanity condemns both the actions of the captains of the world and their own silent allowance of these actions.

The political theme continues as Vere, the "martinet" as the author suggests he is, has the men beat to quarters an hour early to get the decks cleared. "With mankind," Vere felt, "forms, measured forms are everything; and that is the real import couched in the story of Orpheus with his lyre spell-binding the wild denizens of the woods." On which statement Melville editorializes: "And this he once applied to the disruption of forms going on across the Channel and the consequences thereof (p. 272). To Vere, then, the sailors under his command (and all people) were no more than the wild beasts. Only so unthinking a man as he could equate himself with Orpheus. But he is just mad enough to think that he can control the beasts with forms. Only so blind a man as Vere could insist that the French Revolution was *only* a breaking up of forms.

In ending the novel Melville says that it should terminate with the death of Billy, but "Truth uncompromisingly told will always have its ragged edges" (p. 274), and it is truth he is seeking. He writes three more chapters. The order in which they are presented is important.

In the first Melville switches to France and tells how the ship *St. Louis* was rechristened *Atheiste*. But his words must be carefully noted. He does not condemn the French. Although this renaming apparently indicated a nasty turn from religion to atheism, the new name was the "aptest" that was "ever given to a warship," because it is applicable to all war, and it is war that Melville condemns. In having this French ship destroy the British captain, the author is predicting the fate of all men like Vere (and Burke) and those countries whose political philosophy such men reflect.

Furthermore, Vere's death is no glorious Nelson's demise, and he was no Nelson; he was in fact the exact opposite. Necessarily then his death is ignominious. He is shot by a commoner (a marine no doubt) from the port-hole of the enemy's main cabin. Then, if this is not sufficient ignominy, he is carried below and laid with the wounded commoners. After his ship has prevailed over the Frenchman he is put ashore at Gibraltar. Thus, rock unto rock.

On the rock, when Vere has been denuded of his own character by drugs, when these drugs have allowed the "subtler element in man" to speak, then and only then does he begin to think about Billy, and he calls his name twice. Melville is not precise whether Vere's words indicate remorse. But the Captain's motivation is of no consequence. These words are retold to the Captain of the marines, the man on the drumhead court who was most understanding of and sympathetic toward Billy. He has outlasted Vere. This kind of man, Melville is saying, always outlasts the Vere kind.

The death of Vere is his complete dissolution and dismissal. Throughout the story Melville has shown that Vere and his kind of people are interested only in facts; they read newspapers, official reports, and men like Montaigne, who "free from cant...in the spirit of common sense philosophize upon realities." In the official report of the case, the last chapter but one in the book, Melville gives a "factual" and "true" report. It is, of course, a gross misstatement of truth. It reports that Budd was actually guilty, that Claggart was an honorable and worthy individual. But, most important, Vere is referred to only in the generalized term "the Captain." His personality has been completely lost. In the chronicle of human events, Melville is saying, such a man does not deserve even being named.

The novel ends, as a book with such a message had to end, with the common sailors. These men preserve the chips of the spar on which Billy has hanged. There was something sacred about it. Such is the treatment accorded all heroes and saviors by such people. But even more important is the ballad which concludes the work. Though this song is written in the first person, significantly it was composed by other "tarry hands" "among the shipboard crew" than Billy's (p. 279). The "I" in the song is more the sailor-author than it is Billy personally. The singer, for example, thinks about the "ear-drop I gave to Bristol Molly." But Billy was surely as innocent of women as Christ and other heroes were. This is merely a stock statement in sailor songs. In other words, Billy is no longer an individual. He has been universalized. He is Every Sailor. A variant reading of this ballad points this up even more vividly:

> In a queerish dream here I had afore(?)
> A queerish dream of days no more.—
> A general number from every shore
> Countrymen, yes and Moor and Swede,
> Christian Pagan Cannibal breed (p. 283, n).

There could be little more thorough mixing of the peoples of the world than here described: black and white and in-between; religious, irreligious and indifferent. The novel has now returned to the Handsome Sailor—the universal savior—of the beginning, this time in a song.

Melville makes his point clear. There are no songs about Vere; none about Claggart. The song is not actually about Billy personally, but about the type of sailor he represents. He is not an unusual sailor. He is not being hanged unjustly. Rather, very much the average sailor under the circumstances, he is hungry and frightened; and once hanged he is slipped under the water in the usual way—the typical sailor of Dibdin's songs. This conclusion should be compared with a statement (made by Derwent) in *Clarel*:

> Suppose an instituted creed
> (Or truth or fable) should indeed
> To ashes fall; the spirit exhales,
> But reinfunds in active forms:
> Verse, *popular verse*, it charms or warms—
> Belies philosophy's flattened sails—
> Tinctures the very book, perchance,
> Which claims arrest of its advance
> (Part III, canto XXI; emphasis mine).

The political "truth uncompromisingly told" of *Billy Budd*—the real climax—is this ballad, this "popular verse": not the death of Billy, not even the dissolution of Vere. The subject of the novel is the common sailor. Melville has made it clear that this common sailor is inseparably attached to the common landsman—together comprising "the people" throughout the world. The novel demonstrates that "the people" have outlasted all the others and everything else in the book. Here, then, is Melville's reply to the Teddy Roosevelts of his age who cursed Tom Paine. Here is Melville's comment on the Conservative-Liberal controversy of his day and of all times. Here is his resounding affirmation of belief in the ultimate triumph of the Rights of Man and of democracy.

This interpretation is vital to an understanding of Melville's final political philosophy. The anxieties and doubtful hopes—the questions— of *Clarel*, evidenced in the quotes above, have been resolved in new affirmativeness and optimism. His voice in this last work is not much different from what it was when he wrote Hawthorne of his "ruthless democracy," of his asserting "unconditional democracy in all things"[20]; nor from what it was in *White-Jacket* when he thundered against flogging "in the name of immortal manhood." Neither is it far from the sentiment of his motto—"Keep true to the dreams of thy youth"—which was pasted to the inside of the writing box on which he composed *Billy Budd*. But it is far indeed from "acceptance." The Melville who had much earlier come to believe in personal annihilation after death had finally come to this attestation of the power and future of democracy, of hope in "immortal manhood."

Notes

[1] Merlin Bowen, *The Long Encounter: Self and Experience in the Writings of Herman Melville* (Chicago, 1960), p. 215.

[2] Milton R. Stern, *The Fine Hammered Steel of Herman Melville* (Urbana, 1957), p. 207.

[3] Wendell Glick, "Expediency and Absolute Morality in *Billy Budd*," *PMLA*, LXVIII (1953), 104.

[4] John B. Noone, Jr., "*Billy Budd*: Two Concepts of Nature," *American Literature*, XXIX (Nov., 1957), 262. See also Ray B. West, Jr., "Primitivism in Melville," *Prairie Schooner*, XXX (1956), 369-385.

[5] Paul Withim, "*Billy Budd*: Testament of Resistance," *Modern Language Quarterly*, XX (1959), 115-127. See this article for a summary of arguments about "acceptance," "resistance," and irony. Though I agree with these findings as far as they go, I think the author stopped far short of their possibilities.

[6] A late identification of Vere with Melville is in R.H. Fogle, "*Billy Budd*: The Order of the Fall," *NCF*, XV (Dec., 1960), 189-205. His argument is not convincing.

[7] F. Farron Freeman, ed. *Melville's "Billy Budd"* (Cambridge, Mass., 1948), p. 131. Hereafter all quotes are from this text and are given in the body of the paper.

[8] John E. Remsburg, *Thomas Paine, The Apostle of Religious and Political Liberty* (Boston, 1880); M.J. Savage, *Thomas Paine: Some Lessons from his Life* (Boston, 1883).

[9] Roosevelt's words were in his life of Gouverneur Morris (Nat. Ed. VII, 421-422). Quoted in E.E. Morison, et al., The Letters of Theodore Roosevelt (Cambridge, Mass., 1951), II, 1158, with the above comment.

[10] Quoted in Naomi Johnson Townsend, "Edmund Burke; Reputation and Bibliography, 1850-1954" (unpublished dissertation, Univ. of Pittsburgh, 1955), p. 55. Melville's attitude toward Holmes was perhaps mixed, but surely he condemned Holmes' touting everything European as being superior to anything American, what Melville thought was Bostonian flunkeyism. See Leon Howard, *Herman Melville, A Biography* (Berkeley and Los Angeles, 1951), p. 158. Though Melville admired some qualities of Emerson, he sorrowed deeply over others, for example, over Emerson's contempt for the masses. William Alger's *The Solitudes of Nature and Man* (1867) quoted Emerson on the subject: "enormous populations, like moving cheese," "the guano-races of mankind," "masses! the calamity is the masses." In his own copy of this book Melville

underscored these lines and added, "These expressions attributed to the 'kindly Emerson' are somewhat different from the words of Christ to the multitude on the Mount.—Abhor pride, abhor malignity, but not grief and poverty, and the natural vices these generate." Quoted in F.O. Matthiessen, *American Renaissance* (New York, 1949), pp. 401-402.

¹¹Merton M. Sealts, Jr., "Melville's Reading," *Harvard Library Bulletin*, II (1848), 147, 390.

¹²*Clarel, A Poem and Pilgrimage in the Holy Land* (London, 1924), I, 31 (Part I, canto VII); hereafter all references are to this edition, given by part and canto in text of paper.

¹³In mythology and folklore the hero always has certain characteristics: 1) he has a supernatural birth or is illegitimate (Billy is the latter; so is Claggart; but there is something supernatural in their births); 2) he is physically and mentally precocious or outstanding (Billy is the former; Claggart the latter); 3) something about his appearance and behavior is uncommon (Billy is extraordinarily handsome, exceptionally good; Claggart is unusually pale, etc.); 4) often there is highlighted a contest between him and his arch antagonist (occurs in this novel); 5) there is something unusual in his death—convulsions of nature, or some kind of acknowledgement by nature of the hero's passing (so it is in this novel). For the multiple paternity of Lincoln see "The Many-Sired Lincoln," by J.G. de Roulhac Hamilton, *American Mercury* (June, 1925), pp. 129-135. (thirteen men are given as his father).

¹⁴*The Encyclopedia Britannica* (11th ed., New York, 1910), V-VI, 556. He became known as, and called himself, "the orator of the human race."

¹⁵Philip S. Foner, ed. *The Complete Writings of Thomas Paine* (New York, 1945). In *Rights*, Part I (Foner, I, 343) Paine said: "Agriculture, commerce, manufactures...by which the prosperity of nations is best promoted, require a different system of government...than what might have been required in the former condition of the world" In Part II (Foner, I, 400) he was even more extensive and explicit: "I have been an advocate for commerce, because I am a friend to its effects. It is a pacific system, operating to unite mankind by rendering nations, as well as individuals, useful to each other." "If commerce were permitted to act to the universal extent it is capable of, it would extirpate the system of war, and produce a revolution in the uncivilized state of government."

¹⁶Thomas H.D. Mahoney, *Edmund Burke and Ireland* (Cambridge, Mass., 1960), p. 139.

¹⁷In the search for sources of and parallels to *Billy Budd*, not nearly enough attention has been paid to the numerous sailor songs of the time, especially to those of Charles Dibdin. Melville knew many of them, more than were in the only book containing Dibdin's songs that he is known to have consulted, Charles McKay's *Songs of England*. For example, two of the songs in *White-*

Jacket—"True English Sailor" and the one sung to the tune "The King, God Bless Him"—which Melville calls Dibdin's, and which are his, are not in McKay. Melville, therefore, must have known another collection of Dibdin's songs. And Melville drew heavily from these songs for the portraits of Billy and Claggart, and—by inverting Dibdin's extreme Tory sentiments—to develop his final political philosophy in the song which concludes the novel. Concerning the universal naivete of sailors, one of Dibdin's pieces (*Sea Songs*, 3rd ed., London, 1852, p. 102), "The Sailor's Maxim," contains the following lines:

> Of us tars 'tis reported again and again,
> That we sail round the world, yet know nothing of men;
> And, if this assertion is made with the view
> To prove sailors know naught of men's follies, 'tis true.
>
> ...
>
> How should Jack practise treachery, disguise, or foul art,
> In whose honest face you may read his fair heart:
> Of that maxim still ready example to give,
> Better death earn'd with honor than ignobly to live.

See further note 19 below.

[18]For example, freedom for man "takes ground on every character and condition that appertains to man, and blends the individual, the nation, and the world." "Whatever the form or constitution of government may be, it ought to have no other object than the general [sic] happiness. When, instead of this, it operates to create and increase wretchedness in any of the parts of society, it is on a wrong system, and reformation is necessary" (Rights, II, Foner I, 398).

[19]Another of Dibdin's songs (*Sea Songs*, 3rd ed., 1852, pp. 157-158) demonstrates further the conventionality of this kind of statement, and the degree to which Melville uses the songs of the common man to develop his political thesis. Entitled "Ben Block" this piece tells of a man sent to sea by his father, leaving behind his sweetheart Kate. A false friend reports that Kate is untrue, and the sailor commits suicide, as the last stanza chronicles:

> Tho sure from this cankerous elf
> The venom accomplish'd its end:
> Ben, all truth and honor itself,
> Suspected no fraud of his friend.
> On the yardarm while suspended in air,
> A loose to his sorrows he gave–
> "Take thy wise," he cried, "false, cruel fair!"
> And plunged in a watery grave.

[20]For this famous letter, see *The Letters of Herman Melville*, ed. Merrell R. Davis and William H. Gilman (New Haven, 1960), pp. 126-131.

Popular Culture:
Notes Toward a Definition

Ray B. Browne

"Popular Culture" is an indistinct term whose edges blur into imprecision. Scarcely any two commentators who try to define it agree in all aspects of what popular culture really is. Most critics, in fact, do not attempt to define it; instead, after distinguishing between it and the mass media, and between it and "high" culture, most assume that everybody knows that whatever is widely disseminated and experienced is "popular culture."

Some observers divide the total culture of a people into "minority" and "majority" categories. Other observers classify culture into High-Cult, Mid-Cult and Low-Cult, or High-Brow, Mid-Brow and Low-Brow, leaving out, apparently, the level that would perhaps be called Folk-Cult or Folk-Brow, though Folk culture is now taking on, even among the severest critics of popular culture a high class and achievement unique unto itself. Most of the discriminating observers agree, in fact, that there are perhaps actually four areas of culture: Elite, Popular, Mass and Folk, with the understanding that none is a discrete unity standing apart and unaffected by the others.

One reason for the lack of a precise definition is that the serious study of "popular culture" has been neglected in American colleges and universities. Elitist critics of our culture—notably such persons as Dwight MacDonald and Edmund Wilson—have always insisted that whatever was widespread was artistically and esthetically deficient, therefore unworthy of study. They have taught that "culture" to be worthwhile must necessarily be limited to the elite, aristocratic, and the minority. They felt that mass or popular culture—especially as it appeared in the mass media—would vitiate real culture. This attitude persists today among some of the younger critics. William Gass, for example, the esthetician and critic, takes the extreme position that "the products of popular culture, by and large, have no more esthetic quality than a brick in the street.... Any esthetic intention is entirely absent, and

Reprinted from *Popular Culture and Curricula*, Bowling Green State University Popular Press, 1972, p. 3-11. Used by permission.

because it is desired to manipulate consciousness directly, achieve one's effect there, no mind is paid to the intrinsic nature of its objects; they lack finish, complexity, stasis, individuality, coherence, depth, and endurance."

Such an attitude as Gass' is perhaps an extreme statement of the elitist critic's point of view. Luckily the force of numerous critics' arguments is weakening such attitudes. Popular Culture has a dimension, a thrust and—most important—a reality that has nothing to do with its esthetic accomplishment, though that has more merit than is often given to it.

This point of view is demonstrated by the talented young stylist Tom Wolfe, who, perhaps writing more viscerally than intellectually, thumbs his nose at the prejudice and snobbery that has always held at arms length all claims of validity if not esthetic accomplishment of the "culture" of the masses.

Susan Sontag, a brilliant young critic and esthetician, is more effective in bludgeoning the old point of view. Far from alarmed at the apparent new esthetic, she sees that it is merely a change in attitude, not a death's blow to culture and art:

What we are getting is not the demise of art, but a transformation of the function of art. Art, which arose in human society as magical-religious operation, and passed over into a technique for depicting and commenting on secular reality, has in our own time arrogated to itself a new function—neither religious, nor serving a secularized religious function, nor merely secular or profane...Art today is a new kind of instrument, an instrument for modifying consciousness and organizing new modes of sensibility.

To Sontag the unprecedented complexity of the world has made inevitable and very necessary this change in the function of art. This is virtually the same attitude held by Marshall McLuhan:

A technological extension of our bodies designed to alleviate physical stress can bring on psychic stress that may be much worse...Art is exact information of how to rearrange one's psyche to anticipate the next blow from our own extended psyches...in experimental art, men are given the exact specifications of coming violence to their own psyche from their own counter-irritants or technology. For those parts of ourselves that we thrust out in the form of new inventions are attempts to counter or neutralize collective pressures and irritations. But the counter-irritant usually proves a greater plague than the initial irritant like a drug habit. And it is here that the artist can show us how to "ride with the punch," instead of "taking it on the chin."

An equally important aspect of popular culture as index and corrector is its role as comic voice. Popular humor provides a healthy element in a nation's life. It pricks the pompous, devaluates the inflated, and snipes at the overly solemn. For example, such organs of popular culture as the magazines spoofed Henry James' pomposity during his lifetime, spoofed his "high" seriousness and in general tended to humanize him.

A more reasonable attitude than Gass' and one that is becoming increasingly acceptable is that held by the philosopher Abraham Kaplan: That popular culture has considerable accomplishment and even more real possibilities and it is developing but has not realized its full potential. All areas draw from one another. The Mass area being largely imitative, draws from the others without altering much. Elite art draws heavily from both folk and, perhaps to a slightly lesser degree, popular arts. Popular art draws from Elite and Mass, and Folk, but does not take any without subjecting it to a greater or lesser amount of creative change. That popular culture has "no more esthetic quality than a brick in the street" or at least no more esthetic potential is a contention refuted by America's greatest writers—Hawthorne, Melville, Whitman, Twain, to name only four—as well as the greatest writers of all times and countries—Homer, Shakespeare, Dickens, Dostoevski, Tolstoi, for example.

Melville provides an excellent case in point. *Moby Dick* is the greatest creative book written in America and one of the half dozen greatest ever written anywhere. Its greatness derives from the sum total of its many parts. It is a blend of nearly all elements of all cultures of mid-nineteenth century America. Melville took all the culture around him—trivial and profound—Transcendentalism and the plumbing of the depths of the human experience, but also demonism, popular theater, the shanghai gesture, jokes about pills and gas on the stomach, etc., and boiled them in the tryworks of his fiery genius into the highest art.

Many definitions of popular culture turn on methods of dissemination. Those elements which are too sophisticated for the mass media are generally called Elite culture, those distributed through these media that are something less than "mass," that is such things as the smaller magazines and newspapers, the less widely distributed books, museums and less sophisticated galleries, so-called clothes line art exhibits, and the like—are called in the narrow sense of the term "popular," those elements that are distributed through the mass media are "mass" culture, and those which are or were at one time disseminated by oral and non-oral methods—on levels "lower" than the mass media—are called "folk."

All definitions of such a complex matter, though containing a certain amount of validity and usefulness, are bound to be to a certain extent inadequate or incorrect. Perhaps a workable definition can best be arrived at by looking at one of the culture's most salient and quintessential aspects—its artistic creations—because the artist perhaps more than any one else draws from the totality of experience and best reflects it.

Shakespeare and his works are an excellent example. When he was producing his plays at the Globe Theater, Shakespeare was surely a "popular" author and his works were elements of "popular" culture, though they were at the same time also High or Elite culture, for they were very much part of the lives of both the groundlings and the nobles. Later, in America, especially during the nineteenth century, all of his works were well known, his name was commonplace, and he was at the same time still High art, Popular (even mass) art and Folk art. In the twentieth century, however, his works are more distinguishable as parts of various levels. *Hamlet* is still a play of both High and Popular art. The most sophisticated and scholarly people still praise it. But *Hamlet* is also widely distributed on TV, radio and through the movies. It is a commonplace on all levels of society and is therefore a part of "popular culture" in the broadest sense of the term. Other plays by Shakespeare, however, have not become a part of "popular" culture. *Titus Andronicus*, for example, for any of several reasons, is not widely known by the general public. It remains, thus, Elite culture.

Wideness of distribution and popularity in this sense are one major aspect of popular culture. But there are others. Many writers would be automatically a part of popular culture if their works sold only a few copies—Frank G. Slaughter and Frank Yerby, for example. Louis Auchincloss also, though his works are of a different kind than Slaughter's and Yerby's, because his subject is Wall Street and high finance, and these are subjects of popular culture.

Aside from distribution, another major difference between high and popular culture, and among popular culture, mass culture and folk culture, is the motivation of the persons contributing, the makers and shapers of culture. On the Elite or sophisticated level, the creators value individualism, individual expression, the exploration and discovery of new art forms, of new ways of stating, the exploration and discovery of new depths in life's experiences.

On the other levels of culture there is usually less emphasis placed upon, and less accomplishment reached in, this plumbing of reality. Generally speaking, both popular and mass artists are less interested in the experimental and searching than in the restatement of the old and accepted. But there are actually vast differences in the esthetic achievements attained in the works from these two levels, and different aspirations and goals, even within these somewhat limited objectives. As Hall and Whannel have pointed out:

In mass art the formula is everything—an escape from, rather than a means to, originality. The popular artist may use the conventions to select, emphasize and stress (or alter the emphasis and stress) so as to delight the audience with a kind of creative surprise. Mass art uses the stereotypes and formulae to simplify the experience, to mobilize stock feelings and to 'get them going.'

The popular artist is superior to the mass artist because for him "stylization is necessary, and the conventions provide an agreed base from which true creative invention springs." It is a serious error therefore to agree with Dwight MacDonald (in *Against the American Grain*) that all popular art "includes the spectator's reactions in the work itself instead of forcing him to make his own responses." Consider, for example, the reactions of two carriers of non-Elite culture, the first of popular culture, the banjo player Johnny St. Cyr. He always felt that the creative impulses of the average person and his responses in a creative situation were immense:

You see, the average man is very musical. Playing music for him is just relaxing. He gets as much kick out of playing as other folks get out of dancing. The more enthusiastic his audience is, why the more spirit the working man's got to play. And with your natural feelings that way you never make the same thing twice. Every time you play a tune new ideas come to mind and you slip that one in.

Compare that true artist's philosophy with that of Liberace, to whom the "whole trick is to keep the tune well out in front," to play "the melodies" and skip the "spiritual struggles." He always knows "just how many notes (his) audience will stand for," and if he has time left over he fills in "with a lot of runs up and down the keyboard." Here in condensed form is the difference between popular and mass art and popular and mass artists. Both aim for different goals. St. Cyr is a truly creative artist in both intent and accomplishment. His credentials are not invalidated merely by the fact that he works in essentially a popular idiom. Given the limitations of his medium—if indeed these limitations are real—he can still be just as great a creator as—perhaps greater than—Rubenstein. It is incorrect to pit jazz against classical music, the popular against the elite. They are not in competition. Each has its own purposes, techniques and accomplishments. They complement each other rather than compete.

Another fine example can be found among the youth of today and their rebellion against what they consider the establishment. They are obviously not a part of the static mass, to whom escape is everything. Instead they are vigorously active, and in their action create dynamic and fine works of art, as examination of their songs, their art, their movies, etc., dramatically demonstrates.

It is also unfair to give blanket condemnation to mass art, though obviously the accomplishments of mass art are less than those of "higher" forms. Liberace does not aspire to much, and perhaps reaches even less. His purposes and techniques are inferior, but not all his, or the many other workers in the level, are completely without value.

All levels of culture, it must never be forgotten, are distorted by the lenses of snobbery and prejudice which the observers wear. There are no hard and fast lines separating one level from another.

Popular culture also includes folk culture. The relationship between folk culture and popular and elite cultures is still debatable. In many ways folk culture borrows from and imitates both.

Historically folk art has come more from the hall than from the novel, has depended more upon the truly creative—though unsophisticated—spirit than the mediocre imitator. "Sir Patrick Spens," one of the greatest songs (poems) ever written, was originally the product of a single creative genius. Today's best folklore-to-be, that is the most esthetically satisfying folklore which is working into tradition today, is that of such people as Woody Guthrie, Larry Gorman and such individual artists.

To a large number of observers, however, folklore is felt to be the same as popular culture. To another large number folklore derives directly from popular culture, with only a slight time lag. To them, today's popular culture is tomorrow's folklore. Both notions are gross and out of line.

Esthetically folk culture has two levels. There is superb folk art and deficient mediocre folk art. Esthetically folk art is more nearly akin to Elite art, despite the lack of sophistication that much folk art has, than to popular. Elite art has much that is inferior, as even the most prejudiced critic must admit. In motivation of artist, also, folk art is close to Elite, for like the Elite artist the truly accomplished folk artist values individualism and personal expression, he explores new forms and seeks new depths in expression and feeling. But there are at the same time workers in folklore who are mere imitators, just trying to get along— exactly like their counterparts in mass culture.

Thus all elements in our culture (or cultures) are closely related and are not mutually exclusive one from another. They constitute one long continuum. Perhaps the best metaphorical figure for all is that of a flattened ellipsis, or a lens. In the center, largest in bulk and easiest seen through is Popular Culture, which includes Mass Culture.

On either end of the lens are High and Folk Cultures, both looking fundamentally alike in many respects and both having a great deal in common, for both have keen direct vision and extensive peripheral insight and acumen. All four derive in many ways and to many degrees from one another, and the lines of demarcations between any two are indistinct and mobile.

Despite the obvious difficulty of arriving at a hard and fast definition of popular culture, it will probably be to our advantage—and a comfort to many who need one—to arrive at some viable though tentative understanding of how popular culture can be defined.

Two scholars who do attempt a definition, following George Santayana's broad distinctions between work and play, believe that "Popular Culture is really what people do when they are not working." This definition is both excessively general and overly exclusive, for it includes much that is "high" culture and leaves out many aspects which obviously belong to popular culture.

One serious scholar defines a total culture as "The body of intellectual and imaginative work which each generation receives" as its tradition. Basing our conclusion on this one, a viable definition for Popular Culture is all those elements of life which are not narrowly intellectual or creatively elitist and which are generally though not necessarily disseminated through the mass media. Popular Culture consists of the spoken and printed word, sounds, pictures, objects and artifacts. "Popular Culture" thus embraces all levels of our society and culture other than the Elite—the "popular," "mass" and "folk." It includes most of the bewildering aspects of life which hammer us daily.

Such a definition, though perhaps umbrella-like in its comprehensiveness, provides the latitude needed at this point, it seems, for the serious scholar to study the world around him. Later, definitions may need to pare edges and change lighting and emphasis. But for the moment, inclusiveness is perhaps better than exclusiveness.

Bibliography

In the briefest bibliography possible, I suggest the following references:

Gass, William H. "Even if by all the Oxen in the World," in Ray B. Browne, *et al, Frontiers of American Culture* (Purdue University, 1968).

Hall, Stuart and Paddy Whannel, *The Popular Arts* (N.Y., Pantheon Books, 1964).

McLuhan, Marshall, *Understanding Media* (N.Y., McGraw-Hill 1964), and *War and Peace in the Global Village* (N.Y., McGraw-Hill 1968).

Shapiro, Nat and Nat Hentoff, *Hear Me Talkin' to Ya* (N.Y. Dover, 1955).

Sontag, Susan, *Against Interpretation* (N.Y., Farrar, Strauss & Giroux, 1966).

Williams, Raymond, *Culture and Society*, 1780-1950 (London, Chatto & Winders, 1960) and *The Long Revolution* (N.Y., Columbia University Press, 1961).

Redefining the Humanities

Ray B. Browne

Before we commit ourselves again fully to an all-out war on illiteracy—so fruitlessly conducted many times in the past—we need to define our terms of what illiteracy and its opposite, literacy, are, and what role they play in society. Clearly literacy, though desirable, is not an end in itself. Literacy is the mechanism which supports the culture, which in turn undergirds the humanities, and in so doing leads to the ultimate goal of happiness and usefulness in life. What then are the humanities? The answer to that question and the demonstrated relationship between the humanities and literacy will, as usual, be both controversial and disturbing to defenders of the educational status quo, to the power brokers in the business of education. Yet that clarification is squirming for recognition in a world that needs to recognize it.

One of the leading spokespersons for the value of the humanities in society is Lynne Cheney, Chairman of the National Endowment for the Humanities. In her *Humanities in America: A Report to the President, the Congress, and the American People* (1988), Cheney issued a thoughtful, generally well-informed and stimulating statement about the way many people see and read the humanities—and a provoking assertion about the way many others *do not* see and understand the humanities and the role of the NEH in promoting them. As is usual in a report of this kind, though the case is well-made, especially to the already-converted, it leaves sections that should be modified, questioned or enlarged, and reversed.

That there is some problem in the failure of the humanities to fulfill their full potential in the United States is clear. To a large extent that fault lies with the people involved, of course, because individuals seldom live up to all expectations. But to another degree the fault lies in definition, in goals the people want to attain. Ms. Cheney gives the consensus definition in her study—that generally used as a working motto by the National Endowment for the Humanities—in emphasizing the depth of the definition. She reminds us that the Romans gave us the word humanities and generally outlined its meaning to them and to their

Reprinted from *The Many Tongues of Literacy*, 1992, with permission from Bowling Green State University Popular Press.

successors through the ages. To the Romans the humanities were "the good arts." She later reemphasizes this depth by telling us again that "in a democratic society, the humanities—those areas of study that bring us the deeds and thoughts of other times—should be part of every life."

Clearly, those are some of the obligations of the humanities, but by no means all, or even the main ones. The others are more contemporary. The Report is viewing the humanities through a telescope turned around backwards. Ms. Cheney follows in the footsteps of her predecessors as Chairman of the NEH in sticking too closely to the definition of the humanities as formulated by the Victorian conservative British poet-essayist Matthew Arnold in asserting that culture is "the best that has been thought and said." Culture and the humanities—by no means the same—are far more than what Arnold thought them to be. His viewpoint was clouded by his seeing reality through his romantic love of the security of the past and his fear of the future. His world was a "darkling plain where ignorant armies clash by night," and his sense of reaching out through the humanities to humanity extended only to his being true to his "love," as he said in his poem *Dover Beach*:

> Ah, love, let us be true
> To one another! for the world, which seems
> To lie before us like a land of dreams,
> So various, so beautiful, so new,
> Hath really neither joy, nor love, nor light,
> Nor certitude, nor peace, nor help for pain;
> And we are here as on a darkling plain
> Swept with confused alarms of struggle and flight,
> Where ignorant armies clash by night. (*Dover Beach*, Stanza 4)

This is hardly a philosophy to lead a nation into the twenty-first century or to drive an agency of the federal government which is dedicated to furthering democracy. The humanities, to survive, must see beyond this narrow and myopic paranoia.

The humanities must reach beyond the esthetics of the three handmaidens of conventional venue—literature, philosophy and history. Esthetics—even the "best that has been thought and said"—should be tested mainly or only on the questions of truth and value not only to the individual but beyond that to humanity. Is the literature appropriate? Is the philosophy sensible? Is the history accurate? Validity rests not on whether something is beautiful, imaginative and self-creating but on whether it bears some resemblance to reality and whether it is applicable to humankind as a whole.

Cheney's *Report* quotes one professor's lament: "Students are not taught that there is such a thing as literary excellence as they were twenty years ago. We are throwing out the notion of good and bad, or ignoring it." As usual, the academic is overstating the case and defending her own philosophy and practice. Literary excellence is fine in its place, no doubt, and it helps many a bitter pill go down. But to think that literary excellence validates some statement which under other circumstances—badly stated—would be recognized as nonsense or mischief is simply blindly simple. Life does not work that way. The *Report* glosses the professor's remarks by reminding us that "These are, of course, legitimate questions, but focusing on political issues to the exclusion of all others does not bring students to an understanding of how Milton or Shakespeare speaks to the deepest concerns we all have as human beings." Again, accurate and perceptive as long as it is not taken too literally. But to understand Milton's statements about our deepest concerns without realizing that his meditations in the divorce tracts were influenced by his unhappy marriage to Mary Powell and that his political thunderings were dictated by his political situation is to simplify complex issues.

So, to many of us the humanities are more than beautiful and "true" statements. The humanities are those aspects of life that make us understand ourselves and our society. They are a philosophical attitude and an approach to thinking and behaving which interpret life in a human context. In other words, the humanities humanize life and living, make it more understandable and bearable and human. In the words of British critic Fred Inglis: "The humanities are the materials with which humanity gains knowledge of itself." There cannot be humanities without some kind of human compassion about the experiences of life, without some kind of "togetherness," or connectedness. If we understand our strengths and weaknesses and our role in the great scheme, then presumably we will have enough intelligence to develop a useful and helpful attitude and action toward our world. If we know the truth—the whole truth—supposedly we will not only be free, but we might also behave sensibly. If we understand the humanities, we might be fully human.

The humanities are without time and limitations. They were important to the Romans, the Greeks before them and the Egyptians before them. But they are not and must not be merely historical statements. Today's humanities are far more important to us than those of the Romans are to us. Nobody should be content to view his or her present-day life through the ignorance, biases and prejudices of the past. One of the goals of education, especially in the humanities, is to develop a healthy—but not reverential—respect for the past while at the same time freeing one from the errors of the past. The old saw these days is that unless one knows the past he will be condemned to reliving it. But the wisdom of the saw should be explicit enough to say that unless we *understand*—not just know–the past we will forever be chained by it. To paraphrase one of our wisest maxims, "Ye shall understand the past and that understanding shall make you free," and presumably wiser.

It is a grave error, as we see it, to believe, as Professor Allan Bloom says in his book *The Closing of the American Mind*, that our role is to fit ourselves into the world of the past. That is the action of an ostrich as he buries his head in the sand and turns his rear to the sun. We don't fit ourselves into Shakespeare's world. Surely if Shakespeare is to live today—should live, deserves to live—his works must be fitted into our world; otherwise he is merely a beautiful heirloom. It is as impossible to go back into history as it is to fit the genie back into the bottle once it has escaped. The humanities are for the living, not the dead.

The *Report* gives a poignant and truthful illustration of this point. Ms. Cheney tells about how a twelve-year-old black girl in Stamps, Arkansas, who had been nourished on Shakespeare, Langston Hughes, Edgar Allan Poe and Paul Laurence Dunbar, determined one day to "render a rendition" of Shakespeare's poetry in her church but was prevented by her grandmother because Shakespeare was not black. The girl's justification was sensible. "I found myself and still find myself, whenever I like, stepping back into Shakespeare. Whenever I like, I *pull* him to me. He wrote it for me.... Of course he wrote it ('When in disgrace with fortune and men's eyes' etc.) for me; that is a condition of the black woman. Of course, he was a black woman. I understand that. Nobody else understands it, but I *know* that Shakespeare was a black woman. That is the role of art in life" (15). How can there be a finer statement of the role of the past in our lives!

Increasingly the various media of education—the transmission of facts and attitudes and the development of thinking and reasoning—are broadening the base and raising the levels of understanding and appreciation of the humanities. Presumably, we are becoming more "civilized"—more humane—and maybe to a certain extent this is a result of our deepening understanding of the humanities.

Frequently, however, this deepening understanding comes *despite* and *against* the teaching of the elite humanities scholars. The *Report* quotes a series of questions by philosopher Charles Frankel which end with the forced connection of two irreconcilable elements: "Will [the images of human possibility in American society] speak to them only of success and celebrity and the quick fix that make them happy, or will it find a place for grace, elegance, nobility, and a sense of connection with the Human adventure?" Now common sense tells us that "grace, elegance," at least, have nothing to do with the humanities; those affectations are important only to life style. And as for the taint of "celebrity and the quick fix"—as rottening as it may appear to be to the social body—few graceful and elegant people turn it down in their search for happiness unless they already have it or cannot hope to acquire it. All those paths of life are as much a part of the "human adventure" as any grace and elegance that Professor Frankel can find. We do ourselves and truth a disservice when we force into the bottle of similarities those elements that chemically won't mix.

They also tend to create a hierarchy in the applicability of the humanities that is repugnant. "The humanities," Professor Maynard Mack of Yale University, once said, "are not really something you can democratize. It's like democratizing surgery. Who wants someone picked up off the streets to operate on him? Well, it's the same thing in the humanities." All analogizing is dangerous, and Professor Mack's is particularly mischievous. The humanities are not like surgery. Not every person has the training and the need to practice surgery upon himself or other people. But every citizen has the Constitutional right and the self-given obligation to practice the humanities.

The humanities, if they do anything, erase the gap between the privileged and unprivileged classes in society. Robert Coles, Harvard psychologist and Pulitzer Prize winner, correctly states that the humanities are necessary companions to us all: "The humanities," he says, "belong to no one kind of person; they are part of the lives of ordinary people, who have their own various ways of struggling for coherence, for a compelling faith, for social vision, for an ethical position, for a sense of historical perspective."

Richard Hoggart, one of Britain's leading contemporary social commentators, speaking in a larger context, quite properly said essentially the same thing: "The closer study of mass society may make us have sad hearts at the supermarket, but at the same time it may produce an enhanced and tempered sense of humanity and humility, instead of the sense of superiority and separateness that our traditional training is likely to have encouraged."

Leslie Fiedler perhaps pushes this reasoning to its logical conclusion because he believes that the humanities broadly conceived and understood can achieve man's greatest challenge, that of bringing us all together again and united into a community which existed before people became separated by class, education, interests and desires.

The growth of the study and power of the humanities, as the *Report* properly points out, has lagged far behind the development of society.

The fault lies not with the humanities but with the academics who profess them. While academics are forming committees—and, I might add, getting large sums of money from the NEH and other Foundations to decide on a proper curriculum and field of study for the enhancement of the humanities—the world is going ahead, as usual far ahead of their academic segments. People, Ms. Cheney reports, "outside the academy are increasingly turning to literary, historical, and philosophical study, are increasingly finding in the 'good arts' a source of enrichment for themselves and their society."

Indeed, they are. And they are reaching far outside those three fields of academic departmentalization of literature, history and philosophy and far beyond the other traditional "good arts." They are reaching out into all aspects of the popular culture for their humanities and finding that all the arts—both "good" and otherwise—have the potential for enriching the lives of us all and, through us, society.

Popular culture is the everyday world around us: the mass media, entertainment, diversions, our heroes, icons, rituals—our total life picture. Although it generally is, it need not be disseminated by the mass media. Most important, the popular culture of a country is the voice of the people—their likes and dislikes, the lifeblood of daily existence, the way of life. In America, presumably, popular culture is the voice of democracy. Like it or not, every American owes it to himself and his society to make a great effort, through formal or informal study, to understand the culture around him or her. He will discover that there are power brokers in elite culture just as in popular culture—most of us have little influence in shaping our culture. Studying the dynamics of culture, often the student will discover, if he can rid himself or herself of blind prejudice, that much of the popular culture is to be appreciated, just as much of the elite is unappreciable.

Actually, of course, there is nothing new in studying popular culture, that is, the culture of the times. As the editors of the *Literary History of the United States* (1955) asserted: "Each generation must define the past in its own terms," as well as the present. And if there is opposition to the new way of looking at the phenomena of life, that is only natural, as John G. Cawelti observed: "Whenever criticism feels the impact of an expanded sensibility it becomes shot through with ideological dispute," and then must be reinterpreted.

Unfortunately, this reinterpretation is often done by specialists instead of by generalists. Ms. Cheney's *Report* quite properly takes up the role of the scholar and his/her specialization in a society which has become so complex and specialized that specialists can no longer communicate outside their own specialization. Medical doctors can no longer understand other doctors outside their areas of specialization. Sociologists can speak only to other specialists in a sub-category. Literary critics who do not understand the jargon of a particular "school" of criticism are deaf and tongue-tied. But the humanities don't flourish in specialities—even among those who specialize in the humanities. The humanities grow in the world of generalities, in syntheses, in questions and answers raised about the purposes and ends—not necessarily in the miles of the road traveled in getting to the ends. But, just as every road consists of the miles separating one point from another, the particulars are ignored at peril.

The ends of the humanities are the whole humanities, not Western humanities, not Black humanities, not Eastern humanities or Women's humanities but *total* humanities. It is true that we are in the tradition of Western civilization and humanities; and undoubtedly, that tradition has many treasures that we should hold dear. But it is myopic and arrogant to assume that the tradition contains all that is needed for us to understand the humanities, no matter how far back we might go. People in the Western tradition are, after all, only a minority of humanity. Individuals throughout the world share in the hopes and aspirations of a common humanity, no matter how widely divergent our ways of living and achieving those goals seem at times to be. On this space-ship Earth we all fly together or we all fall together.

Often we give credit to our ancestors' ways of life and wisdom that they could not possibly have had. Plato, our godfather, flourished in a slave society and despised democracy. To realize his shortcomings does not mean that we toss all of him out with the shortcomings; it merely means that we do not slavishly accept his wrong assumptions and incorrect conclusions. There can be no doubt that the amount of information on virtually all fronts that was available to the "giant humanists" of the past was not sufficient to allow them to come to irrefutable generalizations about everything. It is our duty to question everything they said and invalidate or revalidate their conclusions. If the classics still speak to us, then we should hear them. If their voice is no longer applicable, it should be ignored.

There is no question that it is imperative that the old concepts be tested and modified to incorporate new approaches, new definitions and new areas of subject matter. Otherwise the humanities—in all their ramifications—will prove misguided and generally inadequate to present-day needs and possibilities. Maybe it will be found that the "eternal truths" that the humanities are supposed to reveal have more effective spokespersons in sources that have not been recognized in the past.

T.S. Eliot recognized the need to be mindful of subjects that one might not find compatible with his thinking. He cried out against popular books as his *bete noir*: "I incline to come to the alarming conclusion," he said in *Essays Ancient and Modern*, "that it is just the literature that we read for 'amusement' or 'purely for pleasure' that may have the greatest...least suspected...earliest and most insidious influence upon us. Hence it is that the influence of popular novelists, and of popular plays of contemporary life, require to be scrutinized." Richard Hoggart, one of today's leading English social observers, comments in a typical British understatement, "Literature at all levels has the unique capacity to increase our understanding of a culture."

Neither observer mentions anything about the "aesthetic" beauty of the literature. Using literary "grace and beauty" as criteria for the value of literature, as Jacques Barzun, one of the defenders of old-time attitudes and values, does, seems therefore all the more off-base. The *Report* quotes Barzun in valuing only the "grace and beauty" of any kind of literature: "Excellence is found in many forms," the *Report* quotes, "some of them unassuming and even fugitive. The specifically literary qualities can grace a detective story by Dorothy Sayers or a farce by Courteline, a ghost story by M.R. James or a poem by Ogden Nash."

Barzun seems always concerned that Gresham's law applies to literature as it presumably applies to economics. But "bad" literature does not drive out "good." There are some 50,000 separate titles of books published in the U.S. annually. Never before have so many books been read. In 1985 there were more than two *billion* copies of books printed—400 percent of the number just forty years before. And that was in a society where ninety-eight of every one hundred homes had television. In total number most of those two *billion* were in popular culture. Which ought to tell the elitists something. If the mountain cannot go to Mohammet, then Mohammet must go to the mountain. And the elite should openly admit what they are actually doing—that is, reading the popular books for pleasure and edification. Just as they are watching television and participating in the other media for pleasure and edification. Sometimes they are bootlegging their enjoyment to themselves. But they fool only themselves, and perhaps the government. There is no need for the elite to dissemble and claim that popular books are the bane of civilization when they read those books and talk about them most of the time. The popular books are, instead, the blessing and the tool of democracy. They spread knowledge and encourage learning.

There can be no doubt that reading stimulates watching television, and that watching television encourages reading. People apparently do not like to live in a quiet, one-dimensional atmosphere. When they pick up a book or magazine to read, many automatically turn on the television set. Likewise, when they turn on the television set many automatically pick up something to read. Further, the television program is likely to stimulate reading in another way: One sees a television show and then gets hold of the book from which the show was made and reads it, just as often one will tune in a television show because the book from which it was made was enjoyable. British crime novelist Ruth Rendell tells how she has seen the television version of her works stimulate people to do all kinds of direct and collateral reading. The media are mutually dependent and supportive. Books, television and movies are only three kinds of media which are mutually helpful one of another.

This means that there should be no sacred domains among the old humanities; they should not be treasured as holy writ and, therefore, be immune to tests of value. They must periodically be asked to revalidate themselves, and if they cannot they must be retired until rejuvenated. Doubtless, many of the old workhorses should be given permanent sabbaticals. They have ceased to have value except as historical markers. The present-day classroom—and research desk—is the one place in society that cannot afford to become a museum of dead ideas and concepts.

Casting out the dead fish from our pond of living ideas is not condemnation of what people have done in the past. It does not invalidate anybody's life's work, anybody's literary or artistic loves, even anybody's evaluation of aesthetically commendable or contemptible materials. Rather, it is a call for intellectuals and other people interested in studying and understanding American life and culture, in its broadest and richest sense, to become broader-minded, more openminded and less exclusive and excluding. Nobody says one has to approve of or like everything that goes on, just as no one has to approve of or like all the "great" works of the arts of the past or the present. Scientists, to our betterment, do not restrict their interests to the "good" things in life. It is foolish for us to pull an ostrich-like hiding of the head and be unaware of the winds that sweep our bodies while the thinking part is in the sand. Such an attitude is dangerous to one's own and the culture's well-being, because in truth American culture continues to grow and develop in its own way pretty much irrespective of the intellectuals' approval or disapproval. Intellectuals may long for the return of the railroad train as a romantic way to travel, but the satellite is flying well and high. It would behoove us to recognize that fact and to bring the humanities into the electronic age. The humanities must prepare us to think our way through the age of instant media. Facts change constantly. "Time dissipates to shining ether the solid angularity of facts," Emerson wrote in his essay on history.

It is undoubtedly a flaw of education to assume that the person who knows a lot of facts is educated. Such a person could do well on *Jeopardy* or *Wheel of Fortune*, but so could an encyclopedia that was trained to speak or a voice-motivated computer. The educated person is not the little Bloomlet or Hirschite who has been cloned in the image of the master, but the person who has refused to be cloned, declined to be satisfied working with the lumber of facts that many educators have handed him, but has instead gone on to imagine and build new concepts and constructions.

The academic's tendency is to be rather open-minded while he does not know much and does not have much to defend. But as he gets more and more specialized, he tends more and more to become proprietary and protective over what he knows, apparently in developing such an attitude fulfilling a deep-felt need within himself. Often, we turn off our listening button and switch on our broadcast button too soon. We learn to "profess" exclusively while we should still be learning what to profess. Such a one-way activity is indeed dangerous, for it is self-defeating. But academia persists in being, by and large in the humanities, the old nest of last year's ideas, not the place where new ideas are generated and welcomed in order to be tested and approved or cast out. Academia should generally use the library as the storehouse of old ideas, for there they need not do any harm. Archives are archives, and the classroom of new ideas ought to be something else entirely. We should never assume that we know something that has not been examined and validated. Academia should be the leading, not the trailing, edge of ideas.

We should remember that Josh Billings, one of our insightful humorists of the 19th century reminded us: "It ain't the things we don't know that makes such fools of us, but a whole lot of things that we know that ain't so." We should always keep an open mind about what are the valuable things we know and the worthwhile attitudes we hold. Otherwise, we insult our intelligence and jeopardize the natural and peaceful development of culture and mankind. The humanities, properly studied and understood, enrich immeasurably our journey and assist us in achieving literacy for all. They also assist us in another equally important way.

They help us recognize the false ways that are constantly placed luringly before us, offering cure-alls and quick-fixes that society can ill-afford to tolerate—much less encourage. The humanities are too important to leave in the hands of the charlatans.

Works Cited

Arnold, Matthew. "Dover Beach." 1867, Columbia HS7131 (1968).

Bloom, Allan. *The Closing of the American Mind.* New York: Simon and Schuster, 1987.

Cawelti, John G. *The Six-Gun Mystique.* Bowling Green, OH: Bowling Green State University Popular Press, 1970.

Cheney, Lynne. *Humanities in America: A Report to the President, the Congress, and the American People.* Washington: National Endowment for the Humanities, 1988.

Hoggart, Richard. *The Uses of Literacy: Aspects of Working-Class Life and Entertainment with Special Reference to Publications and Entertainments.* London: Chatto & Windos, 1957

Inglis, Fred. *Popular Culture and Political Power.* Sussex: Harvester-Wheatsheaf, 1988.

Spiller, Robert, Willard Thorp, Thomas H. Johnson, Henry Seidel Canby. *Literary History of the United States.* New York: Macmillan, 1953.

Popular Culture:
Medicine for Illiteracy
and Associated Educational Ills

Ray B. Browne

Statistics on the rising tide in functional illiteracy in the United States are staggering. Some reports indicate 13% of Americans are not literate. Other figures state more precise numbers: 20-27 million Americans are "seriously illiterate," 40 million are "marginally illiterate" and 4 million adults are studying to learn to read and write. Even if all these figures are too high, on a personal level, illiteracy is crushing. Young people as well as older persons are intimidated by their illiteracy and the fact that the literate condescend to them. Sometimes the reaction is violent. Young people fight and kill when insulted about their illiteracy. British crime-writer Ruth Rendell centered one of her novels on a housekeeper who was illiterate and flashed out and murdered her employers because they kept leaving her notes that she could not read. Society, as well as the individual, is deeply and seriously wounded by the illiteracy of its citizens. Thomas Jefferson quite properly felt that a country cannot have a democracy if its citizens are not literate.

In a world of such mischief created by illiteracy, it is time that educators turned to radical cures for this disease and its fellow-horsemen of a potential apocalypse, school drop-outs, indifference to education and under-education (fade-outs) if they can be found. As many of us have been pointing out for years, such a radical cure is available in the educational value to be found in popular culture.

Popular culture is the practical—pragmatic—Humanities. So it can be used as a tool to assist us in education. It can be utilized in many ways to overcome illiteracy, to keep people in school, to encourage life-long learning and to energize our educational system and the materials we teach.

Reprinted from *Journal of Popular Culture*, Winter 1987, Vol. 21, No. 3. Reprinted with permission.

As a healthy preamble it can be used to counter the hocus-pocus of academia that presents literacy—and education in general—as a magic that one can achieve only after a long and arduous investment of time and labor. This pretentiousness quite understandably puts many people off. The current, 1987, business of celebrating the Bicentennial of the U.S. Constitution is an excellent case in point. In one effort, the Commission on the Bicentennial Educational Grant Program has recently solicited grant applications for "the development of instructional materials on the Constitution and Bill of Rights" for use in elementary and secondary schools because there is a "lack of citizen knowledge about the Constitution and American History." To correct this lack of knowledge, the Commission proposes funding institutes where thirty or more social science teachers will be taught by "two Constitutional scholars" giving a series of lectures and being aided by two "master teachers." Note the language: "Two Constitutional scholars" and two "master teachers." Now everybody knows that words and labels are cheap and meaningless. But a great deal of harm can be done when a government agency is so pretentious that they set about teaching tax-paying citizens—not to mention public school teachers—about *our* governing document in such phony language. Paternalism does indeed die hard. Apparently the educators in Washington still do not want the people in this country to understand the Constitution on their own. It must be spoonfed by Constitutional scholars and Constitutional historians. Perhaps it might be threatening to have people understand the Constitution rationally in the light and language of 1987. Undoubtedly the Constitution, like education in general, could profit by a little less pretentiousness surrounding it. That is, it should be viewed in its popular culture setting, in the setting of the people whose life it guides and controls.

Popular culture is the everyday lifeblood of the experiences and thinking of all of us: the daily, vernacular, common cultural environment around us all, the culture we inherit from our forebears, use throughout our lives and then pass on to our descendants. Popular culture is the television we watch, the movies we see, the fast food, or slow food, we eat, the clothes we wear, the music we sing and hear, the things we spend our money for, our attitude toward life. It is the whole society we live in, that which may or may not be distributed by the mass media. It is virtually our whole world.

Though popular culture is to many people the monster that has caused the problems of functional illiteracy and lack of interest in solid education in the first place, it is really—viewed disinterestedly—merely an environment, a force, a background and foreground and a means of communication and entertainment. It can and should be used as a key to open the possibilities of proficiency in the use of conventional language, especially by those whose use of the language of the media—the main disseminating force of popular culture—is very high but whose utilization of the printed word is generally weak and undeveloped.

The principle I am proposing is that pragmatically one begins with the known and proceeds to the unknown, that one uses what he/she already knows in order to learn something unknown. I propose that educators, recognizing this principle, use it in getting people of all degrees of proficiency and unproficiency in the printed word to expand their capabilities.

That the popular culture around us is known, that it occupies most of the time of nearly all of us and that therefore properly channelled it can be the single most powerful force to encourage and drive people toward a goal seems to go without saying. The sticking point will be in getting interested people on all levels of education to accept popular culture as a worthwhile and effective tool in teaching instead of as a distracting and weakening diversion, and in motivating them to act on this knowledge. In education, as elsewhere, we all need scapegoats to lay the blame on for faults we see in society and what we might secretly admit is our own failings to accomplish the jobs we would like to achieve. To paraphrase Lincoln, if we would make some progress in a task, we must first recognize the means by which the progress might be made, and then we should persevere in our goals. I suggest that we know that experience has taught us that in the teaching business we proceed from the known to the unknown, that we use every device we can in that teaching process, that the popular culture around us is well known, and that therefore we should use it as educational devices in promoting literacy and love of education and learning.

Popular culture is in fact being used successfully in many areas, especially among pre- and early-schoolers in the highly useful *Sesame Street* and *Mr. Rogers' Neighborhood*, and in numerous computer and non-computer children's games which are teaching children vocabulary and simple sentences. It is also being used in the continued education of senior citizens. What is involved is basically the rudiments of communication. Once the basics have been established, the same principles should be used to build more vocabulary, more complicated sentences and more sophisticated communication. In other words, the popular culture can be used to establish the basics of communication and, as I shall argue later on, in the continued growth of literacy, sophisticated communication and to lure people into a love of learning and education. In other words, I am suggesting that popular culture can be a kind of textbook for beginners in all fields of learning. It can begin at the beginning. It can develop into all kinds of sophistication, and it can spur interest in every aspect of life and learning known to man and woman.

The beauty of using the popular culture is the motivation it provides if it is used as a spur to learning instead of an end in itself. Sometimes the tendency is to use the popular culture as a goal, as entertainment, but it is very easy to switch from entertainment to instruction, from passive acceptance of communication to participatory communication, if educators merely make the effort.

Some people in the television medium recognize this potential and are willing to put their money where their mouth is. Bill Moyers, for example, in 1987 gave up a lucrative position with CBS and settled with PBS for one-tenth his CBS salary because he wanted to do more "think" pieces for television. As reported by the Associated Press, April 26, 1987, Moyers said, "Television is a wonderful medium for teaching, as Mister Rogers has proved, as MacNeil-Lehrer has proved, as any carefully crafted documentary proves. It's a wonderful medium for teaching." Moyers essentially summed up the educator's opinion when he said: "The world is endlessly fascinating, and journalists are beachcombers permitted on the shores of other people's ideas and experiences, and they're all around you."

The lure of popular culture to people is constantly brought to our attention. Children spend more time watching television than they do in the classroom. Add to this all the extra time they spend absorbing popular music, eating, dressing, going to the movies, talking about all these activities, and you have most of every day of most people's lives. That is, popular culture is a constant classroom in which education can take place virtually eighteen hours a day. The trick is to make passing the time of our lives, of entertainment, into an educational exercise. All people like to be entertained. The literate and sophisticated want to be entertained, the illiterate want to be entertained. The entertainment of the literate does not differ much in kind from that of the illiterate, only in degree. Both kinds of people want desperately to communicate, and the communication of both does not differ in kind, only in "sophistication." Generally speaking, both have the same experiences in our everyday culture. They go to the same movies, watch the same television, sing the same songs, share the eating and dressing experiences. We are all locked in the America of our day. It seems logical therefore that the literate and the illiterate use the experiences they share, the motivations they have in common, to bring both groups together in communication and shared American life.

We have always prided ourselves on being a practical people. America has always been the land of the tinkerer, the craftsman, the people who can do things, build tall buildings, develop faster means of communication. People have always developed skills because they have seen those skills as being practical and useful. The much-vaunted high literacy rate of the nineteenth century in America developed because people needed to communicate, wanted to develop a sense of community, longed to rise in the social and financial world, and realized that the proper way to accomplish those goals was through the leading communication medium of the time—the printed word.

Despite what may at times seem to be the contrary, Americans still want to communicate; they yearn to develop a sense of community, and they surely lust after social and fiscal upward mobility. Communication among people is more desperately needed today than it has ever been before. In a world which seems forever fragmenting into more and more islands of interest and abilities, people simply are yearning to find the ties that bind them together. Everybody is searching for bonding with other people.

Few people in the United States today are not able to understand and communicate in some of the various media of popular culture. Some cannot handle the printed word but can easily understand and use the various other symbols promulgated by the media. Since literacy is a term which applies only to an old-fashioned technology, we should expand the term to include the ability to understand and use the vocabularies and structures of other media, the symbols of communication such as television, radio, movies, popular music, rapping, jiving, fashions, vernacular architecture, fast foods, etc. That is, *literacy* should include *mediacy*.

One becomes proficient in the communication symbols because one needs to. So it has always been. In the folk community, people learned to communicate because it was necessary. They learned the visual media— home and community activities, farming, everyday needs and means— because they realized that the visual media contained elements that they needed to understand in order to get along.

It is likewise easily demonstrable to the populace at large today that they need to understand and be able to communicate the symbols used in everyday communication in media other than those in which the communication occurs. In our compartmentalized world, the media tend to create islands of in-groups which can understand and communicate in a specific language without being able to communicate outside that particular group. Such people are *mediate*—that is, can understand the language of a particular medium—but may not be able to handle other languages and specifically not the printed word, the one language common to them all. Thus several "languages" may be requisite for communication.

The lure to be held out to people learning other languages of communication can be entirely pragmatic, selfish and self-serving. One gets along better and more easily in life, one gets farther ahead, one becomes happier if he/she understands and uses the dominant symbols of communication, which at this time happen to be the written word.

An excellent case in point was the ability of Americans to use the dominant means of communication in the middle of the nineteenth century. Although only 60% of adult Britons were literate in 1851, over 90% of America's white population was. There were many forces driving Americans toward literacy—the need for family cohesion, the church, schools, etc.—but the main ones were, of course, private: ambition, loneliness, hunger for knowledge and self-improvement. People did not learn to read and write primarily because they were told to. They learned because it was demonstrated to be for their personal benefit.

But for the past fifty years or so, it has not been demonstrable that the only—even the preferred—way of getting ahead in America is through the print medium. Technology has invented new means of one's surviving—even flourishing—and has provided people with choices. They could become literate or remain illiterate in the conventional medium yet still get ahead.

Many people have chosen illiteracy because the road to literacy in the conventional medium has seemed too difficult to accomplish. The seeming difficulty of achieving literacy in the printed word is, of course, an illusion, often created by people who for one reason or another thought and taught that it was difficult, in other words promulgated by people who themselves had an entirely false notion of what literacy is and does.

Literacy is a democratic tool available to and usable by all. It develops in and is expanded by the latest tools of democracy, that is the latest gadgets of technology. The printed word was, after all, printed by technology. Now there are other technological tools developed which promote different kinds of literacy, in other words *mediacy*. No longer is the printed word the key to survival. Television, movies, music, and all the other manifestations of the culture around us, are reestablishing an oral and visual culture in which literacy in the printed word is not absolutely necessary. Naturally the clash between the old and the new is traumatic.

What we have is one technology pushing out another and older technology, with the practitioners of the old clinging to it because they have not worked out a way to manage and manipulate the new. Practitioners of print literacy have reason to recognize the force of the new technology. The cost in emotional and financial terms to change from print technology to electronic technology will be staggering. It is hard to imagine a world that is visually and symbolically, and numbers, oriented, pretty much devoid of conventional printed words, depending on a different kind of mediacy. We can hardly imagine and cope with a world that uses the standard means of communication flashed on the computer screen. How can we even contemplate a world that virtually ignores the old forms of literacy? The answer is of course that the clash is made to seem more dangerous that it really is. There are around us several worlds of communication and all are compatible, all can be interfaced, can speak to one another. Scientists and mathematicians, musicians and medical doctors operate in the worlds of symbols peculiar to their trade while at the same time living in the world of the printed word. But the mutual incomprehensibility among the several jargons creates areas of expertise, and one that suffers most is the area of composition-literacy.

It is a peculiar fallacy that has become almost a truism that says that educators in composition-literacy are the ones who are responsible for developing that competency because effective composition equals literacy, or that literacy comes only with artful composition. So other educational departments that use literacy as a tool in their communication often opt out of the teaching of literacy because they were not formally trained and therefore feel themselves not competent to teach and develop composition-literacy, a feeling of inadequacy historically promoted by composition teachers. Such teachers, having installed themselves as sovereign in the teaching of literacy, have pretty much shamed members of other literate groups into withholding their assistance. Professors of history, sociology, technology, dance, education, etc., may not be able to write sentences which please their colleagues in English departments, but they communicate. Responsibility for keeping English as the coin of the realm is theirs also. After all, their sons and daughters need to communicate. On Spaceship Earth we all communicate or we fly off course. But when the English departments try to enlist the assistance of their colleagues in other departments, often they are met with shrugs of shoulders: Literacy is somebody else's problem.

To a real degree, the English departments have caused their own trouble. Historically, teachers of composition-literacy have worked under the assumption that they are out to train people to craft well-turned, grammatically correct and graceful sentences, paragraphs and essays. This attitude was built on the assumption that in order to recognize and appreciate great literature, one must be able to write "great" compositions. In other words one writes like the "masters," imitating them in style as well as thought.

Such reasoning is flawed from the beginning. In the first place there may be some correlation between the ability to write the well-crafted sentence and essay and the appreciation of "great" literature, but the relationship is vague and tenuous. The refutation is glaringly and embarrassingly self-evident; most literary scholars, who probe most deeply into the meanings of literature, write anything but the well-crafted and graceful sentence and paragraph. They manage to communicate, but not much more.

The purpose of all media is communication. Electronic media communicate very well. As a medium of communication, television is not a "vast wasteland" not a "boobtube," nor a "glass teat," as people have variously called it. Nor is the medium of rock music pornographic. Other manifestations of popular culture are not evil forces trying to destroy civilization merely for the riches of unprincipled people. Some people may use them for devious and dangerous purposes. But like computers, television and music, and other media, are merely means of communication that demand "literacy," that are perhaps more important than, and surely just as natural as, the printed word, and—worse yet to some people—will ultimately replace the printed word. In other words, the *mediacy* of the new media of communication will eventually replace that of the old. The guardians of the old-style "literacy" can go with the flow or be washed over by it.

Washed over by it they will be, provided the keepers of the conventional literacy do not realize the threat and adjust to it. There seem to be two choices: keepers of the conventional literacy can use the communication capabilities of the other media and in so doing maintain literacy for all people in the conventional printed word; or ignore and despise the more advanced electronic media and in so doing guarantee the continued erosion of conventional literacy in the present forms and eventually its disappearance or anachronistic status as a minority practice. It is conceivable that a hundred years from now—or even less—conventional literacy in language will have disappeared because it is no longer useful to the general public.

That is not to say, however, that users of the conventional literacy must capitulate to the new, even before it has arrived. On the contrary. But it should be to our interests to realize that the finest tool in the retention of the old form of literacy is in fact the very electronic media that might eventually replace it. That is, the best way to retain the old literacy is to use the popular media and the popular culture they disseminate as a means of teaching it.

People interested in promoting written literacy should understand that experiencing anything gives a basis for communicating. Communication is analogical. One experiences something in one medium, becomes interested, and wishes to have similar experiences in other media. One "reads" something in television and turns to the medium of print in order to supplement his knowledge, excitement and enjoyment. Unfortunately, of course, one who is excited by television or some other electronic medium frequently is denied access to the treasures of the printed word because he does not understand it.

Here is where the promoter of written communication can take advantage of the media. All forms of communication in the modern vernacular world can be springboards for conventional literacy. The key is getting people to realize that the printed word is the common language—the *lingua franca*—that they all need.

The electronic media provide access to and enrich the print medium. They open up myriads of opportunities to stimulate the mind and capabilities of students which then can be translated into the print medium. Students respond to the stimuli provided by rock music, by questions of youth behavior as catalogued in the media, by questions of morality, ethics, teenage and adult behavior, by the symbolism in such American phenomena as the fast-food industry, shopping malls, rituals, icons and fetishes. Some of the most exciting and useful courses taught in high school and college level composition courses have been sports-oriented: the literature of sports, sports in American culture, the history of sports. The media fairly bulge every day with subjects that excite and invite the thoughtful student and teacher: the commercialization of Christmas, sex-education in public schools, combatting the spread of AIDS, abortion, televangelism, the role of the elderly in society, pet therapy, the positive and negative images of such television shows as "Dallas" and "Dynasty." The Popular Culture Department of Bowling Green State University recently ran a successful state-wide writing contest among eleventh-grade high-school students on "Should Rock Lyrics be Censored?" Uncountable instructors in composition classes have always used current events and other popular culture subjects as topics for compositions. The range of stimulating topics is boundless.

One medium foolishly ignored is the comic book. Everyone knows that in Mexico, Central and South America, the People's Republic of

China, and elsewhere, comics are used to teach reading and writing as well as political ideology. In Japan, according to a recent AP article, children, women and business executives read comics all the time. According to one expert, comics exert as much influence over school kids as school itself does. Increasingly comic books are being used to simplify and augment textbooks. How-to comic books are becoming more and more popular, covering all kinds of education and activities. Japan, like America, is a very visual-oriented society. With a claimed 100% literacy rate, does Japan know something about teaching literacy that we refuse to accept? It seems so. Let me give you an example.

At Bowling Green State University we have created the Popular Culture Library and are archiving as much popular culture as we can. One of the largest collections is our comic book archive. Years ago when we were just getting started, a man from Toledo called one day and said that he would like to contribute his collection of comic books to our archives. He brought down several thousand comics—a station wagon full. Six months later he brought down another thousand, and sometime later another large collection. Being curious about where he was getting his books, I asked him where he got them and why. His answer was very poignant—touching—and significant. He said that he worked for Toledo Edison as a lineman, and he simply liked to read. So he bought as many comic books as he could. Now I would suggest that in that man's simple statement lies the whole kernel of an American educational system: a person so desiring to read that he would spend all available cash for the opportunity. There lies the seed for education and one of the media.

Providing access to literacy through these various media does not mean that anybody who teaches composition through the popular culture must undergo a shriveling of his own talents, his own life, his own tastes, if that is the result of such association, though I surely doubt that it is. The teacher should be able to maintain a distance between his private tastes and his professional ones. Using the various popular culture media merely means that in a democracy, one teaches from democratic premises, with democratic assumptions, from and through democratic media, for democratic ends. That means that the instructor should never be embarrassed by or condescending to the degree of literacy or illiteracy one finds or to the means of eradicating that illiteracy. Everybody has to begin sometime at the beginning.

All people, no matter how humble, have the democratic right to access to the valuable and useful experiences of the past and present in order to improve or make more enjoyable their own lives. They cannot, in our democracy, properly be denied the tools of access to those experiences.

Which, of course, brings up an informative parallel. Asian-American children are doing so well in schools and colleges that questions are being raised as to whether they are smarter than other American kids. The statistics are impressive: Asian-American kids usually score some 30 points higher than other Americans on the Scholastic Aptitude Test, 520 out of a possible 800. Although Asian-Americans constitute only 2.1% of the American population, they make up 11% of the freshman class at Harvard; 18% at MIT; 25% at Berkeley. Does that mean that Asian-American kids are smarter than other American kids? Though the jury is still out on that verdict, there is every reason to believe that success depends more on motivation than native intelligence. Asian-American kids simply work harder.

University of Michigan psychologist Harold W. Stevenson feels that "they work harder largely because they share a greater belief in the efficacy of hard work." Stevenson added: "Japanese mothers gave the strongest rating to the idea that anyone can do well if he studies hard." Stevenson might have added that parents know very well that if students do not succeed early they will be condemned to a life in which they never can achieve the highest goals in their society. In Japanese society, success is built from one of the three elite universities and one's capabilities to matriculate in one of these schools are fiercely competitive and established early. Chinese mothers strongly agree in this particular work ethic. A typical Stanford Chinese student's comment was, "In the Chinese family, education is very important because parents see it as the way to achieve. With that environment it's natural to study. My friends are that way too. It's not a chore. They know the benefits."

Are we to conclude from these statistics that all other American students are stupider than the Asian-Americans? That their parents are stupider? Hardly. The evidence demonstrates that the Asian-Americans work harder. They are "merely entertained" less than the other American kids. So what should we do? Being realistic, we may as well confess that television and the other aspects of American entertainment and popular culture are not going away. One inalienable right that we are prepared to fight for is the "American Way" of life—and that way consists mainly of our popular culture. Since we are not going to put technology back into the undeveloped stage, why not use it to further our designs to create and promote conventional literacy? If Asian-American kids learn because their family tradition expects it of them, why don't we get the other American kids to learn because it is so easy and one uses the most enjoyable media to learn from, and because American society expects it of *them*? And rewards them for it. If the American way of life is so much fun, we should use it to learn to get even more fun out of it. The American way of life can become even more pleasurable and profitable for many more if educators use that means of pleasure and profit to promote literacy in the conventional forms.

Yet educators, people who presumably lead in the world of ideas, continue to face backwards, to remember the "good old days" when they were acquiring their wisdom and to teach wrong-headed ideas. Little wonder that American higher education is falling apart. For example, in 1987 Allan Bloom, professor in the Committee on Social Thought at the University of Chicago, published a book entitled *The Closing of the American Mind*. Picturing modernity as the enemy of the classics, and therefore of learning in particular, Bloom (*Chronicle of Higher Education*, May 6, 1987, p. 96) railed against television, "pop psychology," popular literature, and nearly everything else that was not written in the misty past. One of his guiding starts for "classics" was the works of Charles Dickens and the unforgettable characters that Dickens created. Apparently little did Bloom know that Dickens was the most "popular" writer of his day, turning out copy while the printer's devil leaned over his shoulder in order to make a living and avoid the debtors' prison. And Bloom, who curses stereotypical thinking, says that one of the great benefits of Dickens' writing is that his characters are "a complex set of experiences that enables one to say so simply, 'He is a Scrooge'," etc. In other words although he uses other words, Bloom desires the ease and convenience of the stereotype, the very rib-cage of popular literature of today.

Bloom stumbles over other dangerous misassumptions about education. One is that democracy helped kill off education: "The democratization of the university helped dismantle its structure and caused it to lose its focus." These are the words of the enemy of the people and of education in general, not of one who understands what education is for. Bloom also voices poisonous nonsense when he thinks of the purpose of education: "The old teachers who loved Shakespeare or Austen or Donne, and whose only reward for teaching was the perpetuation of their taste, have all but disappeared," he complains. Prof. Bloom apparently forgets that Shakespeare's plays were written for the very practical purpose of making the author a living on the stage, and Austen's and Donne's had their practical purposes. But mainly Bloom's words reflect the mentality of Matthew Arnold of the nineteenth century and merely demonstrate that many academics instead of wanting to generate free and innovative thinking for the twentieth century want to clone themselves and the past. An educational system that wants merely to clone itself and its history is going to be condemned to reliving the past. The frightening thing about Bloom's thinking is that apparently it is honey to many other academic bees who see in it salvation for their troubles. But it is more likely a Siren's song lulling unwary academics into a mess of troubles because it preaches against use of all modern thinking and theories, and surely against popular culture as one of the tools of instruction, with working with what one has.

In using popular culture to promote literacy, sometimes instructors have to be understanding and work from very little. For example, if a student in "composition" would rather perform on his guitar, if he would rather sing a song than write an essay, he should be encouraged, and the performance should be accepted as a "composition." If an "essay" consisted of a collage of pictures of rock 'n' roll stars, it should be accepted. From these parallel beginnings, actual literacy in conventional language can be encouraged. The person who sang a rock song or performed on his guitar could be induced to talk about what he had done, and then urged to write down his thoughts for those people not in class. The person who pasted up the collage could be asked to form some kind of connection, historical or cultural, between the pictures, and thus in effect to some "writing" that would promote his literacy. Acceptance of the different language is useful in bridging the gap between the two or three media, and through acceptance students are assured that the instructor lives in and appreciates the world that they are concerned with. The communication, the empathy, the understanding form a two-way street, and two-way communication.

With these purposes and techniques in mind no plan should be too low to begin on, and no idea should be assumed to be above the reach of the print illiterate until it has been proved to be so. Many Americans may have difficulty with even the simplest words and sentences. But these people are not necessarily stupid or unteachable: they simply have not yet learned the art of language use, and they have not learned because for one reason or another they have not been properly motivated. To teach such people, educators need liberated and active minds looking for ideas of today and tomorrow that will excite and motivate the minds before them. The field of these ideas remains constantly present.

There is no reason for the American educator to think that he will have to stop using the media when he has accomplished literacy in the print medium, that the potentials are short-lived and soon exhausted. Functional literacy through the media is only a beginning. This accomplishment can be like a person holding a piece of candy just out of the reach of a hungry child. As the child crawls toward the candy, it can be pulled back continuously—until, in theory at least, the child has become an adult. The bon-bon of media education can likewise be continually pulled back until the learner is accomplished in advanced degrees of literacy and knowledge, until he is, in fact, what we might call "educated." Properly presented the entertainment of life is an unending source of knowledge and training.

The point is to realize the possibilities and to get to implementing them. Illiteracy, drop-outs, fade-outs (arrested learners) are problems that should be attacked directly, not obliquely. Thus on the matter of effective education in the United States, William Bennett, the Secretary of Education, should not be grandstanding by teaching history or philosophy to 8-year-olds in schoolrooms. He should be out on the streets of Detroit—and Washington and every community in the U.S.— asking drop-outs and fade-outs and illiterates why they are not in the classroom. He should be concerned with the very basics of long-range education—that is, keeping students in classrooms long enough for them to learn, then teaching them something while they are there. The task is to get them into situations conducive to our purposes and goals. As everybody knows, the people are learning, but they may not be learning what we think is of primary importance. But there is no doubt that the Prof. Blooms of academia can do a great amount of mischief if they continue to rely exclusively on the "classics" for wisdom and then do not understand them.

Academics are often uncomfortable in the presence of the multitude of ideas that the media and popular culture provide because they need the feeling of safety and assurance guaranteed by the old restrictions. Such people prefer the snugness found in the old forms of expression to the potentials latent in the new and unrestricted possibilities. Some see merit in the cliche being circulated by many of today's politicians of going "back to basics." Indeed there is much merit in the concept, other than the deceptive alliteration, provided we do not mis-remember what the basics are. The basics are age-old means of communication about the phenomena of life. The media of communication have been modernized and brought up to date every time the medium of communication has changed. When copying of texts by hand, one by one, gave way to rapid printing, the "basics" became tied to printing. When mechanical typewriters gave way to electric machines, nearly everybody happily changed machines and the "basics" underwent yet another technological advance.

Entertainment is also "basic" in nearly everybody's life, one of the primary drives which socialize society. Through the years the media entertainments have changed radically. Though many people like to cling to some aspects of the "old" entertainment, perhaps claiming that they are superior to the newfangled ones, most people have moved happily into the forms provided by the electronic media.

Society like technology in a literate world moves inexorably forward. But it moves along a trail which includes the past. In truth, popular culture *is* that past as well as its present. Popular culture has never left the basics—it *is* the basics, the fundamentals, the everyday, and indeed it should be so used. Only the technology of popular culture changes. Technological genies do not go back into bottles once they have been released. The practical and sensible thing, then, is for educators to realize the importance and opportunities of the technological society we live in and to utilize its equipment in the teaching of print literacy. The opportunities are great—and the penalties for failing are heavy and costly. Too costly, in fact, for us to afford. Either we go with the media or they go without us.

So popular culture which on one hand seems to be destroying conventional literacy is actually providing people with the greatest and easiest access to practical functional literacy, to the basics, to getting people to remain in school, and to luring people into continued education long after their formal years are finished, if we will only realize the opportunity and take advantage of it.

Never before have so many people had such easy access to so many means of getting to the top and fulfilling the American Dream of success. That these media are not utilized to develop mediacy and love of learning constitutes one of the great and needless shames of our country and our time. Utilization of popular culture in this way would not, of course, cure the whole trouble. The literacy and education provided might not be of the casebook variety and might not be conventional literacy and education. But it would be communication, it would be functional literacy, and it would keep the human mind busy on "worthwhile" subjects. There would, of course, still be many people who would not or could not become literate in the conventional sense, who would, for one reason or another, not be interested in learning and using the mind. perhaps the illiterate and the half-educated, like the poor, will always be with us in certain numbers. But literacy builds on its own accomplishments, just as education feeds on education. Literacy breeds love of learning; education breeds more love of education, and of literacy. Learning through popular culture is no panacea. But this approach would surely help alleviate the problem of illiteracy, of drop-outs and fade-outs and would provide bases for further development. Any assistance should be welcome and tried. After all, half of the American Dream is better than none—for individuals *and* for society.

Ray B. Browne
Bibliography

Compiled by Maryan Wherry

Books

Popular Beliefs and Practices from Alabama. Ed. Ray B. Browne. Berkeley: U of California P, 1958.

The Burke-Paine Controversy. Ed. Ray B. Browne. New York: Harcourt, 1963.

The Celtic Cross: Studies in Irish Culture and Literature. Eds. Ray B. Browne, William John Roscelli and Richard Loftus. West Lafayette: Purdue UP, 1964.

The Indian Doctor: Frontier Pharmacology. Indianapolis: Indiana Historical Society, 1964.

Critical Approaches to American Literature. 2 vols. Eds. Ray B. Browne and Martin Light. New York: Crowell, 1965.

New Voices in American Studies. Eds. Ray B. Browne, Donald M. Winkelman and Allen Hayman. West Lafayette: Purdue UP, 1966.

Frontiers of American Culture. Eds. Ray B. Browne, Richard H. Crowder, Virgil L. Lokke and William T. Stafford. West Lafayette: Purdue UP, 1968.

Popular Culture and Curricula. Eds. Ray B. Browne and Ronald J. Ambrosetti. Bowling Green, OH: Bowling Green State U Popular P, 1969.

Themes and Directions in American Literature. Eds. Ray B. Browne and Donald Pizer. West Lafayette: Purdue UP, 1969.

Challenges in American Culture. Eds. Ray B. Browne, Larry N. Landrum and William K. Bottorff. Bowling Green, OH: Bowling Green State U Popular P, 1970.

Mark Twain's Quarrel with Heaven, "Captain Stormfield's Visit to Heaven" and Other Sketches. New Haven, CT: College and UP, 1970.

Teach-In: Viability of Change. Eds. Ray B. Browne and B.D. Owens. Bowling Green, OH: Bowling Green State U Popular P, 1970.

Crises on Campus. Eds. Ray B. Browne, Russel B. Nye and Michael T. Marsden. Bowling Green, OH: Bowling Green State U Popular P, 1971.

Melville's Drive to Humanism: Humanism in the Works of Herman Melville. West Lafayette: Purdue UP, 1971.

Heroes of Popular Culture. Eds. Ray B. Browne, Marshall W. Fishwick and Michael T. Marsden. Bowling Green, OH: Bowling Green State U Popular P, 1972.

Icons of Popular Culture. Eds. Ray B. Browne and Marshall W. Fishwick. Bowling Green, OH: Bowling Green State U Popular P, 1972.

Instructors Manual to Accompany "The Popular Culture Explosion": Experiencing Mass Media. Eds. Ray B. Browne and David Madden. Dubuque, IA: Brown, 1972.

Popular Culture and Curricula. Eds. Ray B. Browne and Ronald J. Ambrosetti. Bowling Green, OH: Bowling Green State U Popular P, 1972.

The Popular Culture Explosion. Eds. Ray B. Browne and David Madden. Dubuque, IA: Brown, 1972.

Popular Culture and the Expanding Consciousness. Ed. Ray B. Browne. New York: Wiley, 1973.

Lincoln-Lore: Lincoln in the Contemporary Popular Mind. Bowling Green, OH: Bowling Green State U Popular P, 1974.

Theories & Methodologies in Popular Culture. Eds. Ray B. Browne, Sam Grogg, Jr. and Larry N. Landrum. Bowling Green, OH: Bowling Green State U Popular P, 1975.

"A Night With the Hants" and Other Alabama Folk Experiences. Bowling Green, OH: Bowling Green State U Popular P, 1976.

Dimensions of Detective Fiction. Eds. Ray B. Browne, Larry N. Landrum and Pat Browne. Bowling Green, OH: Bowling Green State U Popular P, 1976.

The Many Faces of Democracy: The Long Push to Democracy. Bowling Green, OH: Bowling Green State U Popular P, 1977.

Icons of America. Eds. Ray B. Browne and Marshall W. Fishwick. Bowling Green, OH: Bowling Green State U Popular P, 1978.

The Alabama Folk Lyric: A Study in Origins and Media of Dissemination. Ed. Ray B. Browne. Bowling Green, OH: Bowling Green State U Popular P, 1979.

Directions and Dimensions of American Culture Studies in the 1980s. Eds. Ray B. Browne and Ralph W. Wolfe. Bowling Green, OH: Bowling Green State U Popular P, 1979.

Popular Abstracts: Journal of Popular Culture 1967-1977, Journal of Popular Film 1972-1977, Popular Music and Society 1971-1975. Eds. Ray B. Browne and Christopher Geist. Bowling Green, OH: Bowling Green State U Popular P, 1979.

Rituals and Ceremonies in Popular Culture. Ed. Ray B. Browne. Bowling Green, OH: Bowling Green State U Popular P, 1980.

Objects of Special Devotion: Fetishism in Popular Culture. Ed. Ray B. Browne. Bowling Green, OH: Bowling Green State U Popular P, 1981.

The Defective Detective in the Pulps. Eds. Ray B. Browne and Gary Hoppenstand. Bowling Green, OH: Bowling Green State U Popular P, 1983.

The Hero in Transition. Eds. Ray B. Browne and Marshall W. Fishwick. Bowling Green, OH: Bowling Green State U Popular P, 1983.

Forbidden Fruits: Taboos and Tabooism in Culture. Ed. Ray B. Browne. Bowling Green, OH: Bowling Green State U Popular P, 1984.

More Tales of the Defective Detective in the Pulps. Eds. Ray B. Browne, Gary Hoppenstand and Garyn Roberts. Bowling Green, OH: Bowling Green State U Popular P, 1985.

Heroes and Humanities: Detective Fiction and Culture. Bowling Green, OH: Bowling Green State U Popular P, 1986.

Laws of Our Fathers: Popular Culture and the U.S. Constitution. Eds. Ray B. Browne and Glenn J. Browne. Bowling Green, OH: Bowling Green State U Popular P, 1986.

The God Pumpers: Religion in the Electronic Age. Eds. Ray B. Browne and Marshall W. Fishwick. Bowling Green, OH: Bowling Green State U Popular P, 1987.

The Gothic World of Stephen King: Landscape of Nightmares. Eds. Ray B. Browne and Gary Hoppenstand. Bowling Green, OH: Bowling Green State U Popular P, 1987.

The Spirit of Australia: The Crime Fiction of Arthur W. Upfield. Bowling Green, OH: Bowling Green State U Popular P, 1988.

Symbiosis: Popular Culture and Other Fields. Eds. Ray B. Browne and Marshall W. Fishwick. Bowling Green, OH: Bowling Green State U Popular P, 1988.

Against Academia: The History of the Popular Culture Association/ American Culture Association and Popular Culture Movement, 1967-1988. Bowling Green, OH: Bowling Green State U Popular P, 1989.

Dominant Symbols in Popular Culture. Eds. Ray B. Browne, Marshall W. Fishwick and Kevin O. Browne. Bowling Green, OH: Bowling Green State U Popular P, 1990.

Old Sleuth's Freaky Female Detective: (from the Dime Novels). Eds. Ray B. Browne, Garyn Roberts and Gary Hoppenstand. Bowling Green, OH: Bowling Green State U Popular P, 1990.

Digging into Popular Culture: Theories and Methodologies in Archeology, Anthropology and Other Fields. Eds. Ray B. Browne and Pat Browne. Bowling Green, OH: Bowling Green State U Popular P, 1991.

Rejuvenating the Humanities. Eds. Ray B. Browne and Marshall W. Fishwick. Bowling Green, OH: Bowling Green State U Popular P, 1991.

The Many Tongues of Literacy. Bowling Green, OH: Bowling Green State U Popular P, 1992.

Continuities in Popular Culture: The Present in the Past and the Past in the Present and Future. Eds. Ray B. Browne and Ronald J. Ambrosetti. Bowling Green, OH: Bowling Green State U Popular P, 1993.

The Cultures of Celebrations. Eds. Ray B. Browne and Michael T. Marsden. Bowling Green, OH: Bowling Green State U Popular P, 1994.

Articles

"Two Alabama Nonsense Orations." *Southern Folklore Quarterly* 17 (1953): 312-15.

"Children's Taunts, Teases from Southern California." *Western Folklore* 13 (1954): 190-95.

"More Circular Tales." *Western Folklore* 13 (1954): 130-33.

"Negro Folktales from Alabama." *Southern Folklore Quarterly* 18 (1954): 123-36.

"Some Notes on the Southern 'Holler.'" *Journal of American Folklore* 67 (1954): 73-78.

"Children's Taunts, Teases from Alabama." *Western Folklore* 14 (1955): 206-10.

"Southern California Jump-Rope Rhymes: A Study in Variants." *Western Folklore* 14 (1955): 1-36.

"Shakespeare in the 19th Century Popular Songbooks." *Shakespeare Quarterly* 8 (1957): 207-18.

"Milton and Dryden in 19th Century Popular Songbooks." *Bulletin of Bibliography* 12 (1958): 143-44.

"The Oft-Told *Twice-Told Tales.*" *Southern Folklore Quarterly* 23 (1958): 69-85.

"American Poets in the 19th Century 'Popular' Songbooks." *American Literature* 30 (Jan. 1959): 503-22.

"The Satiric Use of Popular Music in *Love's Labour's Lost.*" *Southern Folklore Quarterly* 24 (1959): 137-49.

"Shakespeare in American Vaudeville and Negro Minstrelsy." *American Quarterly* 12 (Fall 1960): 374-91.

"Popular and Folk Songs: Unifying Force in Garland's Autobiographical Works." *Southern Folklore Quarterly* 21 (1961): 153-66.

"Superstitions Used as Propaganda in the American Revolution." *New York Folklore Quarterly* 17 (1961): 202-11.

"Mark Twain and Captain Wakeman." *American Literature* 33 (1961): 320-39.

"Billy Budd: Gospel of Democracy." *Nineteenth-Century Fiction* 17 (1963): 321-37.

"The Burke-Paine Controversy in Irish Popular Songs." *The Celtic Cross.* Eds. Ray B. Browne, William John Roscelli and Richard Loftus. West Lafayette: Purdue UP, 1964. 80-97.

"Huck's Final Triumph." *Forum* (Winter 1964). Rpt. in *Critical Approaches to American Literature.* Vol. 2. Eds. Ray B. Browne and Martin Light. New York: Crowell, 1965. 97-108.

"Introduction" to Sut Lovingood's "Marrying a Substitute." *The Lovingood Papers.* Vol. 3. Ed. B.H. McClary. Knoxville: U of Tennessee P, 1965.

"The Political Symbolism in *Benito Cereno.*" *Critical Approaches to American Literature.* Vol. 1. Eds. Ray B. Browne and Martin Light. New York: Crowell, 1965. 309-25.

"Popular Theatre in *Moby Dick.*" *New Voices in American Studies.* Eds. Ray B. Browne, Donald M. Winkelman and Allen Hayman. West Lafayette, IN: Purdue UP, 1966. 89-101.

"The Affirmation of 'Bartleby.'" *Folklore International.* Ed. D.K. Wilgus. Hatboro, PA: Folklore Associates, 1967. 11-22.

"Israel Potter: Metamorphosis of Superman." *Frontiers of Popular Culture.* Eds. Ray B. Browne, Richard H. Crowder, Virgil L. Lokke and William T. Stafford. West Lafayette, IN: Purdue UP, 1968. 88-98.

"'The Wisdom of Many': Proverbs and Proverbial Expressions." *American Folklore.* Ed. T.P. Coffin, III. U.S. Information Services: Voice of America Forum Lecturers, 1968. 217-28.

"Popular Culture: Notes Toward a Definition." *Popular Culture and Curricula.* Eds. Ray B. Browne and Ronald J. Ambrosetti. Bowling Green, OH: Bowling Green State U Popular P, 1969. 1-12.

"The Uses of Popular Culture in the Teaching of American History." *Popular Culture and Curricula.* Eds. Ray B. Browne and Ronald J.

Ambrosetti. Bowling Green, OH: Bowling Green State U Popular P, 1969. 123-36.

"Popular Culture and (Canadian) History." *Journal of Popular Culture* 4 (Spring 1971): 1023-25.

"Epilogue." *Heroes of Popular Culture.* Eds. Ray B. Browne, Marshall W. Fishwick and Michael T. Marsden. Bowling Green, OH: Bowling Green State U Popular P, 1972. 186-88.

"The Uses of Popular Culture in the Teaching of American History." *Social Education* 36 (Jan. 1972): 49-53.

"Academicons—Sick Sacred Cows." *Icons of America.* Eds. Ray B. Browne and Marshall W. Fishwick. Bowling Green, OH: Bowling Green State U Popular P, 1973. 292-301.

"The Historian and Popular Culture." *New Approaches to American History.* Ed. Ray B. Browne. New York: Dodd, 1973.

"Can Opener." *Journal of Popular Culture* 9 (Fall 1975): 353-54.

"Whale Lore and Popular Print in Mid-Nineteenth Century America: Sketches Toward a Profile." *Prospects* 1 (1975): 29-40.

"Inside Look." *Journal of Popular Culture* 10 (Fall 1976): 493-94.

"'Two Loves Have I' or The Relationship Between the JPC and the PCA." *Journal of Popular Culture* 10 (Fall 1976): 490-92.

"Popular Entertainments: Summing Up." *American Popular Entertainments: Papers and Proceedings of the Conference on the History of American Popular Entertainment.* Ed. Myron Matlaw. Westport, CT: Greenwood, 1977. 293-97.

"Libraries at the Crossroads: A Perspective on Libraries and Culture." *Drexel Library Quarterly* 16 (July 1980): 12-23.

"Ritual and the Humanities 'Intellectual.'" *Rituals and Ceremonies in Popular Culture.* Ed. Ray B. Browne. Bowling Green, OH: Bowling Green State U Popular P, 1980. 338-49.

"Ritual One." *Rituals and Ceremonies in Popular Culture.* Ed. Ray B. Browne. Bowling Green, OH: Bowling Green State U Popular P, 1980. 1-18.

"The Seat of Democracy: The Privy Humor of 'Chic' Sale." *Journal of American Culture* 3 (Fall 1980): 409-16.

"Up from Elitism: The Aesthetics of Popular Fiction." *Studies in American Fiction* 9 (Autumn 1981): 217-31.

"Bad Blood on the Potomac." With Alicia R. Browne. *Clues* 3 (Fall/Winter 1982): 7-10.

"Academic Fetishes: Articulated Skeletons." *Objects of Special Devotion: Fetishism in Popular Culture.* Ed. Ray B. Browne. Bowling Green, OH: Bowling Green State U Popular P, 1983. 215-26.

"Hero with 2000 Faces." *The Hero in Transition.* Eds. Ray B. Browne and Marshall W. Fishwick. Bowling Green, OH: Bowling Green State U Popular P, 1983. 91-106.

"The Repressive Nature of TV Esthetics Criticism." *Journal of American Culture* 6 (Fall 1983): 117-22.

"Sherlock Holmes as Christian Detective in *The Case of the Invisible Thief.*" *Clues* 4 (Spring/Summer 1983): 79-91.

"Don't Touch, Don't Do, Don't Question—Don't Progress." *Forbidden Fruits: Taboos and Tabooism in Culture.* Ed. Ray B. Browne. Bowling Green, OH: Bowling Green State U Popular P, 1984. 1-6.

"Lincoln in the Bosom of Familiarity." *The Hero in Transition.* Eds. Ray B. Browne and Marshall W. Fishwick. Bowling Green, OH: BGSU Popular Press, 1984. 308-22.

"Popular Culture as the New Humanities." *Journal of Popular Culture* 17 (Spring 1984): 1-8. Rpt. in *Federation Review* 8 (Sept./Oct. 1985): 10-14.

"Class Reunions as a Folk Festival." *Journal of Popular Culture* 19 (Summer 1985): 107-13.

"The Heroic World of Judson Philips." *Clues* 6 (Spring/Summer 1985): 79-96.

"Interview with John Ball." *Clues* 6 (Fall/Winter 1985): 147-50.

"The Affirmation of the Humanities." *Humanities in the South* 64 (Fall 1986): 1, 6.

"The Border Through Canadian Detective Field Glasses." *Journal of American Culture* 9 (Spring 1986): 7-10.

"The Frontier Heroism of Arthur W. Upfield." *Clues* 7 (Spring/Summer 1986): 127-45.

"Popular Culture: Medicine for Illiteracy and Associated Educational Ills." *Journal of Popular Culture* 21 (Winter 1987): 1-15.

"The Rape of the Vulnerable." *The God Pumpers: Religion in the Electronic Age.* Eds. Ray B. Browne and Marshall W. Fishwick. Bowling Green, OH: Bowling Green State U Popular P, 1987. 183-90.

"Joan Hess's Humanistic Silk Stockinged Sleuth." *Clues* 9 (Fall/Winter 1988): 29-36.

"Popular Books and Popular Culture." *Symbiosis: Popular Culture and Other Fields.* Eds. Ray B. Browne and Marshall W. Fishwick. Bowling Green, OH: Bowling Green State U Popular P, 1988. 22-33.

"Popular Culture as the New Humanities." *Symbiosis: Popular Culture and Other Fields.* Eds. Ray B. Browne and Marshall W. Fishwick. Bowling Green, OH: Bowling Green State U Popular P, 1988. 1-9.

"Popular Culture: Medicine for Illiteracy and Associated Educational Ills." *Symbiosis: Popular Culture and Other Fields.* Eds. Ray B. Browne and Marshall W. Fishwick. Bowling Green, OH: Bowling Green State U Popular P, 1988. 10-22.

"Interview with Ralph McInerny." *Clues* 10 (Spring/Summer 1989): 117-34.

"Redefining the Humanities." *Pennsylvania English* 13 (Spring/Summer 1989): 16-28.

"Redefining Literature." *Journal of Popular Culture* 23 (Winter 1989): 11-21.

"Evolution of Book as Symbol." *Dominant Symbols in Popular Culture.* Eds. Ray B. Browne, Marshall W. Fishwick and Kevin O. Browne. Bowling Green, OH: Bowling Green State U Popular P, 1990. 20-29.

"Ross Macdonald: Revolutionary Author and Critic; Or the Need for the Oath of Macdonald." *Journal of Popular Culture* 24 (Winter 1990): 101-11.

"Folk Cultures and the Humanities." *Rejuvenating the Humanities.* Eds. Ray B. Browne and Marshall W. Fishwick. Bowling Green, OH: Bowling Green State U Popular P, 1991. 24-34.

"The Many Tongues of Literacy." With Arthur G. Neal. *Journal of Popular Culture* 25 (Summer 1991): 157-86.

"Non-Work Time and the Humanities." With Michael T. Marsden. *Rejuvenating the Humanities.* Eds. Ray B. Browne and Marshall W. Fishwick. Bowling Green, OH: Bowling Green State U Popular P, 1991. 16-23.

"The Traveller and the Humanities." *Rejuvenating the Humanities.* Eds. Ray B. Browne and Marshall W. Fishwick. Bowling Green, OH: Bowling Green State U Popular P, 1991. 135-48.

"A Lion's Share of Tourism in the 21st Century" in *Visions in Leisure and Business.* Ed. David Groves. Bowling Green, OH: Appalachian Associates. Vol. 12.2 (Summer 1993): 1-11.

"Why Should Lawyers Study Popular Culture?" in *The Lawyer and Popular Culture: Proceedings of a Conference.* Ed. David L. Gunn. Littleton, CO: Fred B. Rothman & Co., 1993.

Translations in Chinese

《美国通俗文化协会与创始人布朗》
　　见《合肥教院学报》1991年第1期

《美国文化协会的诞生与发展》见
　　《合肥教院学报》1991年第3期

《美国通俗文化协会的国际化》见
　　《东南文化》1996年第5期

《美国通俗文化研究评述》见《世
　　界史研究动态》1992年第12期

《布朗和美国通俗文化运动》见《合
　　肥教学报》1993年第2期

《美国通俗文化出版社的诞生与
　　发展》见《合肥教院学报》1993
　　年第2期

Book Reviews
Journal of Popular Culture, 1971-1993; over 200 reviews.
Journal of American Culture, 1978-1993; over 60 reviews.
Clues: A Journal of Detection, 1980-1993; over 400 reviews.

EPILOGUE

✦

Epilogue

Ronald J. Ambrosetti

In September 1967, on a crisp autumn evening in northwest Ohio, while much of the country was focused on the erupting issues of Vietnam, civil rights and political change, a fledgling graduate student walked uncertainly into a graduate course at Bowling Green State University. The course was an introduction to research methods, with a rotating battery of the graduate faculty. On this particular evening, the guest professor was a new arrival from Purdue University. The class, already somewhat inured to the obligatory performances thus delivered, settled in for a perfunctory tour of American literature and the current research materials and methods. What, in fact, happened that night should happen for every graduate student and every graduate program in American higher education. Professor Ray Browne never once used the words "bibliographic tool;" he did not bring a list of library "compass readings." Instead, Ray Browne opened his own mind to 25 graduate students, who in turn opened their own minds to the substantive issues of research and scholarship in American literature, American Studies and popular culture. Ray Browne spent a couple of hours that night by describing the paths of his own scholarship—in a very real way he eschewed the superficial conduits of library research and explored the connective networks of ideas and approaches. Most importantly, Ray Browne addressed the graduate students in concrete terms; he opened his presentation with a lengthy discussion of Herman Melville's *Billy Budd*. Ray Browne's approach to the Melville novel was grounded in the confluence of folklore and popular culture. Ray Browne persuaded a collection of young minds that the Melville novel, and indeed any expression of oral or literate culture, is a nodule at the connective tissue of a variety of influences and forces in a culture. The investigation of folklore and popular culture happened to be Ray Browne's specific and erudite approach to a literary text; his deep structure in the pedagogical lesson that night was twofold: literature is often rooted in the vernacular materials of a culture and the scholar must pursue the whole spectrum of those materials in an egalitarian spirit. Since that evening in 1967, Ray Browne has spent the past 26 years in teaching and validating this lesson to the wide array of academic disciplines which have attempted to ground their lofty theories in the ethnographic and holistic *praxes* of a multiplicity of learning and teaching constituencies. Myth and symbol do exist in the speech of the quotidian interactions of normal men and women; popular culture *is* reflective of folklife, which *is* reflective of literature—whether it is the spoken literature of African-American hip-hop, the mythic dimension of Caribbean dub poetry, or the syntactic ebb and flow of the deep rhythms of Faulkner's mythical South.

In his 1974 book on Abraham Lincoln, entitled *Lincoln-Lore*, Ray Browne opened his Preface with an astute encomium to Lincoln as perhaps the greatest of all American popular heroes:

> Lincoln probably more than any other President of the United States saturated the consciousness and subconsciousness of the American popular mind, that is, of the people in general. The reason is obvious. In time of great national crisis people focus their minds on the President as the center of the storm. He becomes, in effect, the cause as well as the agent for the cure. The Civil War was an internal struggle and, therefore, double intense.
>
> The degree to which our sixteenth President dominated people's thoughts on this popular level can well be gauged by the noisiness and the forms this reaction assumed.

My vignette at the start of this essay should now assume a second relevance. Ray Browne and "the popular culture movement" did not present themselves as adventitious and external events in the flux of the turbulent American experience in 1967; using his own tenuous and egalitarian qualities, Ray Browne established himself as the Lincoln of the Ivory Towers in the second American Civil War, which was the culture wars of the 1960s. In his 1989 history of the movement, *Against Academia*, Ray Browne has chronicled both the landmark achievements and the heartbreaking disappointments that he and his wife, Pat, have encountered in the quarter-century of enterprise in journal publication, national association leadership, and the long-wished-for recognition in the Federal educational circles. As in the case of Lincoln's opponents, the noisy and trembling adversarial obstructionists often give more tribute in their condemnations than the conspicuously absent praise.

As the graduate student in the first part of this essay, I have always considered my intersection with Ray Browne on that night in 1967 as an event fortunate for both my personal and my professional conduct. Not long after that first semester in graduate school, I was drafted out of the academic and into an alien and brutal environment. Upon my taking leave of Ray and the Teaching Assistantship in his and Pat's Journal office, Ray's parting words were: "Never forget where you have been and where you belong." In the long days and months later, I cherished these words as a compass on a dark and hostile terrain. In retrospect, I believe that Ray Browne has given these same words to an academy with an array of disciplines that many times lose their way in the irrelevant and the self-serving. Ray has comported his own life and work along the axis of those words; he is an egalitarian compass to a profession that occasionally could use some direction.

Contributors

Ronald J. Ambrosetti is the Associate Dean of Arts and Sciences at the SUNY College at Fredonia. Except for a Fulbright year in Portugal as Senior Lecturer in American Studies in 1981, he has been a faculty member and former chairperson of the Department of English at Fredonia since 1976. He has just completed a manuscript for MacMillan-Twayne in the English Authors Series on Eric Ambler.

John G. Cawelti is author of *Apostles of the Self-Made Man, The Six-Gun Mystique, Adventure, Mystery and Romance, The Spy Story* and other studies in Popular Culture. He is Professor of English at the University of Kentucky.

Thomas Cripps is University Distinguished Professor at Morgan State University. In addition to numerous essays, he has written *Slow Fade to Black: The Negro in American Film, 1900-1940* (Oxford, 1977); *Black Film as Genre* (Indiana, 1978); and *Making Movies Black: The Hollywood Message Movie from World War II to the Civil Rights Era* (Oxford, 1993), and the script for the prize-winning film, *Black Shadows on a Silver Screen* (*Post-Newsweek*, 1976). He has held many fellowships, among them a Guggenheim, Rockefeller, Woodrow Wilson, and has been a resident fellow at The National Humanities Center, The Smithsonian, and the Villa Serbelloni in Italy.

Dennis Hall is a Professor of English at the University of Louisville, where he serves as Director of Composition. He also edits *Studies in Popular Culture.*

Harold E. Hinds, Jr. is Professor of History and Director of Latin American Area Studies at the University of Minnesota-Morris. He is co-editor of the annual journal *Studies in Latin Popular Culture*, the *Handbook of Latin American Popular Culture* (1985), co-author of *Not Just for Children: The Mexican Comic Book in the late 1960s and 1970s* (1992), and currently at work on an edited volume devoted to popular culture theory and methodologies.

Carl Bryan Holmberg is an Associate Professor of Popular Culture at Bowling Green State University whose interests include horror fiction, social gatherings, the environment and men's studies. This paper is the result of an ongoing research project begun over 20 years ago concerning the relationship between media and culture. Carl also serves as Executive Secretary and Program Director for the Midwest Popular Culture and Midwest American Culture Associations and wants you to feel free to net with him at cholmbe@andy.bgsu.edu.

M. Thomas Inge is the Robert Emory Blackwell Professor of Humanities at Randolph-Macon College in Ashland, Virginia. He is the editor of the three-volume *Handbook of American Popular Culture* (Greenwood Press, revised and enlarged edition, 1989) and author of *Comics as Culture* (University Press of Mississippi, 1990) and *Perspectives on American Culture: Essays on Humor, Literature, and the Popular Arts* (Locust Hill Press, 1994). He has been a Fulbright Lecturer in Spain, Argentina, Russia, and the Czech Republic.

Marty S. Knepper, Professor of English at Morningside College, teaches an American Popular Culture seminar with John Lawrence. A former President of the Popular Culture Association, she has written papers and articles on detective fiction, film, and women's studies.

John S. Lawrence is Professor of Philosophy at Morningside College, Sioux City, IA 51106. With Robert Jewett, he is co-author of *The American Monomyth* (Doubleday, 1977; UPA, 2nd ed., 1987); with Bernard Timberg, he is co-editor of *Fair Use and Free Inquiry: Copyright Law and the New Media* (Ablex, 1980; 2nd ed., 1989).

Judith Yaross Lee is Assistant Professor of Interpersonal Communication at Ohio University, where she teaches theory, rhetoric, and historiography. In addition to essays on popular American writing in *American Literature and Science* (ed. Scholnick, 1992), *Literature and Technology* (ed. Schachterle and Greenberg, 1992), *Studies in American Humor*, and *American Heritage of Invention and Technology*, she has written *Garrison Keillor: A Voice of America* (University Press of Mississippi, 1991) and co-edited *Beyond the Two Cultures: Essays on Science, Technology, and Literature* (Iowa State University Press, 1990). She is presently at work on studies of e-mail and *The New Yorker*.

Michael T. Marsden is Dean of the College of Arts and Sciences and Professor of English at Northern Michigan University. The author/editor of numerous articles and books, he is also the Co-Editor of the *Journal of Popular Film and Television.*

Jay Mechling is Professor of American Studies at the University of California, Davis. He received his undergraduate education in American Studies at Stetson University and his graduate training in American Civilization at the University of Pennsylvania. He edited *Western Folklore* for five years and is chair of the California Council for the Humanities.

Marilyn Ferris Motz is Associate Professor in the Department of Popular Culture at Bowling Green State University. She is author of *True Sisterhood: Michigan Women and Their Kin, 1820-1920* and co-editor of *Making the American Home* as well as author of articles on nineteenth- and early-twentieth-century private expressive forms such as diaries, photograph albums, letters and gardens. She was one of the organizers of the conference on "The Future of Popular Culture Scholarship in the Twenty-First Century" at which earlier versions of the articles in this volume were presented.

John G. Nachbar is Professor of Popular Culture at Bowling Green State University and co-editor of the *Journal of Popular Film and Television.* He studied under Ray Browne as a doctoral student and has been a colleague of Browne's in the Department of Popular Culture since 1974.

Tim Orwig is Director of the Learning Center at Morningside College and author of *A Centennial History of Morningside* (1994).

Richard Gid Powers has written *G-Men: Hoover's FBI in American Popular Culture, Secrecy and Power: The Life of J. Edgar Hoover,* and the forthcoming *Not Without Honor: The History of American Anticommunism.* He is a Professor of History at the Graduate Center and the College of Staten Island, City University of New York.

Joseph W. Slade is Professor of Telecommunications at Ohio University. He has held NEH, Hagley Museum, and Gannett Fellowships, and taught at several institutions, including the University of Helsinki, where he was Bicentennial Professor of American Studies in 1986-87. His *Thomas Pynchon* (1974), the first book-length study of the novelist, was reissued in 1990. He is co-editor of *Beyond the Two Cultures: Essays on Science, Technology, and Literature* (1990), and author of *Pornography: A Reference Guide* (forthcoming from Greenwood Press) as well as several dozen articles on literature, film, technology, broadcasting, and culture.

Stephen Tatum is Associate Professor and Chair of English at the University of Utah. He is the author of *Inventing Billy the Kid*, as well as articles and essays on Western American literature, film, and history.

Maryan Wherry is a Ph.D. candidate in American Culture, Bowling Green State University, Bowling Green, OH. She is currently with the University of Maryland, European Division, Würzburg, Germany.

.

www.ingramcontent.com/pod-product-compliance
Lightning Source LLC
Chambersburg PA
CBHW031501270326
41930CB00006B/191